About the Author

Pascal Ménoret, researcher and Arabist, developed a deep understanding of Saudi society during an extensive period in Riyadh, beginning a few days after September 11, 2001. He is the author of several publications in French on Saudi politics and society.

The Saudi Enigma

A History

—————

Pascal Ménoret

Translated by Patrick Camiller

ZED BOOKS
London & New York

WORLD BOOK PUBLISHING
Beirut

DAVID PHILIP
South Africa

To the memory of Gérard Lebrun
To the future of my students in Riyadh

The Saudi Enigma was published in 2005
in Lebanon, Bahrain, Egypt, Jordan, Kuwait, Quatar, Saudi Arabia and United Arab
Emirates by World Book Publishing, 282 Emile Eddeh Street, Ben Salem bldg, PO
Box 3176, Beirut, Lebanon, www.wbpbooks.com

in Southern Africa by David Philip (an imprint of New Africa Books),
99 Garfield Road, Kenilworth 7700, South Africa

and in the rest of the world by Zed Books Ltd, 7 Cynthia Street, London N1 9JF, UK,
and Room 400, 175 Fifth Avenue, New York, NY 10010, USA

It was published in French as L'Énigme Saoudienne
by La Découverte in 2003

www.zedbooks.co.uk

Copyright © Éditions La Découverte 2003
Translation copyright © Patrick Camiller 2005

The English-language edition of this book has been published with the support of
the Centre National du Livre of the French Ministry of Culture.

The right of Pascal Ménoret to be identified as the author of this work
has been asserted by him in accordance with the Copyright, Designs
and Patents Act, 1988

Designed and typeset in Monotype Joanna
by Illuminati, Grosmont, www.illuminatibooks.co.uk
Index: ed.emery@britishlibrary.net
Cover designed by Andrew Corbett
Printed and bound in Malta by Gutenberg Press Ltd

Distributed in the USA exclusively by Palgrave Macmillan, a division of
St Martin's Press, LLC, 175 Fifth Avenue, New York, NY 10010

A catalogue record for this book is available from the British Library
Library of Congress Cataloging-in-Publication Data available

ISBN 9953 14 070 7 Pb (Lebanon)
ISBN 1 84277 604 5 Hb (rest of world)
ISBN 1 84277 605 3 Pb

Contents

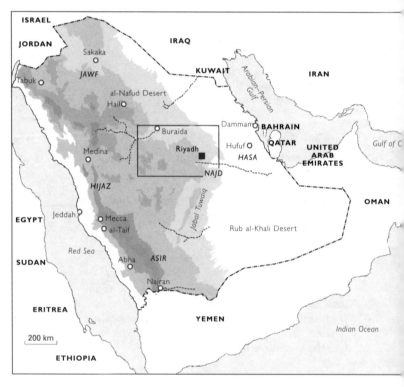

Saudi Arabia (physical)

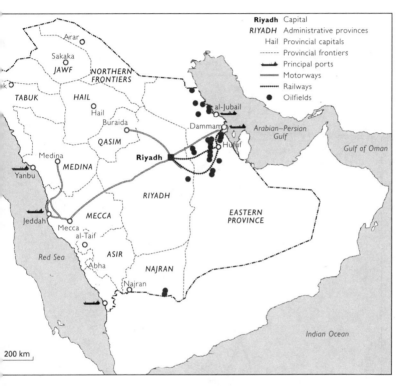

Saudi Arabia (administration and economy)

Najd

Motorways
Main roads
Oases

50 km

Afif
Hudaija
UPPER NAJD
Bijadiya
Nifi
Dukhna
Ras
al-Bukairiya
Riyadh al-Khabra
Badai
Midhnab
QASSIM
BURAIDA
UNAIZA
Dawadmi
Ruwaida
Shaqra
WASHM
Zilfi
Ghat
Majma'a
SUDAYR
Huraimala
Ghatghat
Muzahmiya
Dhurma
Uyaina
Dir'iya
ARID
Hair
RIYADH
HARIQ
Hawta bani Tamim
Dilam
KHARJ
YAMAMA

Foreword

No country in the world, with the possible exception of Tibet, has been the object of such misrepresentation and mystification as Saudi Arabia, a country of more than 15 million people, site of a quarter of the world's known oil reserves, and location of the two holiest cities of the Muslim religion, Mecca and Medina. As with many of the myths and confusions that beset the understanding of the contemporary Middle East, this misrepresentation of Saudi Arabia is sustained from two sides, by a combination of mercenary public relations writers and sectarian enemies from without, and vacuous official scribes from within. From the outside come images of the desert, of inordinate wealth, of unparalleled repression, and from the inside come the often self-righteous and declamatory products of various official ministries and diwans of disinformation, all under the aegis, and on the payroll, of a state that allows no resident independent foreign correspondents and where the press itself remains controlled to a fine degree. The result is that the outside observer, Arab or Westerner, Muslim or other, knows, and often can know, very little about how this country really runs, what its people think, and, perhaps most importantly, how it is, like any other country in the world, subject to change, some of it very rapid, from within and without.

The available literature on Saudi Arabia is, in large measure, of little value, being either mystified travel writing, focusing on deserts, in which only a small minority of the population of the country, let alone of the Arabian Peninsula as a whole, actually live, or officially inspired histories and biographies of the Saudi family and state. There is not, to my knowledge, a single serious study based on adequate statistics of the Saudi economy, of the structures of power and influence within the state, of the social classes of Saudi Arabia, of the ethnic and social composition of the major cities (Mecca, Medina, Jeddah, Taif, Riyadh, Dammam) in which most Saudis live. Of available books in Western languages that merit study the list is small: two good histories, one by a Russian writer (Alexei Vassiliev, *The History of Saudi Arabia*), one by an anthropologist and member of a former ruling family (Madawi al-Rasheed, *A History of Saudi Arabia*); two of historical sociology by a Saudi sociologist, Mai Yamani (*Changed Identities: The Challenge of the New Generation in Saudi Arabia*, and *Cradle of Islam: The Hijaz and the Quest for an Arabian Identity*); a general study by an independent Marxist writer, Helen Lackner (*A House Built on Sand*), and that is largely it. Those who rule the country, and make a pretence of pluralism and openness, ensure that concrete issues are not discussed or investigated, while those who, from outside, make money from the country, notably oil companies, banks and contractors, have just as little interest in the truth. All is misrepresented in propaganda and by the four ideological blankets that between them smother the realities of the country – oil, religion, monarchy and desert.

It is, therefore, all the more welcome to read this study by Pascal Ménoret, refreshing in tone and methodology as much as it is in substance. Finally, we have a book by someone who has a robust social science approach to what is a modern and fast-changing society, who has lived in, and thought a lot about, the country, who does not fall into conspiracy theory, who avoids the anti-Saudi banalities of the outside world as much as the pieties of the regime, who, in a word, tells us how the country actually works. What emerges above all from this book is that, against all the mystification and nonsense to which we have long been treated, Saudi Arabia is, in many ways, a modern and comprehensible country. It is modern in the sense that the state was created in recent times, in the 1920s, and, later, transformed by oil revenues, that it has benefited from the backing of a major outside power, the USA, that this state does more or less what other states do, namely centralize power and promote a mythical national ideology, and that the society, as much as others in the Middle East or elsewhere, responds both to the state and to the international context in ways that change over time.

Ménoret provides a fascinating and persuasive account of the rise of the Saudi state. He shows that it served not to strengthen, but to weaken, tribal forces, in order to consolidate the state, and that oil revenues, from the 1970s to the 1990s at least, served to forge a new economy and society. Not everyone will be persuaded by his argument about the role of colonialism in shaping the modern Saudi state, but his account of how this state and society were produced is superior to any other yet produced. Of great importance in understanding, and demystifying, Saudi Arabia is his account of how the state has promoted a particular self-serving account of its own history and of Saudi identity that belies the variety and pluralism inside the country. He also cuts to the heart of the misuse of the concept 'Islam' as something that can explain how the country actually works. He goes so far as to challenge the conventional view of the Saudi regime, as a coalition of the tribal Al Saud elite with the religiously authoritative descendants of the eighteenth-century reformer Mohammad Bin Abd al-Wahhab, the Al Sheikh, and, instead, argue that the core of the regime has, till now at least, been based on an alliance of the Al Saud, the Najdi centralizing warriors, with the merchants of the Hijaz. Among other myths briskly dispensed with is that there is, in any accurate sense, such a thing as 'Wahhabism', a frequently used misnomer for the strict Hanbali variant of Islam that is official in the country, and that Saudi money has promoted abroad.

Ménoret is equally informative, and measured, when it comes to the present. He shows that over the past decade, as population has risen, tensions have grown within Saudi Arabia and that a mood, but not an organization, of opposition has developed within the country. People there want to know where the oil money has gone, where the jobs are going to be created, why the ruling family has been so close to the USA. 'Saudization' of the economy has largely been a failure, because no one in the private sector wants to employ Saudi nationals. The Saudi governing elite, a group of old men who run the country, have responded with spasmodic reforms, followed by sudden reverses. Great promises of economic liberalization to the outside world and to the private sector, and claims of political change, have been followed by stagnation, and regression.

Into all this has stepped al-Qaida and the crisis following 11 September 2001. External criticism of the state has increased, not a little of it deploying stale anti-Arab prejudices, and obscuring the role of Western states and greedy contractors in creating the present situation. At the same time an armed opposition, making intermittent but well-planned and targeted attacks, has emerged within the state. All of this has been compounded by something everyone in Saudi Arabia, ruler and ruled alike, is well aware of, the regional crisis comprising popular insurrection in Palestine, the war in Iraq, and the marked deterioration in relations between the Arab world and the USA. The regional initiatives of the Saudi government, such as an opening to Iraq in 2002 and the Arab–Israeli peace plan of the same year, have come to nothing, spurned by the USA and Israel, and at the same time failing to win broad Arab support.

While surveying the multiple pressures to which Saudi Arabia is now subjected, Ménoret believes that the country should be left alone by the rest of the world to find its way through the current crisis. All who know the country, and who believe that a reformed Saudi Arabia is, for everyone, Saudi or not, preferable to a violent and disorganized fragmentation, can only hope that his advice is heeded.

Professor Fred Halliday,
London School of Economics

Introduction

One can grasp a people only in its qualities.

Nicolas Bouvier

Coming as they did after an inconclusive decade, the attacks of 11 September 2001 seemed to restore a degree of ideological consistency to the contemporary world. In the early 1990s the West had seen its *raison d'être* disappear with the fall of the Soviet bloc. Decked out with military equipment, strategic doctrines and dualist conceptions, it found itself alone facing a world that had suddenly become illegible. One bright September morning, a new resolve appeared in the skies above New York and Washington, and certain Westerners hastily spoke of 'the absolute event, the "mother" of all events, the pure event concentrating all events that have ever taken place'.[1] The enemy, back in play, was attacking. And he was not attacking any old target but the United States itself, the global policeman, whose power bloc had gone unchallenged since the disintegration of the Soviet Union.

The attacks of 9/11 made it possible to read the 1990s as the incubation period of a new enemy, when peripheral conflict had turned into murderous assault and a resurgent fundamentalism had developed into a flare-up of violence. Opening the new century with an attack on the inner sanctum of the free world, Islamism seemed to be ushering in an uncertain and nightmarish strategic era, where an enemy unafraid of death might strike anytime, anywhere and in defiance of all logic.

So, 9/11 was not only the 'mother of events' but held the key to the strange wars to come; it was the first conflict of the twenty-first century. The enemy had to have a spokesman, and Osama bin Laden came forward as the new Hermes periodically informing the West of the thoughts and ambitions of godlike Islamist terrorists. The enemy had to have a rear base, and this was provided by the mountains of Pakistan and Afghanistan, a maze of lost valleys on the outer edges of the empire once carved out by Alexander the Great. Finally, the enemy had to have a model or guide, and that was Saudi Arabia, the world's leading oil exporter and traditional ally of the United States in the Middle East. The expression of a new world, containing an unfamiliar geopolitics and unprecedented risks, 9/11 appeared as both apocalypse and epiphany.

Going beyond the logic of security

What factors can explain, as fully as possible, the attacks of 11 September 2001? To read the Western press and most of the essays published on the question,[2] it is self-evident that Saudi Arabia is the principal guilty party and that the causes of 9/11 are purely Islamic: Saudi Arabia consciously or unconsciously funded global Islamism, which borrowed from the kingdom its ultra-violent fundamentalist ideology of 'Wahhabism'; the contradiction between Saudi Arabia's support for Islamists and its alliance with the United States led the Islamists to attack the very heart of infidel America; and, as if to rub the point in, fifteen of the nineteen kamikazes were Saudi citizens. Washington therefore decided to reconsider its alliance with Riyadh. The preventive war against Iraq in the spring of 2003 is the most striking expression of the change in American policy, whose chief operational base in the region is now no longer Riyadh but Baghdad.

This version of events does not correspond to the reality. First of all – at a formal level – this typical media account makes light of the first rule of historical caution: namely, that any historical event has a complex causality, which can only dogmatically be reduced to a single factor. To see the Saudi kingdom as the real power behind 9/11, because of the Islam professed there, is to operate more as an inquisitor than a researcher: it is to name a guilty party, instead of seeking an explanation for what has happened. Such an approach, smacking of the courts and the police, has nothing in common with scientific objectivity and the uncovering of real political causes, but in Europe and the West it has contaminated a whole production line of discourses relating to Islamism in general and Saudi Arabia in particular.

Next – at the level of *objective content* – it is possible to identify Saudi Arabia as the 'origin of Islamism' (the title of a book published in 2001) only by painting Saudis in a way that is at best a caricature and at worst a complete distortion. Or, rather, what is involved is a twin image: on the one hand, the replete bourgeois who slips money to Islamic foundations without caring too much whether it will be spent on a hospital, a Koranic school or the activities of a terrorist group; and on the other, the young Saudi, indoctrinated and at a loose end, who goes to fight in Afghanistan, Chechnya or Bosnia, or flies off to New York or Washington. The main purpose of this book is precisely to show that, between these two totally reductionist extremes, Saudi society displays an infinite number of possible variations, gradations and attitudes.

It is common to explain Islamism as the simple product of cultural, economic or social causes. Cultural: Islamist violence against the West and its Arab allies is contained in the Koran itself. Economic: the backwardness of the Muslim world stirs to revolt the uncultivated and starving masses. Social: wealthy religious upper classes combine with countless numbers of young people to produce violent and financially powerful Islamist movements. Saudi Islamism refutes these three narratives, however,[3] and we admit to having looked in Arabia for more than just Arabia. We have sought there an image of contemporary Islamism, with its special features, its presuppositions and its characteristic forms of behaviour. Beyond mechanically determinist causal explanations, whether cultural, economic or social, we have tried to discover the actual reality – if only to know what we should fear from it and what we can hope.

Finally – at a *methodological* level, which is perhaps that of the main insight guiding this work – we may say that to adopt the same discourse as one's object of study is not the surest way of achieving objectivity. We do not come closer to the truth by applying Islamic causality to an Islamic movement or regime, nor do we account for the behaviour of those active in them by repeating various 'Islamic' concepts that they employ (*jihad* in the name of Allah, the issuing of a *fatwa*,[4] a sentence of *takfir*,[5] a campaign to introduce the *sharia*,[6] and so on). Indeed, we would be tempted to say that the opposite is the case. When Galileo turned his gaze away from planetary motion and constructed an *abstract representation*, objectivity took a decisive step forward. When Copernicus refused to accept the data of perception and demonstrated that the earth revolves around the sun, his revolution laid the basis for our present-day science. The scientific approach and method consisted of abstracting from the way in which the object itself appeared, of closing one's ears to the 'discourse of the object' and concentrating on the causes behind it. After it had founded nearly all the sciences of which the West is so proud, this salutary revolution eventually extended to the field of Orientalism. Unfortunately, however, it has not yet led to a radical overhaul of Saudi studies.[7]

In trying to explain self-styled religious movements or states in terms of religion alone, various authors have failed to realize that this makes them accomplices of their object of study, allies of the object of their denunciation; that they are using the very instrument they consider illegitimate and wielding the very discourse that gives weight and credibility to those they attack. This paradoxical complicity culminated in the mirror images of George W. Bush and Osama bin Laden, who used the same kind of apocalyptic language to appeal for holy war or a war of Good against Evil. Everyone agrees that, behind Bush's discourse, real political, social or economic forces are giving it life. So why should we refuse the same multiple causality to the discourse of bin Laden? And why should we not take the Islamic discourse of Saudi leaders as a mere communications trick, designed to make credible a content that is anything but religious?

It might be said in reply that, since Islam furnishes the vocabulary used by institutional players (the Saudi state) or Islamist oppositional movements, and since Islam is the principal medium of the Saudi people's identity, it is right to accord it great importance. This argument is correct as far as it goes. But the importance of Saudi Islam does not justify the use of essentially religious instruments to analyse it. What would we think of a book on the IRA that did not rise above Catholic rhetoric to highlight the historical mechanisms underlying Irish nationalism? Or a book on Japan that did not go outside the narrow limits of Shintoism, on the grounds that it is still the official imperial doctrine? Or a book on the America of George W. Bush that did not shake off the biblical imagery with which the discourse of Republican hawks is sprinkled?

We must learn to free ourselves from a purely religious level of explanation, even if that is the register which the key Saudi players themselves invoke and master. We shall therefore avoid taking at face value the Islamic discourses of government and opposition, and try to do justice to geographical, historical, political, social and economic explanations. These may be much less dazzling, and the path to them may involve a much steeper climb, but we hope that they will bear greater and more reliable fruit as a result.

Osama bin Laden and Saudi Arabia

The discourse of Osama bin Laden, which has been cautiously reported in the media since the mid-1990s, is representative of the Islamist network to which he has given a name, a face and a voice. For, while the rhetoric he uses is Islamic, his actual arguments do not really remind us of a religious preacher touched by grace.

Talking to the British journalist Robert Fisk in 1996, bin Laden made it clear that for him religious discourse is like the packaging on a washing powder: a cosmetic element of marketing and communication. In these interviews, he first of all traces the history of the Saudi kingdom from its refoundation in 1902 by Abdelaziz Al Saud to the second Gulf War in 1991:[8]

> The regime started under the flag of applying Islamic law, and under this banner all the people of Saudi Arabia came to help the Saudi family take power. Abdul Aziz did not apply Islamic law; the

country was set up for his family. Then, after the discovery of petroleum, the Saudi regime found another support – the money to
make people rich and give them the services and life they wanted
and to make them satisfied.[9]

According to bin Laden, it was by holding high the banner of
Islam that Abdelaziz was able to bring the majority of Arabs in
the Peninsula into a single kingdom. This source of legitimacy was
then abandoned when the ruling family sank enough roots in the
country to dispense with a religious reference, and the oil wealth
enabled it to stand instead on the ground of modernization. Thus
the House of Saud invoked three successive sources of legitimacy:
first Islam, then a traditional popular allegiance to their dynasty,
and finally modernization activity made possible by oil revenue.
In other words, for the spokesman of al-Qaida, royal power and
money were the opium that dulled the religious aspirations of the
Saudi people.

In the eyes of bin Laden, the policies of the Saudi royal family
during the second Gulf War strikingly revealed this methodological
agnosticism. After it was announced that Iraqi troops had invaded
Kuwait, and while US Defense Secretary Dick Cheney was convincing
Saudi officials that Saddam Hussein was about to march into Saudi
Arabia,[10] King Fahd agreed to American military intervention and
asked the grand mufti of the kingdom to give the US military
presence his religious blessing. Here is what bin Laden says about
this:

> When the American troops entered Saudi Arabia, the land of the
> two holy places [Mecca and Medina], there was a strong protest
> from the ulema and from students of the sharia law all over the
> country against the interference of American troops. This big
> mistake by the Saudi regime of inviting the American troops
> revealed their deception. They had given their support to nations
> that were fighting against Muslims. They helped the Yemeni com-
> munists against the southern Yemeni Muslims and are helping
> Arafat's regime fight Hamas. After it insulted and jailed the ulema[11]
> eighteen months ago, the Saudi regime lost its legitimacy.[12]

For bin Laden, then, the Saudi regime is not motivated by Islamic
considerations. In 1994, during the civil war in Yemen, Riyadh gave

its support to the socialist regime in the South, thereby demonstrating that it did not feel for those in power in Aden the kind of revulsion that a pure Islamic state ought to feel for an atheistic Marxist system. The support given by the Saudi royal family to Yasser Arafat, sometimes against the Palestinian Islamist opposition, testifies to the same pragmatism. And, in the wake of the second Gulf War, Islamist movements more or less everywhere in the Muslim world publicly expressed their abhorrence of the Saudi regime. Because of its excessive materialism and pragmatism, 'the Saudi regime lost its legitimacy' and therefore cannot be held up as a bandleader or even an icon of world Islamism.

There is no doubt that bin Laden's rhetoric is Islamic. But what about the content of what he says? The continuation of his interview with Robert Fisk gives us some idea of this:

> The Saudi people have remembered now what the ulema told them and they realize America is the main reason for their problems. The ordinary man knows that his country is the largest oil producer in the world, yet at the same time he is suffering from taxes and bad services. Now the people understand the speeches of the ulemas in the mosques – that *our country has become an American colony.* They act decisively with every action to kick the Americans out of Saudi Arabia. What happened in Riyadh and Khobar[13] [when twenty-four Americans were killed in two bombings] is clear evidence of the huge anger of Saudi people against America. The Saudis now know their real enemy is America. ... *The war declared by America against the Saudi people means war against all Muslims everywhere.* Resistance against America will spread in many, many places in Muslim countries. Our trusted leaders, the ulema, have given us a fatwa that we must drive out the Americans. The solution to this crisis is the withdrawal of American troops ... *their military presence is an insult to the Saudi people.*[14]

What bin Laden is really saying is that Saudi Arabia is in the situation of a colony; that the Americans have robbed the Saudi people of their wealth and their potential for economic development; and that the monarchy's sizeable revenue from oil exports is no longer enough to offset a budget deficit that has become structural as a result of massive expenditure on an ineffective defensive arsenal as well as the hefty bill for its security ($70 billion) that it had to pay following the first Gulf War in 1991.[15] That war was apparently directed against Iraq on behalf of Saudi Arabia, but bin Laden's view is that it was really waged against Saudi Arabia on behalf of the United States. Whereas the media war, the image war, was launched from the skies above Iraq, the *economic* war, the reality behind the war, unfolded within the Saudi financial apparatus and to the detriment of the Saudi state.

Bin Laden's dialectical inversion is worthy of the writings of the early Marx: the Gulf War, 'which [contrary to appearances] was waged by America against the Saudi people', becomes the starting point for a total mobilization against the United States. Robert Fisk concludes his own remarks by arguing that bin Laden 'wanted an end to the dictators installed by the Americans, men who supported United States policy while repressing their own people. And I had the impression that for millions of Arabs it was a strong message.'[16] It was strong because it was cast in the bronze of a clear argument, simply and effectively anti-imperialist; strong because it was soaked in an Islamic rhetoric more accessible to the vast majority of Muslims than all the discourses imported from the West (including the discourse of anti-imperialism itself); strong because bin Laden's 'man in the street' spoke neither English nor French and because the language of human rights or scientific socialism was as alien to him as the language of the Koran is to the Parisian man in the street; and strong because it touched a hugely sensitive chord in the Arab world, one that makes people quiver at any mention of the double standards whereby the United States gives to Israel and Kuwait but takes from the Palestinians and Lebanese, defends the oil emirates but turns a blind eye to the massacre of Iraqi Shiites ten or twenty miles from Kuwait City, fails to say what it does or to do what it says.

It seemed necessary, at the beginning of this book, to touch again on the significance of the events on 11 September 2001, which catapulted the kingdom of Saudi Arabia into the world headlines. We by no means take what bin Laden says at face value, but simply suggest that it may tell us more accurately than the diatribes of Western journalists and academics the real state of mind of those 'God-obsessed people', who may not be as obsessed as all that. The preliminary hypothesis coming out of this discussion will be that the attacks in New York and Washington were neither unprecedented events nor the first war of the twenty-first century. On the contrary, they were the last battle in the twentieth-century wars of decolonization. And, for Osama bin Laden, that means nothing other than the decolonization of Saudi Arabia itself.

A suburb of the West

Thus, instead of explaining Saudi Arabia by Islamism or vice versa, we prefer to limit ourselves to as accurate an account as possible of contemporary Saudi Arabia. We shall avoid the discourse of those who trace an unbroken cause-and-effect relationship between the religion and elites of Saudi Arabia and the kamikazes of 9/11. That kind of conception – 'Saudi contradictions had to find their solution in the picture windows of the World Trade Center' – can operate only as a *post factum* reconstitution and has no scientific value. It is a maximalist argument which, in our view, should be banished from serious analysis. Nor is there any room for the minimalist line taken by some Saudi leaders after 9/11: namely, that the group of deranged individuals who organized the attacks had no connection with the political and social situation inside their country. Neither an automatic result nor an isolated event: what, then, is the true relationship between 9/11 and Saudi Arabia?

In bin Laden's view, it was one episode in a war of national liberation. Does this mean that Arabia is that 'protected dictatorship' of which a former French diplomat to Riyadh wrote in the mid-1990s?[17] At the heart of what President Eisenhower called 'the most important strategic zone in the world', because of its key position bridging Asia, Africa and Europe and its huge oil deposits, Arabia has aroused covetous looks from the United States since the 1920s. The alliance of the kingdom with the American superpower, signed and sealed in 1945 through a marriage of convenience, led in 1990 to a military occupation that was supposed to end with the second Gulf War but actually continued until April 2003. Yet the history of foreign domination in Arabia did not begin with the discovery of oil: between the eighteenth and twentieth centuries, Egyptians, Ottomans, French and British all attempted for various reasons to gain control over the country: whether the holy cities of Mecca and Medina, the southern marches of the Ottoman Empire, a strategic position on the route to the Indies, or an emblem of Arab purity and intransigence.

After 1933 the classical domination of the British Empire gradually gave way to the new-style domination of the United States, more economic and financial than directly political. This 'mild colonization' manifested itself in the recycling of petrodollars and the 'energy cushion' mechanism whereby Arabia, being able at any moment to flood a tense world market, ensured that oil prices remained within a certain range. It was also apparent in the economic backwardness of a country which, despite its new-found wealth, failed to escape its dependence on oil and did no more than the rest of the Arab world to diversify its economy.[18]

Rather than a 'protected dictatorship', then, Saudi Arabia appears as a suburb of the West, a production space deprived of the lasting fruits of its wealth, a zone of turbulence subject to Western policies which, in pursuit of strategic stability and the struggle against terrorism, have been massively geared for more than fifty years to security and police considerations. Arabia is a suburb of the West also because it is the object of symbolic as well as political and economic violence – that is, violence whose victims sometimes serve as auxiliaries, freeing their oppressors from any awareness of the domination they exert. Saudis suffer from this domination all the more since they hold, but are unable to use, the wealth and energy power that could be the instrument of freedom. This paradoxical frustration may be the reason why Saudis have clung more tenaciously than Arabs elsewhere to ideological forms that explicitly reject Western modernity, while they themselves have lived in close contact with it.

The strange proximity of Western modernity and a violent re-action against it is particularly shocking for Westerners, who do not understand how it is possible to consume in a Western way without adopting the values of the West, to study in the West without embracing its *Weltanschauung*, to both admire and hate Western civilization, to castigate its faults while sharing its aspirations. Generally seen as collusion between imported modernity and indigenous tradition, between consumerist society and 'Wahhabi' Islam, this proximity is further analysed as the main 'contradiction' of the Saudi kingdom – which eventually found its resolution in the attacks of 11 September.

It is against this simplistic explanation that the present book is directed. The first part explores the historical roots of contemporary Saudi identities, in the complexity of their regional, cultural, economic and religious components, and systematically contrasts external perceptions with the reality they address but do not always attain. The second part then looks at how not one but several political, administrative and economic powers came into being, and at how, in the course of the twentieth century, the dynamics of opposition to the regime overlapped with tribal, nationalist, socialist, communist and finally Islamist conceptions of the problems facing the country. The third part, devoted to a reading of the contemporary economy and society, tries to show at work the forces that the second part has painted on a historical canvas. How does modernity manifest itself in Arabia? How does it manage to escape the symbolic and real violence of the West? What is Saudi modernity? These are a few of the questions to which we have tried to find answers.

An inexperienced writer feeling his way around in the world of publishing knows more than anyone else to whom he owes the courage he pretends to flaunt. He owes it first of all to François Burgat, who never stinted on enthusiasm and advice and on several occasions offered him the hospitality of the Centre français d'archéologie et de sciences sociales in Sanaa, Yemen. All thanks for his boundless encouragement, his communicative energy and his immensely stimulating reading of texts.

The author also – above all! – owes his determination to his students and friends in Riyadh, who accompanied, guided and loved him at the beginning or end or throughout this work. He hopes that he has proved worthy of their confidence.

Antoine Aviat, Laurent Bonnefoy, Grégoire Carrier, Stéphane Durin, Jean-Baptiste de Froment, Stéphane Lacroix, Baptiste Lanaspèze, Nauf al-Mayman and Hélène Thiollet read, criticized, attacked, consoled, corrected and supported. Their incisive advice was very precious, and their presence, patience and indulgence quite indispensable.

Very many thanks to Houda Ayoub, Jean de Boishue, Hosham Dawod, Bruno Foucher, Muriel Genthon, François Gèze, Alain Gresh, Abdallah al-Khalifa, Claude Lorieux, Sabrina Mervin, Anne-Marie Moulin, Bernard Poletti, Sophie Pommier and Pascal Taranto for their encouragement, shared enthusiasm, generous assistance and sensible advice, which – he hopes – helped the author to grow a little.

Finally, the author would like to express his gratitude to a number of researchers he has never met, his elders who gave rhythm to his life and to the writing of this book; their pioneering theses reinforced his own conjectures, and their research gave some consistency to his hypotheses. The author stood on the broad shoulders of Kiren Aziz Chaudhry, Mamoun Fandy, Madawi al-Rasheed, Modj-ta-ba Sadria and Alexei Vassiliev. Everything true here is due to them; only for the errors does the author claim all the responsibility.

PART I

The construction of identities

I

The island of the Arabs

Deceived by the loquacity of the Arabs, Europeans
have at all times formed a fantastic opinion of that
unknown and calamitous land.

Charles Doughty

The other country

In one of the finest novels ever written on immigration, Ibrahim
Abdel-Meguid tells the story of Ismael, an Egyptian who went to
work in Saudi Arabia.[1] From his first contact with the 'other country'
until his final separation from it, Ismael goes through the stages of a
veritable odyssey leading from refusal to acceptance, from voluntary
detention to freedom, from solitude to love.

When he arrives in Tabuk, a small town in north-western Arabia,
Ismael is determined to keep apart from things and people, shut up
within his own little treasury of silence. But he gradually comes into
contact with other immigrants – Egyptians, Pakistanis, Sri Lankans,
Yemenites, Thais – then with Saudis, especially Mansur, an arche-
typal young idler from the golden years of the oil boom, who
carries around his boredom and disdain wherever he goes, with a
young monkey on his shoulder as a protective genie. In the end
Ismael succumbs to the charm of Arabia's mysterious geography
and shimmering apparitions. Literally enchanted, he finds salvation

through women: the American Rosemary, the Egyptian Aida and especially the Saudi Wadha, whose very name ('the evident') indicates that she will show her lover the hidden face of Arabia, the country where one loves, sins and lives. If Saudi Arabia 'makes you forget your father and mother', Ismael understands at the end of the novel that this very forgetting is an illusion, that the kingdom is enchanted only because 'nothing makes you forget anything'. 'Tabuk does not make you forget either father or mother.... In fact, it is strangers who come here in search of oblivion.'[2]

In a sharp break with uncritical academic literature on the rigorist influence that the Saudi regime dreams of exercising in the Muslim world, Abdel-Meguid shows that although you can try to save your soul in Arabia you can also lose it there, that Arabia only really offers what you take to it. Just like a photographic developer, it is an opaque liquid medium where a worker passing through encounters nothing other than himself. Abdel-Meguid therefore shows that, far from being the soil of absolute Islamic truth, Arabia is the land of distorted images, of the plausible and the illusory. He is the anti-Lawrence of Arabia: whereas the British officer sees only black and white, heaven and earth, holiness or sin, the Egyptian writer perceives minute differences and imperceptible nuances. Gradations and variations are everywhere, as in the glistening 'red-ochre mountains rising in tiers' around Medina, which are like 'a silent, motionless guardian protecting the city from the vicissitudes of time'.[3]

The land we are about to enter is therefore not one of those places that can be criss-crossed in a weekend or a week, rucksack on your back, camera around your neck, guidebook in your hand, with the satisfaction that you will be able to return home with a clear opinion about it. Arabia is not a tourist destination, and for good reason: there is no sense of disorientation here, except in the vastness of its expanses; not even much exoticism, except for the sight of women in black and men wrapped in white and red. It is all motorways, expressways, giant roundabouts, rest areas, packed restaurants, airports, café terraces, urban flowerbeds, sprawling city suburbs. Constantly thrown back on himself, a foreigner feels surprised to be hating himself and the country that treats him so harshly. In any event, with the exception of writers, who by nature keep a watch on themselves, everyone returns from Arabia as in a dream, exhausted and happy despite everything to find a tangible reality again. The 'magic kingdom' has kept itself hidden, and a prize is due to anyone who can give the key to the dream in a few pages.

We therefore need to take a few precautions. Let us first say that, from London to Paris and Washington, from Peshawar to Kuala Lumpur and Dacca, from Cairo to Casablanca and Damascus, Saudi Arabia is seen as an isolated country whose exceptional nature can be summed up in two words: Islam and oil. The image is of a monstrous uncreated country stretching its Islamic and financial tentacles over a large part of the globe. Separated from the Middle East by a belt of deserts, cut off from the world by the seas surrounding it on three sides, the 'Island of the Arabs'[4] and Saudi Arabia (which occupies four-fifths of the peninsula) appear to be a land outside human time. A deafening silence stretches across the centuries separating its two momentous revolutions: the birth of Islam in the seventh century and the discovery of oil in the twentieth. 'Arabia sleeps for a thousand years and triggers a catastrophe each time it awakes' – this witticism of a Riyadh intellectual summarizes rather well the illusions and fears that surround the Saudi hydra, a land forgotten by men, where, from time to time, God strikes the earth with his fist.

Islam and oil are at the root of the contradictory, fear-inducing image that Arabia presents to outsiders. It is the home of Islam, the launching pad for Arabization of the Middle East, the land of origins and authenticity celebrated by every Arab who claims to come from one of the two lines of Arabhood: Adnan and Qahtan.[5] At the same time, however, Arabia is the land of the *nouveaux riches*, the Arab country closest to the United States and to American policy in the Middle East. The Western world, the Muslim world and the Arab world are curiously agreed on these few points: Arabia is at once mythical origin and fallen reality. As one Lebanese journalist put it, 'Arab intellectual circles have for too long cultivated stereotypes about Saudi society, seeing it as a mixture of Bedouinhood and surface modernity. These prefabricated ideas do the country an injustice.'[6]

Nevertheless, when the origin appears to make a comeback in reality, when the myth seems broken through degeneration, when

Islam makes use of oil money, everyone concurs that it is necessary to eradicate if not Saudi Arabia itself, then at least the 'simplistic, bellicose and totalitarian' Islam that it supports,[7] and the oil that serves as ammunition for this weapon. In a work that appeared in 2002, the director of France's Observatoire des pays arabes, Antoine Basbous, made himself the herald of this overhasty view:

> To measure and ward off the threat hovering over the world, it is necessary to turn to Saudi Arabia.... How will America treat an ally whose ulema glorify and fund the total war that is being waged against it? How can a country be 'neutralized' when its subsoil holds a quarter of the world's reserves of black gold? These are some of the questions posed for the West.[8]

The fantasies of outside perception

What accounts for this stubborn failure to know Saudi Arabia? Why has this country, one of the most Westernized in the world, remained a 'black hole' for Western elites?[9] Why did America open its eyes wide after 9/11, pretending to have only just discovered that Saudi Arabia was not merely a 'big gas station to be pumped and defended but never to be taken seriously as a society'?[10] What accounts for this ignorance – when thousands of Americans have been living in Arabia since the 1950s; when the British have been regularly visiting the region for nearly two centuries; and when Western countries do big business with the kingdom, sending to Riyadh or Jeddah their experts, weapons, goods, turnkey factories, teachers and diplomats? The Saudi writer Ahmad Abodehman confidently claimed in the late 1990s that 'others understand us much more than we do ourselves'.[11] It is sad to see how wrong he was, now that 'others' have turned Arabia from a miraculous horn of plenty into something more like a monster.

We must therefore consider more closely how other nations have perceived Saudi Arabia since the 1950s, and identify the underlying errors of perspective that led the West to make such a mistake. How are Saudis seen outside the kingdom of Saudi Arabia? Whether viewed from the West, the Muslim world or the Arab world, they present roughly the same features, and this very convergence is a good example of the real isolation in which Saudi Arabia has been kept, despite the intense economic, cultural, human and financial exchanges in every direction.

Saudis are seen culturally as *Bedouins*, religiously as *fundamentalist Muslims* and socio-economically as *nouveaux riches*. In a book published in early 2003, a French journalist made these three features the backbone of Saudi identity. The picture he draws of Abdelaziz Al Saud, the founder of the present Saudi state, is particularly terse and mistaken: 'A Bedouin to the core of his being, he passionately loved the vast desert that was his domain. A strict Muslim, he had no need of any rhythm in his life other than that of the five prayers'[12] – whereas, in fact, Arab chroniclers of the nineteenth century tell us that the Saudi royal family had settled urban origins and should not be confused with any Bedouin tribe.[13] According to the same author, not only the royal family but 'the vast majority [of Saudis] are legitimist fundamentalists'.[14] Finally, 'easy money has transformed a Bedouin tribe into a multinational of waste.... Nothing is more difficult than to save money you own but have not earned.'[15]

The portrait is complete. Uncouth, fanatical and wealthy, the Saudi people seems at first sight to have all the ingredients of an explosive cocktail. For the ostensible identities are mutually exclusive: there is a contradiction between those whose identity is indexed to local particularisms (tribalism, for example) and those whose identity refers to a global pole (Islam or the market); and there is a second contradiction between those who define themselves in terms of Islam and those who prefer to identify themselves as capitalists. These two contradictions – local and global, Islamist and modernist – supposedly provide the keys for a reading of Arabia. The Saudi people, sunk in tribal particularism, finds universal expression only in a narrow and violent Islam, while the elites, suddenly grown rich on oil, travel from capital to capital unaware of the volcano on which they are sleeping. It is easy to infer from this picture that Arabia displays 'a fragile equilibrium between cosmopolitan elites and one of the world's most reactionary populations'.[16]

Contradiction between Bedouins, fundamentalists and nouveaux riches, contradiction between traditionalists and modernists: Saudi

Arabia is a country where people are always claiming to detect contradictions, and it is not easy to unravel such a nexus of problems without cutting right through them. The genealogy of 9/11 is supposedly clear: it was the remote resolution of Saudi contradictions, or Saudi Arabia's export of its own problems. Did 9/11 sound the knell for the whole messy business? Did it mark the sudden dissolution of all of Saudi Arabia's contradictions? Or did those contradictions not exist, rather, in the gaze that the West and the rest of the world turned on the kingdom? We are more inclined to accept the second hypothesis, so little does the picture drawn from afar and above correspond to reality.

Are Saudis Bedouins? This notion, repeated ad nauseam in every little article on Arabia, would bring a smile to the face of the most severe-looking Saudi and bring down lasting ridicule on anyone who echoed it at a dinner in Riyadh or Jeddah. It is wrong to think that Saudis can be defined by their tribal origin: the urban populations of Najd and Hijaz have been detribalized for a number of centuries. The idea that they are all Bedouins is absurd, since Arabia has traditionally been inhabited by Bedouins and settled populations: nomads, oasis or coastal plain farmers, city merchants and craftsmen. The outside imagination has kept a place only for the Bedouins, more exotic and infinitely more unusual in our eyes than the farmers, small breeders, craftsmen and shopkeepers who always formed the bulk of the population until the 1930s, until the foundation of the Kingdom of Saudi Arabia and the discovery of oil.

The supposedly Bedouin character of Saudis seems after all to correspond to an axiological judgement, and ethnographic description of the Bedouins is often no more than a disguised normative discourse: the Bedouin is surly, keeps his women locked up, is unfit for work, and so on. 'With a few rare exceptions,' we read in Marchand, 'Saudis are completely incapable of operating within a private company geared to performance and profit.... A Bedouin and poet in his soul, each Saudi dreams of himself as a chief and is loath to occupy anything other than a managerial position. He is rarely capable of it.'[17] As a counterweight to their gratuitous spite, Saudis are allowed a love of poetry and that convivial spirit which accompanies the 'legendary' hospitality of the Bedouins. But the

'Bedouin argument' essentially serves to cover up the hatred or contempt lurking in the vivid colours of exoticism. Not only does the exoticism involve an ethnological distortion; its covert moral judgement is too crude to be really convincing. It is rather like saying the French spirit is derived from the 'turbulent behaviour' of the Gauls, or the German spirit from the coarseness of the Germanic tribes. In short, the strategem does not work.

The Saudi, then, is not a Bedouin, even if Bedouin identity has in certain places remained all the more alive for no longer corresponding to any economic, political or social reality. In other words, what Saudis retain from Bedouinism (an uncluttered image, a memory of great inter-tribal epics and a poetry inspired by them) bears no relationship to the way in which Westerners conceive of Bedouin life (violence, misogyny, sloth); Bedouinism is an object of collective memory, not a structure still shaping social and political relations.

Next, are Saudis really fundamentalists? Before 9/11 Saudi Islam was described as rigorist and literalist; since 9/11, in the Western imagination, Saudis are not just highly conservative Muslims but have come to occupy the place left vacant by the Bolshevik with a knife between his teeth or the capitalist octopus strangling the world. Not merely savages, they are also dangerous Islamists whose financial power fills the coffers of many a radical movement, many a tendentious mosque, many a terrorist network. A Saudi hand is supposedly at work everywhere: from the Algerian Islamist movements to the Palestinian Hamas, from Osama bin Laden in Afghanistan to Omar bin al-Khattab in Chechnya, from black Africa and Malaysia to French city suburbs and American ghettoes. Arabia would seem to be one of those boxes in which one shuts up a devil, and which, once opened, surprises us by the terror it causes.

The crudeness of this demonization of Saudi Arabia has already been mentioned in the introduction. But it is interesting to note that the argument governing the accusation of fundamentalism varies with the identity of those who put it forward. In the West it is readily thought that Saudi Arabia, being the cradle of Islam, is also the centre of the Muslim world, and that this 'factory of terrorists' is the source of all the global Islamist networks. If this idea is widely shared by Westernized Arab elites, especially in the Western-protected 'democracies', the reason is often that the regimes in place prefer to blame Islamist opposition to their rule on outside causes, instead of attributing it to real popular aspirations or the bankruptcy of their own policies:

> The refusal by all these regimes to recognize the profoundly endogenous character of the Islamist upsurge has led them, and their [Western] allies, to attribute an excessive role to intervention by their neighbours.... In Egypt, when it is not the confrontation between Muslims and Copts that produced Islam, it is supposedly the immigration to Saudi Arabia.[18]

In the Arab and Muslim worlds, Saudi Arabia is regarded as a pro-Western and pro-American country. It is also perceived as a religious centre, because of the presence of the two sacred mosques in Mecca and Medina, but Saudi policy is seen through a prism that has nothing to do with religion and everything to do with its pro-Western orientation. In this reading, if fundamentalism does owe something to Saudi Arabia, it is more because of the alliance between Riyadh and Washington than because of a strictly Islamic option on the part of its rulers.

Abdolhassan Bani Sadr, president of the Islamic Republic of Iran between 1980 and 1981, well represents a widespread view in the Arab world that fundamentalism is a Western idea which the Saudis – rather unwillingly, given the great danger of a backlash – have merely put into practice.

> As Benazir Bhutto said, the idea for the Taliban was British, the management American, the money Saudi and the groundwork Pakistani! ... The function of fundamentalist discourse, as part and parcel of the ruling power, is to allow that power to say that violence is exported from the non-Western world to the West, whereas in reality the West is the source of the violence that is turned against it.[19]

Although Arabia is fundamentalist in each version, it is so in dia-metrically opposite ways: for the West, it is by nature and tradition the cradle of terrorist Islam; for Arabs and Muslims, it is fundamentalist only in its subordination to the West.[20] In any event, the gap between Western and Muslim or Arab perceptions of the fundamentalist phenomenon should make us extremely cautious; at least it has the merit of showing up the inanity of one-way readings and essentialist analyses of Islam. The opposition between a 'bad' Islam of the Saudi desert and a 'good' Islam of coastal regions (the Mediterranean, for example) is only a myth so long as it rests on a metaphysics or an ethics rather than a precise social and historical analysis. As we pointed out in the introduction, it is precisely when we speak of religion that we must be most wary of the religious mode of argument affected by Western Islamologists, political analysts and journalists, which prefers incantation to evidence, the pleasure of diatribe to the labour of proof.

Finally, is the Saudi a nouveau riche? Or, in other words, is the only link between Saudis and nature the extraction of wealth they do not deserve? If Arabia is a vast desert unsuitable for endogenous economic development, then the discovery of oil could appear to Saudis only as a blessing, and to Westerners only as an injustice. Alas, the capitalist economy is in Europe and the United States, so can it be right that its main source of fuel is in Arabia?

To define Saudis as nouveaux riches, to mock their bad taste and lavish spending, is to give vent to this original resentment and perplexity at the whims of a thoroughly unjust nature. But it is also, in the end, to establish a continuum between the Bedouins and present-day Saudis. The Austrian Orientalist Sprenger once described the Bedouin as 'a parasite of the camel',[21] whose precarious condition and infertile land had condemned him to pillage and to a nomadic hunter-gatherer existence, clinging to an animal that provided him with milk, meat, leather, wool, urine and even, in case of extreme thirst, gastric fluid. And, if the Bedouin is a parasite of the camel, the emir oozing wealth and sensuality is a parasite of the West. This limpid equation follows from a picture of Arabia as the 'country where the primal role of the land has been lost to light and sky'[22] – and now to the subsoil and the wealth it holds. Saudis therefore could not recognize the primacy of the land: that is, of labour.

In the conception we have just outlined, the picture-book Bedouin differs only in degree from the Saudi living today. Both benefit from wealth produced by the labour of others – the others being, according to the period, Anglo-American oil corporations or the

immigrant workers who continue to supply Arabia with half its
manpower. In keeping with a work ethic that owes a great deal to
certain Protestant formulas, today's Saudis – and Semites in general
– are unworthy because their wealth does not come from labour.

A text by Hegel, who practised Orientalism without realizing
it, is emblematic for this idea of an unworthiness generated in the
wastes:

> With his herds Abraham wandered hither and thither over a
> boundless territory without bringing parts of it any nearer to him
> by cultivating and improving them. Had he done so, he would
> have become attached to them and might have adopted them as
> parts of his world. The land was simply given over to his cattle for
> grazing. The water slept in deep wells without living movement;
> digging for it was laborious; it was dearly bought or struggled
> for, an extorted property, a necessary requirement for him and his
> cattle [– a good that can only be dominated and with which it is
> impossible to play].... He was a stranger on earth, a stranger to the
> soil and to men alike.[23]

Nothing ties the man of the desert to a particular territory; his
life slips by, but on land lacking any thickness, which can be neither
turned over nor cultivated and is but the shapeless correlate ('boundless') of the senseless movement that it supports. No property is
possible, since man cannot put his stamp on the world and is content
to move among things that remain alien to him. Here, in a caustic
reversal, it is only animals that can really enter into contact with
nature. The extraction of water (it could also be oil) does involve a
certain domination, but nature at such depths is dead: it impresses
its necessity on human beings without allowing them to play with
it and so prove their own freedom. Forced to dig laboriously for
water, they can neither create nor transform their environment: they
remain a cog in nature, unable to exert their will over it. They can
buy nature or conquer it by force, but they cannot transform it.
Abraham is thus a stranger because of his idle relationship to the
world, an idleness that is paradoxically the corollary of laborious
toil. It is toil, not work, because nothing in his activity corresponds
to another goal than his own self-preservation; nothing permits him
to free himself through his own activity.

Replace Abraham with 'Bedouin' or 'nouveau riche', and Hegel's text provides the skein of an economic interpretation of traditional Arabia, according to which its infertile soil chained people to necessity and exempted them from all work. It is but one step from this Orientalist vision to the idea that Arabs are eminently unworthy to give form to matter, to create something new, to deserve their wealth. That step is gladly taken by certain economic readings of the rentier state,[24] which identify a state that draws its revenue from oil as an idle state and a nation that imports its goods and labour as a nation of incompetents; Saudi Arabia ends up an economic excrescence of the West. Behind the hackneyed image of Saudi philistinism, then, lie a formidable political theory and an apparatus for the justification of the West's exploitation of Saudi wealth.

Contempt for history

Beyond their various factual errors, these three definitions of Saudi identity concur in their essentialist grounding of Saudi politics and society, whether upon a culture (Bedouinism), a religious form (fundamentalism) or an economic phenomenon (miraculous wealth). Eminent specialists in the Middle East (Georges Corm, in particular[25]) have pointed to the dangers of such readings, which are as absurd as an attempt to interpret the whole of the French Republic in terms of the revolutionary Terror, or monarchy as a strict application of theories of divine right, or socialism as a practical implementation of the writings of Marx, Engels and Lenin.

It is therefore astonishing that many recent works on Saudi Arabia throw all caution to the winds and, instead of reforming the vague ideas we have about the country, are anxious to make them grow and prosper. The essentialism of these authors is also evident in their scant regard for history and geography – in fact, most of the books dealing with Saudi Arabia are unconscious works of history and geography, and this allows their authors to make such crude mistakes as to think of the Saud family in Bedouin and tribal terms.

The Bedouin – the first fantasy in the outside perception of Saudi Arabia – is reduced to an ahistorical 'type' with clear-cut moral characteristics, a type to which contemporary Saudis (whether

Bedouin or settled by origin, nomadic, rural or urban by tradition) are expected to conform. Similarly, the smug accounts of Saudi rigorism set out to display its deeply reactionary side:[26] Saudi fundamentalists thus appear as inveterately backward-looking towards the early days of Islam (the age of the Prophet's companions) or, closer to our own time, the middle of the eighteenth century, when the first Saudi state was formed through an alliance of the 'sabre' and the 'turban', military force and religious authority. In any case, Saudi Islam is presented as fundamentally medieval.

Most of the literature presents Saudi Islam as a ragbag of disparate quotations from the Koran, school textbooks and theological or moral pamphlets written by contemporary ulema.[27] It is rather as if, to explain the attitude of Israelis to their Palestinian neighbours, one were to keep quoting the most violent passages from the Torah and holding aloft the least accommodating statements by such and such a member of the Israeli far right. The reasoning seems to be that, if the fundamentalist quest for a model in the darkest past leads Saudis to erase history, why not erase history ourselves and make Saudi Islam an essence in the heaven of ideas?

Finally, with regard to the nouveaux riches, the argument is that they could not have a history because they were born with the oil wealth that submerged Saudi Arabia in the last third of the twentieth century. With no past, no culture and no education, the rich Saudi's only history is that of his frenzied consumption of everyday goods and luxury items. As to intellectuals – the writers, academics and students – it is so difficult to fit them into any of the above three categories that they are usually passed over in silence.

Unfortunately, those who direct their gaze at Saudi Arabia from outside tend to pass without warning or justification from one explanatory key to another, evoking either the overwhelming force of Saudi references to the past or, on the contrary, the lack of a historical culture. It is regrettable that this reading uses totally diverse prisms, without ever justifying them or reporting their joint use. Yet it is impossible to read Arabia as if it existed only in the past or were totally devoid of historical background. The two frameworks, though quite incompatible with each other, rest upon the same disregard for time and history.

As Ibn Khaldun wrote in the fourteenth century about the method-ology of Arab historians:

> They are content to weave on the same loom as their predecessors. They take no account of the changes that the march of time brings to circumstances and customs. Their presentation of past dynasties and events is as empty as a sheath without a blade, and their science is insubstantial since we cannot tell from it what is true and what is false.[28]

Do we not hear today that, for a Muslim, the passing of time is of no significance, or that history has no meaning and is cancelled by destiny? But also that Muslims are fatalistic and that nothing has changed in this respect with the sudden flow of wealth? Do various authors not show that a nouveau riche becomes mired in the eternal present of consumption and idleness, where nothing is transformed or created except new needs requiring immediate satisfaction? Or, finally, is there not a belief that Bedouins, with no attachments or place they can call home, are trapped inside a thick layer of tradition like an insect in a block of amber?

How is the contradiction to be resolved? Mostly it is not resolved at all, and here lies the root of the incoherence of Western accounts of Arabia. The opposition between tradition and modernity is simply left in place – between a necessarily stifling tradition and a modernity that is naturally devoid of memory. Saudis are thought of as being caught in a crossfire, between a reactionary official clergy obsessed with the birth of Islam and amnesiac businessmen or modernists glued to satellite television. This time criterion is then used to distinguish two strongly pronounced attitudes: 'Bedouin' or 'funda-mentalist' traditionalism and 'Western-style' modernism. No interest is shown in the fact that, for example, Bedouin traditionalism is a recent invention and does not correspond to anything in the lived experience of Saudis of Bedouin origin, not to speak of other Saudis. Nor is it imagined that the city is anything but an imported novelty, whereas in fact urban civilization in Arabia goes back to early antiquity and is a structuring element in Saudi, Arab and, more generally, Muslim identity.

Only history can allow us to unravel the tangle of meanings, to distinguish between the traditions of real experience and the

traditionalism invented by modernity, or between genuine modernity and a modernism that is only a servile imitation of Western
behaviour. The first thing to be done, therefore, is to acknowledge
the right of Saudi Arabia to a history.

The abolition of geography

This also means giving its due to Saudi geography, which is too often
obscured beneath the fable of Arabia as a 'kingdom of the sands'
lacking density or diversity, a desert suddenly inundated with riches.
The geography is in fact an unconscious history: the only criterion
by which it operates is the discovery of oil, so that the history of
Arabia and its physical and human geography are divided into two
great periods: before and after petroleum. Before, the age of surface
and desert. After, the age of subsoil, oil and gas. A whole set of
images plays upon this opposition – from the photos showing a
desert crossed by camels and cadillacs, to others of an immaculately
dressed Bedouin with flashy sunglasses. We must have done with
this idea of a featureless milieu from which oil and dollars one day
gushed forth, have done with a miraculous conception of space and
time, with the 'miracle among the sands' to which Saudi Arabia is
too often reduced.

   The desert has also often been the background for conceptions
of Islam, as the opening sentence in a famous work of geopolitics
well illustrates: 'Islam was born in the desert.'[29] The presupposition
is all the stranger as the city-dwelling Prophet Mohammed felt
nothing but contempt for the Bedouins and those who lived in the
desert, and he could receive the revelation only in the great trading
towns of Hijaz that were already imbued with Jewish and Christian
monotheism.[30] Yet, from Hegel to Planhol, the derivation of Islam
from the harshness of the desert has become a trope of Orientalism
and, more particularly, of culturalist explanations applied to the
Arabian Peninsula. 'From a crude and undifferentiated raw material,
the desert brought forth the three most consummate human types
of the Arab world: the warrior, the poet and the saint':[31] Abdelaziz
Al Saud, Imrul-Qais[32] and the Prophet Mohammed, who, out of
formless matter, created political, literary or religious form.

In a desert metaphysics with rather blurred contours, various authors have therefore painted a picture of a truly non-terrestrial Arab land, a mineral universe to which a molten sky imparts the harshness and simplicity of slowly wrought materials, a mythical country where spirit gives form to matter through the movement of armies, the movement of poetic composition and the movement of the divine word. As no sense of belonging could distract men from their empty contemplation, it seems inevitable that the great monotheisms should have been born there. Nature itself having fallen silent, absolute desert had to pour forth the most awesome of monotheisms, Islam, the roughest of languages, Arabic, and the most violent of empires, the Saudi state.

The imagined anthropology of Saudi Arabia is therefore based upon a fantastic geography of uniform desert wastes, one that makes it possible to reduce Saudi identities to the simple equation of 'life in the desert'. In reality, however, Arabia is made up of very different regions in which several populations exist alongside one another, bordered by desert that occupies no more than a third of the land surface. The rest consists of oases, mountains, wadis, steppe, high plateau scrubland, and Mediterranean-type countryside on the Hijaz heights. The mountain climate in the south enables a few forests to flourish in Asir, while in the north Tabuk is on the edges of the olive-growing zone. The coasts also present great diversity: in the east, palm-fringed beaches and tamarisk forests further inland; in the west, wadis sloping sharply away from Hijaz and providing sufficient irrigation for traditional crops to create some of the appearance of a sub-tropical Burgundy.

The Arabian Peninsula is not so much desert as a huge plateau sloping from west to east – from the peaks of Hijaz and Asir (3,133 metres at the Jabal Sauda, the 'Black Peak') to the shimmering sandy shores of the Arabian–Persian Gulf, where ruined Portuguese and Turkish forts look out across a shallow sea to the high mountains of Iran. This huge plateau, the traditional centre of the Peninsula, is called Najd (Arabic for plateau and, by extension, a road on the side of a plateau). Najd is certainly arid but not a desert region: large wadis cut through it, the most notable being the Rummah wadi in the north (which has its source in the Medina area and flows a thousand kilometres down to join the Shatt Al Arab in Iraq), the Hanifa and Sahba wadis in the Riyadh area, and the Dawasir and Najran wadis in the south; Najd is also bisected in the middle by a huge limestone cuesta, the Jabal Tuwaiq ('small garland mountain'), which is a kind of backbone and reservoir of the Arabian interior. Endowed with subterranean reserves of water that well up to the surface, further freshened by rain and stream water, Najd has been an agricultural region since early antiquity, with an economy traditionally organized around irrigated crops, animal breeding, crafts and trade. It is therefore not easy to see how anyone can write:

> Sixty years ago, the economy of Saudi Arabia greatly resembled what it must have been like in the Middle Ages: tribes of Bedouin nomads raising camels and goats in the centre of the country, and embryonic trade on the edge of the Yemeni mountains.[33]

Today, most Saudis live in the four major populated areas:[34] Najd in the centre of the country, the oil-producing Hasa in the east, Hijaz on the Red Sea in the west, and Asir in the south-west. These areas straddle several geographical regions: mountain and plateau in Najd; desert, oasis and coast in Hasa; mountain and coastal plain in Hijaz and Asir. Bedouin civilization first emerged in the steppe, desert and homogeneous areas on the edge of these four major' regions; sedentary civilization spread in the cracks, the intersections, the heterogeneous spaces. Thus, in 1932 oil started to gush forth in a country that was made up of several historically and geographically constituted countries, and not by some miracle from the nothingness to which so many have tried to reduce it.

One of the aims of this book is to resituate Saudi Arabia in its true history and geography, without resorting to the crude images that filter through abroad. The history will be considered especially in Chapters 2, 3 and 4, in connection with Saudi Islam and the construction of the state. Human and political geography will be the theme of Chapters 6, 7 and 8 and the Conclusion, in connection with the large-scale urbanization of contemporary Saudi society and the geopolitics of Saudi Arabia.

An unattainable national identity?

The interpretive frameworks we have just been considering mainly serve to obscure the question of Saudi national identity, in accordance with a common tendency among Orientalists to 'ethnicize' or 'Islamicize' political analysis of the contemporary Middle East. This reduction of politics to one of these factors (Bedouin ethnicity or Islamic religion) often conceals political motives: Western policy in the Middle East has traditionally sought to play off different ethnicities and religions against one another. Why should this not also be the case for Saudi Arabia, when, as we shall see, the contemporary Saudi state is partly the result of British imperial support for the House of Saud?

Nowadays, political or geopolitical analysis that tends to play off regions against each another (Najd and Hijaz, for example) or religions against each another (Shiites and Sunnis) often has behind it a project to partition Arabia. In December 2002 a report circulating in Washington precisely argued for the dismemberment of Saudi Arabia into three states (Hijaz, Najd and Hasa), invoking either religious differences (Hasa is traditionally Shiite), cultural-historical factors (Najd and Hijaz have traditionally been 'distinct') or economic considerations (Hasa, in the east of the kingdom, is the oil-producing region). Such discourses, though ostensibly scientific, actually serve a disguised strategic purpose. Sometimes this is cynically recognized to be the case, as when a French expert living in the United States wrote:

> We [the United States] could easily occupy the oil fields, most of which are in the Eastern Province; all we would have to do is dig up the invasion plans dating from the 1970s. The operation would only take a few days. Then we would see what to do; the province might be turned into a new state or annexed to Bahrain.[35]

The conventional and sometimes dangerous images we have just been considering locate the key to Saudi identity in the local culture (Bedouin tribalism) or a global culture (Islam plus a rather narrow capitalism), but rule out any notion that Saudi identity might be defined in national terms. The common denominator in these three readings of Arabia is thus the impossibility that Saudis should ever think of themselves as Saudi. A conservative Saudi thus becomes a Bedouin or an Islamist, while a modern-minded Saudi will be a nouveau riche or a globalized capitalist. In any event, the issue of national identity is obscured, since there is no idea that Saudis might see themselves otherwise than through a supranational (Islam, world economy) or infranational (Bedouin, ethnic or regional affiliation) referent.

In these readings, a Saudi is never really Saudi but always something more or something less: globalized Islamist, neocapitalist or, on the contrary, Najdi, Shiite or Bedouin. It may be granted that Saudis are beginning to think of themselves as a nation, thanks to the bodily reflex involved in such phenomena as identification with the national football team. But that does not mean they are allowed any national identity. How could it be otherwise? Are we not speaking of a dictatorship, a regime in which liberties are absent, national sentiment is by definition non-existent, and people are 'completely lacking in what a Westerner calls political awareness'?[36] Are we not speaking of disparate provinces (Hijaz, Asir, Najd and Hasa) that the British only recently squeezed together within artificial frontiers? The very idea of a Saudi 'nation' is suspected of being an ideological construct, an image that the regime, for the sake of form and propaganda, pinned to a reality consisting of particularisms either inherently unsurpassable or sublimated in a global entity. Hence the metaphor: the Sauds are sitting on a cauldron filled with various ingredients, some of them more than a little toxic. Saudi Arabia would thus seem to be the opposite of a melting pot in which a new identity can be built. Between regionalism and globalization, what can be the status of Saudi national identity?

Chapter 2 will examine the Islamic reference and its complex relationship with national sentiment. For the moment, however, let us assess the regional, religious and cultural divisions to which so many authors try to reduce the Saudis. What is a good point of entry into the issue of Saudi identity? If Arabia is that 'deeply divided' country of the Orientalist imagination, which are the most pertinent criteria of division? The interpretive frameworks that we shall now consider are more elaborate than the previous group:

they reduce Saudi Arabia to two principles, not just a single one (Bedouin, religious or economic). We may call these frameworks 'dualist', since they perceive in the complex play of Saudi identities an opposition between two forces: Bedouin and sedentary, Sunni and Shiite, Najd and periphery.

Bedouin and sedentary

Saudi Arabia has traditionally been made up of a Bedouin and a sedentary population, *badu* and *hadhar*: literally 'those who suddenly appear' (and just as suddenly disappear) and 'civilized people'.

In the fourteenth century, in his *Discourse on World History*, Ibn Khaldun showed that 'Bedouin and sedentary are natural groups, for whom necessity becomes a [cultural or political] law':[37] no Bedouin spirit, no sedentary spirit and no mythology about Arabhood, therefore, but a simple statement that the sedentary and Bedouin ways of life are two adaptations to two necessities, two distinct natural environments. Nomad mobility takes possession of a poor and vast territory; sedentary immobility makes it possible to belong to a richer and less extensive land.

If environment is the natural criterion for a distinction between the two groups, what is the social criterion? Should we say that the Bedouins but not the sedentary population are characterized by tribal organization? That would not be correct, because there are sedentary tribes. Or is the criterion economic activity: pastoralism among the Bedouins, agriculture and commerce among the sedentary population? That does not seem to be true either: pastoralism was also practised by the sedentary population; Bedouins were crucial players in the large-scale caravan trade and often owned arable land, which farmers cultivated in return for the payment of tribute. The distinguishing social criterion seems, rather, to be the power that Bedouins traditionally held over the sedentary population, since the large Bedouin tribes long had the advantage of superior force, territorial depth, mobility and speed. Necessity 'became law', both for men of the steppe and for oasis farmers, and this necessity was for a long time expressed in Bedouin social, political and symbolic domination over the sedentary population. Is this interpretive key applicable to contemporary Arabia? Is it relevant to a definition of Saudi identity?

First of all, the Bedouin–sedentary division has never been clear-cut: the two populations did not only live alongside each other but very often overlapped. Periods of exile and settled existence corresponded to the alternation of drought and plenty, so that any member of the sedentary population could find his way back into the desert, and many a Bedouin settled down for a time or even for good. The principle of adaptation to necessity governed these to-and-fro movements, and the richness of the soil remained the ultimate criterion for the reach of landed property. If rainfall became scarce, the tribes extended their *diras* (tribal territory) as far as Syria and the plains of the Fertile Crescent; but a return of the rains led the tribe to retrench around the newly recovered plenty. At the same time, sedentary victims of a lean year would also drift northward, abandoning their rooted way of life, whereas fat years would see the population of Najd oases swell with an inflow of Bedouins attracted by greater affluence.

Second, the meaning of the two terms has varied considerably over time. Today, only a Bedouin ascendancy gives distinction to a Saudi – although he will heap scorn readily enough on those who have actually remained Bedouins. It is good form to be descended from nomadism, but also to have left it firmly behind. This is the case particularly in the towns. In the countryside, the boundary between Bedouin and sedentary is open to novel kinds of reconstitution, as in those Wadi Dawasir oases 700 kilometres south of Riyadh, where well-born Saudis call themselves 'Bedouin' – whether they are of Bedouin or sedentary ancestry, former nomads or long-settled village people – and describe as 'sedentary' not only Arab or Asian immigrants but even other Saudis who for one reason or another have settled in the Wadi.[38] The noble connotation has remained uppermost, but here 'Bedouin' paradoxically means 'rooted' or 'propertied', while 'sedentary' refers to those who own nothing but their labour-power and have to move around in order to live (more or less equivalent to 'immigrants' or 'proletarians'). Town-dwellers, on the other hand, are content with a few conventional remarks that conjure away history by fixing it in a broadly painted image. For, whatever some say, the great historical turning point is not the oil-driven victory of the Arabian desert over the cities of the Mediterranean and the Fertile Crescent but the revenge of the Arabian town-oases over the desert of the Bedouins.

As we see, it is impossible to apply the 'traditional' dialectical concepts of a Bedouin–sedentary division and 'asabiya (group spirit, tribal solidarity), without contextualizing them and tracing the changes resulting from social practice. In any event, the recomposition of these concepts means that we cannot use them without a prior critique, nor identify distinct geological layers within the Saudi imagination, as if the premodern state (in which the Bedouin–sedentary distinction did operate) had left a few scattered outliers of traditionalism where camel-riding Bedouins are so backward that they differ little from those observed by Ibn Khaldun seven hundred years ago.

As our contemporary reading of the terms 'Bedouin' and 'sedentary' has shown, we have to conceptualize the distinction between the two on the basis of an objective social, economic and political situation, and not conceptualize the social, economic and political reality of Arabia on the basis of concepts borrowed from Ibn Khaldun. Georges Corm made this point before us: 'Islam, Bedouinhood, 'asabiya as popularized by Ibn Khaldun and gleefully adopted by present-day anthropologists: these are the recurrent themes used to explain the repeated failure of state modernity in the Middle East.'[39]

Third, the Bedouin–sedentary distinction was – contrary to a widespread view – challenged by state-led modernization and the huge shift to sedentarism in the course of the twentieth century. Beginning in the 1910s, the government pursued a policy of eliminating the strong tribal counterweights to its power, assisted in this by the setting of frontiers between the areas previously opened up. To block the movement of tribes was to force them into a settled way of life; to bring them under common law was to diminish their prestige and to prevent them from more than sporadically disturbing public order to their own benefit.[40] It was therefore not the Bedouin–sedentary division that stymied the development of political modernity, but the administrative modernity of the Saudi state that got the better of the Bedouin population and thereby cancelled the traditional opposition between Bedouin and sedentary.

Sunnis and Shiites, Najd and periphery

Does the religious division have any meaning? Saudi Arabia, a country with a Sunni majority, also has a sizeable Shiite minority estimated at between 5 and 10 per cent of the total population. The Sunnis are themselves divided into Hanbalites in Najd and Shafeites, Malikites and Hanafites on the west coast of Arabia.

We should first note that, although Saudi Arabia is an Islamic state, the state religion is not defined as Sunni or Shia and still less in terms of one of the four schools of Sunni Islam (Hanafite, Malikite, Shafeite and Hanbalite). It is Islam *tout court*. Much as the state has watered down the figure of the Bedouin to provide Saudi national identity with one simple referent, so has it reduced religion to its lowest common denominator, Islam, with the declared aim of combating *fitna* (disunity, secession, break-up of the national community). The oppression of religious minorities that has been part of the process is a frequent source of concern for human rights organizations – although the violence against Shiite tombs in Hijaz and mosques in Hasa ceased a long time ago, and the regime often chooses to turn a blind eye to Shiite or Sufi religious practices.[41] Are the religious divisions superimposed upon geographical divisions? It is generally thought that the central province of Najd is Sunni Hanbalite, the western province of Hijaz is Sunni Shafeite, Malikite and Hanafite (therefore oppressed by Najd Islam since its annexation by Al Saud in 1926), and the eastern oil-producing province of Hasa is mostly Shiite.

These divisions (religious and geographical) should nowadays be put in perspective. For the barrier that long separated Sunnis from Shiites – a barrier reinforced by Saudi official mistrust of the big Iranian neighbour – no longer really exists anywhere else than in people's minds. Since the late 1990s Riyadh has pursued a new economic opening towards Tehran, and inside Saudi Arabia an agreement in 1993 between members of the Shiite Islamist opposition and the central government has led to the appointment of first one, then two Shiites from Eastern Province to the Majlis al-Shura, the Saudi consultative assembly. Finally, on 21 June 2003, Crown Prince Abdullah and the Sunni ulema of Najd recognized the existence of confessional diversity. This by no means implies that Shiites occupy a comfortable position within the majority Sunni state, but the two communities do now rub shoulders – even if they do not truly mix – in the same ruling circles, the same newspapers and universities.

The Sunni–Shia distinction has therefore lost much of its significance, especially as Shiites have for some time no longer been a geographically defined community: Saudis from all parts of the country have flooded into the Eastern Province, which contains the oil reserves, and Shiites have now lost their demographic preponderance there.

Is the division between Hanbalite Islam in Najd and Shafeite, Malikite and Hanafite Islam in Hifaz more consequential? There is something seductive about the picture of a rigorous Islam of the interior and a coastal Islam more open to outside influences (especially those coming from Egypt). Yet such characterizations no longer have any purchase since the aeroplane totally opened up Najd, to the point where Riyadh is a more cosmopolitan city than the highly cosmopolitan Jeddah itself. Besides, internal migration has made any distinction ineffectual, and it would be more useful to distinguish between degrees of religious practice than between Sunni theological schools. Finally, and most important, the opening of Najd Islam itself to Egyptian influences (especially the Muslim Brotherhood) has helped quite considerably to narrow the gap between Shafeite and Hanbalite.[42]

More generally, whereas the four major regions managed to preserve their quite distinct cultural identities until the 1970s, regional divisions have lost much of their significance since the oil boom of 1973 and the ensuing economic growth, galloping urbanization and massive flight from the countryside. Saudis are perhaps the most mobile Arabs inside their own country, because of the high-quality roads and cheap petrol, but also because of the recent dispersion that has separated current place of residence from traditional family roots and caused large numbers of people to spend time on the move. Thus, today's Saudis tend to define themselves more in terms of Saudi or Muslim identity, or even membership of the Gulf Cooperation Council,[43] than by their regional origin.

The disjuncture between Najd and periphery has nevertheless become an obligatory reference in Saudi studies, especially since 11 September 2001. Attempts have been made to show that the Saudi kamikazes, mostly from the 'Yemeni' province of Asir that was annexed to Najd in 1920, had radicalized as a result of their unenviable social position and insults to their regional identity. In reality, however, not only did regionalism play much less of a role than supranational Islamic identity in the mental genesis of the terrorists, but they had a high level of education and were reasonably affluent. A micro-economic reading of their actions is therefore not very convincing.

In view of the modernization of Arabia, the dividing line no longer runs between Najd and the periphery but between the large cities (Riyadh, Jeddah or the eastern metropolis of Dammam/Khobar/ Dhahran) and their respective peripheries, between the urban areas in general (85 per cent of the population) and the countryside.[44] It therefore seems misguided to explain 9/11 in terms of the encounter between Islam and regionalism, or indeed to read the Islamist opposition as the end result of religious, social, economic or regional causes. Rather, it should be understood as a fully fledged *political movement*: that is, a movement whose impulses are general and not deducible from any particularisms.

All the theories about supposed divisions actually breed determinism – a sense that it is impossible to understand the relationship between people and their society in terms of freedom, since Saudi identity (whether expressed within or against the state) can be reduced to a one-sided cultural, religious or economic determinant. Such analytic frameworks are no less essentialist than the ones we considered earlier, since they overdetermine one criterion to the detriment of all others, one opposition to the detriment of all possible compositions. Against all essentialist reductions of Saudi society, it will be necessary for us to read the country's politics in *political* rather than exclusively social, economic, religious or cultural terms.

Modernity and tradition

Let us return to the question we posed at the beginning of this chapter: why is Saudi Arabia so little known? Why are the frameworks used in the West for analysis of the kingdom so remote from its social, economic and political reality? Arabia shares with the rest of the Middle East the sad privilege of being at once the closest region to the European West and the one least understood by it. But this is not a sufficient explanation.

We also need to build into the picture the real ways in which Saudi Arabia is closed in on itself. This is not just a matter of its highly finicky visa policy or its close watch on journalists; after all, since 9/11 openness has become a general slogan and Saudis have never before seen so many Western journalists and Islamologists on their soil. But this openness does not mean that the many prejudices held by Westerners have vanished overnight – on the contrary, they do not seem to have been given up in any of the books published since 9/11 on Arabia.

The administrative closure of the kingdom to Western intellectuals and journalists does not therefore explain everything. A more powerful factor would seem to be the probability of *symbolic* closure, which has continued to manifest itself in the projection abroad of an *image* that does not correspond to social and political reality. Bedouinism? Islam? These really are the twin pillars of the image that the Saudi regime wishes to give of the country, as if a few crude icons were enough to *keep the West at a safe imaginative distance.*[45] It is, to say the least, paradoxical that the concepts used by the West to criticize Saudi Arabia are the very ones that the Saudi regime has forged for symbolic defence of the country under its sway; or that the West sees Arabia through a fog of culturalist or Islam-centred explanation that it likes to denounce but that remains the only one at its command.

This objective alliance between Western journalists and those they constantly hold to blame is sufficiently curious to be noted and borne in mind. The symbolic closure of Arabia that it highlights could therefore not disappear *pari passu* with the administrative closure. On the contrary: it may well be the case that the opening of Saudi

Arabia is producing a fresh outbreak of clichés about the subject, as in those over-visited countries about which travellers repeatedly pass on the same banalities and the same misconceptions.

We have already noted the paradox that the defective knowledge of Arabia is especially bound up with the fact that, for the last fifty years, it has housed one of the largest communities of Westerners outside the West. The problem is that these Westerners mostly live there as in a conquered land with which you just do not associate, reproducing at a distance of a few decades the reflexes of French people living in the Algiers area or the protectorate of Morocco. Unfortunately, then, the Saudi symbolic closure is matched by a no less pronounced Western closure. How many Europeans leave Arabia after a twenty-year stay without knowing more than a dozen words of Arabic? How many work, love and dream in Arabia without ever working for Arabia, loving Arabia or dreaming of Arabia? The resonance of the model of the 'little white man' explains a lot of misunderstandings. This attitude is more disturbing when it no longer comes from honest employees or engineers but from experts who claim to be bringing to light the truth about the country.

A journalist or academic arriving in Riyadh to learn the country's secrets must therefore immediately avoid all the traps, beginning with the trap of friendship. Whether he speaks French, Spanish, Portuguese, Italian, English or German, he will always come across Saudi intellectuals who are familiar with the ways of the West and can hold forth in his own language – often serving up phrases that have lost their edge through frequent repetition. Then there is the trap of the cities, which only gradually reveal themselves in a series of long walks, and which cannot be compared to blocks of Americanization transplanted to the desert. And finally he has to negotiate the trap of opaque, difficult, highly coded social relations, which require long familiarity before they can be roughly deciphered. For a European or American passing through, everything is new and magical, nothing really legible or understand-able. Rather more serious is the attitude of well-known experts who, having published texts on Arabia from afar and above, feel they have to visit the country to check what they have put together behind the doors of their office in New York or Paris. All this means that the opening-up process will be long, paradoxical and possibly counter-productive.

The difficulty of mutual understanding is certainly bound up with the long proximity between Arabia and the West. For the Western gaze, Saudi modernity is evidently a purchased import, and tradition is just as evidently endogenous and *sui generis*; or, in other words, modernity is Western and tradition is Islamic or tribal. Hence the endless journalistic and academic clichés counterposing Islamic allegiances and alliance with the United States, or West-worshipping modernists and Islamist traditionalists, or simply the rich and the poor. The lack of understanding perhaps has to do with a failure to imagine that modernity can be endogenous to Arabia and actually be conveyed there by Islam − that *Islam can stand in opposition to tradition*. There is a similar failure to imagine that *tradition can be imposed from outside* (by the state, by a ruling ideology, etc.), instead of being a visceral reaction to the West.

What can modernity be like in Arabia? In our view, it *already* manifests itself in the overcoming of the social and religious divisions, the economic, regional and ethnic divisions whose anachronistic character we have demonstrated above. It would be hard to end this chapter without quoting a passage by Ahmad Abodehman, a writer who, despite − or perhaps because of − the fact that he is originally from Asir and not really identifiable as a eulogist of the Saudi government,[46] brings out the true meaning of modernization Saudi style and the unprecedented opening that political and administrative centralization represented for the provinces.

The action takes place in the 1960s, when a communal religious school has just been opened by the education minister in the Asir village where Abodehman was born:

> The opening of the school overturned all the norms of village life. 'They' forbade us to carry a knife;[47] 'they' forced us to cut our nails, to wear shoes, to wash often, to obey the teachers from neighbouring Egypt, Jordan or Syria. Whereas the village had wanted to make of me a man in whom I would recognize nothing of myself, the kind of life conjured up at school was more in keeping with my inner life. I discovered myself completely within it; I was suddenly the best. At school I found what the village and

tribe had tried to erase: my reality. There the language[48] was different, richer, vaster than all the fields. There I felt in touch with
words, all words: I read them, wrote them, imagined them. There
we were simply boys.[49] ... School gave me a soul and a language.
I compiled a dictionary of all the words I had never heard in the
village and all that had previously had only a very limited meaning.
The words we learned were like so many voyages: the finest were
those offered us by poetry, history and geography. 'World' was one
of those I liked most.... Fathers suspected the school of making us
cowardly, and suspected the [Riyadh] government of storing up an
unhealthy future for the tribes.[50]

Those who still think of Arabia as a mixture of Islam and tribalism
plus a sprinkling of modernity may find it hard to imagine that a
religious school should open up children to the wider world and
involve radical criticism of tribal traditions. But, at the risk of being
accused of over-optimism, we would argue that the way outlined
by Abodehman is the one we should follow, in the hope of understanding Arabia better than it understands itself.

2

What is Wahhabism?

> The Wahhabi sect still arouses serious concerns,
> and everything to do with its origins and existence
> excites great curiosity.
>
> Le Moniteur, 9th Brumaire, Year XIII

In the first half of the eighteenth century, central Arabia underwent a religious reformation and a political revolution within the space of a few years. The religious reformation was the one that Muhammad ibn Abd al-Wahhab[1] started in the Hanbalite Islam of the central Arabian Peninsula; the political revolution resulted from his alliance with Muhammad ibn Saud, the prince of a modest oasis in Lower Najd.

The reforms of Muhammad ibn Abd al-Wahhab

The religious reform movement known as Wahhabism was the first to appear in modern Islam. Orientalists point out that the renewal of Islam, driven by interpretation (ijtihad) of the sacred texts of the Koran and Sunna (collections of the Prophet's deeds and words), had exhausted itself by the fourteenth century, its last great figure being Taqi al-Din bin Taymiyya (1263–1328).[2]

There were a number of reasons for this closure of Islam around a fixed corpus of texts and set of customs. The most important, no doubt, was that the successive capitals of Islam (Baghdad, then Istanbul) disseminated a form of religion which was more and more akin to dedicated service of the ruling caliph or sultan. In this connection, Ottoman rule in the Middle East strengthened the technocratic and narrowly procedural tendency of state Islam, so that the destiny of the Arab peoples, though no longer spurred on by religious fervour, continued to be written in the language of Islam and to embrace its codes and directions. These peoples no longer had a history of their own; they were at best one peripheral area of an empire that stretched across three continents and, at its eastern limits, bordered on the Chinese world.

In its archaic inflexibility and ceaseless pursuit of autonomy, the movement known as Wahhabism was a reaction to the imperial Islam of the Ottomans and thus an original affirmation of Arab nationalism. This first reform of modern times opened a new history in which, from the nineteenth century on, numerous fresh starts were attempted in the Arab and Muslim world. It also gave one Arab people an endogenous history, and, above all, it placed Arabia back in world history, after its eviction from it in the eighth century and the shift in the centre of gravity of Islam to the plains of the Fertile Crescent.

Muhammad ibn Abd al-Wahhab was the son of a qadhi (judge) from Uyayna, a small town in Lower Najd that has by now been swallowed up as a suburb of Riyadh. Born in 1703, he studied Koranic sciences with his father, made the pilgrimage to Mecca, continued his studies for a while in Medina, then travelled in the lands bordering on Arabia, to Basra, Baghdad and perhaps Kurdistan and Damascus. It was doubtless in Basra, an Ottoman dependency, that he began to preach – and in any event he was soon banished from the town by the religious and political authorities. After his return to Najd in the 1730s, he went to be with his father in Huraymala, a few dozen kilometres north of Uyayna, where he wrote the Kitab al-Tawhid (the Book of Monotheism). It was during this period that his ideas began to spread in Najd and he became a celebrated figure there; his religious positions sparked off an animated debate.

A great deal has been written about the Book of Monotheism, some likening it to a collage of quotations with no driving spirit of its own, others to a violent diatribe filled with the crude simplicity and fanaticism that many in the West, following the first European travellers to the region, ascribed to the inhabitants of central Arabia. The content of the book does indeed have nothing original: it is a collection of quotations from the Koran and the Sunna. The content of the Book is the revealed word. Abd al-Wahhab was not really a commentator; he compiled quotations in the manner of the craftsmen of classical Arabic literature (*adab*), whose talent it was to have mastered the art of palimpsest, the rewriting, copying and exposition of texts handed down to them.

In the same way that classical Arabic literature is passed on by the word of mouth whose native freshness it seeks to transcribe, so is the Book of Monotheism shot through with the transcendence of divine quotation. Abd al-Wahhab's original contribution comes down to his ordering of quotations and his constant, often imperative, appeals for meditation in the résumés at the end of each chapter, which serve as much to jog the memory as to set out a spiritual exercise.

From appeal to appeal, from quotation to quotation, the rhythm carrying the book along is one of orderly meditation. Although the chapters in the *Kitab al-Tawhid* do not, like Descartes's *Metaphysical Meditations*, follow the path of individual consciousness towards the truth, they show how fragmentation of the revealed truth should arouse personal effort (*jahd, jihad*) on the part of the believer. Textbook, reference book and combat manual, the *Kitab al-Tawhid* is written in a hurried, urgent language. Its call for inner *jihad*, for struggle against obscurantism and idolatry, has only one aim: to liberate Muslims from false gods, idols or images; to take Islam back to pure contemplation of the one God; to restore to religion its radical transcendence.

The content of the *Kitab al-Tawhid* is therefore very simple and may be summarized in one short sentence: 'The distinctive feature of divine worship consists in monotheism.'[3] This bald theme is the basis for all the preaching against deviance and illicit adoration, spurious royalty and corrupt power, and the calls for a reform that will be not only religious but political and even semantic.[4] The oneness of God is here the touchstone of all conduct, all custom, all tradition: it becomes the only genuine tradition. The invention of a guided history, delivered from the restless wandering of customs and the arbitrariness of illegitimate rule, consists in this movement of *preservation* and return to self.

This movement of renewal has been compared to a dogmatic and intolerant closure, and special emphasis has been laid on Abd al-Wahhab's sweeping rejection of all innovation (*bid'a*), in keeping with the austere tradition of the Hanbalite school to which he belonged.[5] However, from a reading of the *Kitab al-Tawhid* and various texts left by Abd al-Wahhab, it would appear that the reason why they strictly define the boundaries of innovation is to keep it to questions of theology. As far as action in the world is concerned, their simple position links up with the flexibility of early Islam: 'Everything useful is not prohibited.'[6] This contrasts with the *Kitab al-Tawhid*'s trenchant statement on theology: only the adoration of God has any value; worship of his creation – trees, standing stones, animals, men, princes, prophets and even Mohammed, the Prophet of Islam – has no value and must be fought against. Some have seen in this only intransigence, failing to notice that the rigidity is wholly theoretical and theological, and that its insistent reference to a transcendent God makes possible one of the first expressions of an ecumenical *rapprochement* between monotheisms: 'The religion of all the prophets is the same religion.'[7] 'Any blame that God addresses to Jews and Christians in the Koran also concerns us Muslims.'[8]

At the practical level of social and political action, however, the main focus is on 'leaders who have gone astray'[9] and the one who 'accords himself the title of king of kings'[10] (the Shah of Persia, but also the Sultan of Istanbul). In relation to them, the prescribed conduct is unambiguous: 'To obey scholars and governors when they prohibit what God has allowed or when they allow what God has prohibited is tantamount to treating them as divinities':[11] that is, committing the sin of *shirk*, in which another divinity is associated with God. Divine transcendence here serves as a measure or gauge. Hanging over kings as well as slaves, princes as well as common mortals, it subjects them to the same body of laws and the same constraints.

This first norm (in the public-law sense in which constitutional principles are the highest or first norm to which all others ultimately refer back) is articulated in a quotation from the Prophet: 'He who satisfies God and displeases men shall satisfy God and men; he who satisfies men and displeases God shall displease God and men.'[12] The basis of all legitimacy must be sought in God and God alone; there can be no balancing between God and men, between divine legitimacy and popular legitimacy, but there is a strict equivalence which means that he who satisfies God gains the adherence of men as well. So, there is no democratic legitimacy, only a guarantee that the demos will assent if God's law is respected. Much as the French Revolution would locate the criterion of all legitimacy in an ideal and transcendent general will, so did Abd al-Wahhab's reform locate the criterion of good government beyond the particular will of this or that ruler, in the ideal and transcendent norm represented by God's law. In either case, the return to self is inseparable from the positing of an absolute norm or gauge or criterion.

The Najd revolution

All the problems are not solved – far from it. Abd al-Wahhab's thought is complex, sometimes contradictory, always shaped by the urgent necessity of restoring Islam in its purity. So far as politics is concerned, the most striking difficulty is to know who decides the content of God's law, who has the right interpretation, the legitimate exegesis. If 'nothing useful is prohibited', yet the prince must follow God's law on pain of losing the support of men, who will advise him on the conduct he should pursue? And, since God's law is set forth in a series of texts that are often contradictory and seldom applicable as such, who will become their interpreter and deliver the practical keys of good governance?

It is certainly a persistent problem, which has been posed for all Islamic states since the original State of Medina – from the Prophet's lifetime down to the revolutionary Iran of today. It means that the keys of religious interpretation are always in human, all too human hands, and that 'struggles for secularization in Islam are not what they are for us'. For 'secularity, in a sense, goes without saying for them [Muslims].'[13] The difficulty also concerns every period in Saudi history, from the preaching of Muhammad ibn Abd al-Wahhab to the manifestoes of modern Islamists, from King Abdelaziz's instrumentalization of the clergy in the 1930s to King Fahd's creation of a consultative assembly (Majlis al-Shura) in 1992. *Who will be the prince's adviser?* Although Abd al-Wahhab freed Najd from the terror that the distant Ottoman Empire could inspire, and from the arbitrary power of unscrupulous kinglets, the awesome question that he bequeathed to Arabia has still not received a satisfactory answer.

In 1740 Muhammad ibn Abd al-Wahhab returned to Uyayna and won the confidence of its prince, Uthman bin Muammar. Abd al-Wahhab's first political experiments certainly went too far in the direction of purification, and the suzerain of Lower Najd, the emir of Hasa on the east coast of Arabia, asked Uthman bin Muammar to put an end, if necessary by force, to the seditious activity. Abd al-Wahhab then took refuge with one of his disciples in Diriya, a few kilometres south of Uyayna, where he managed to gain the ear of Prince Muhammad bin Saud for the further pursuit of reform.

Abd al-Wahhab's first directly political act was to abolish the tax on agricultural produce in the emirate, and to replace it with revenue from holy war (jihad) against other Najd emirates.[14] It is in this fiscal and budgetary measure that we should see the real contract between Abd al-Wahhab and the Saudis, not in the celebrated – but somewhat implausible – exchange of vows:

> Muhammad ibn Saud greeted Muhammad ibn Abd al-Wahhab and said, 'This oasis is yours, do not fear your enemies. By the name of God, if all Najd was summoned to throw you out, we will never agree to expel you.' Muhammad ibn Abd al-Wahhab replied, 'You are the settlement's chief and wise man. I want you to grant me an oath that you will perform jihad against the unbelievers. In return you will be imam, leader of the Muslim community, and I will be leader in religious matters.[15]

The promise does not primarily concern either the legitimacy of Muhammad ibn Saud or his future power over the community of Muslims, even if Abd al-Wahhab's descendants have continued (with the exception of a few decades) to occupy the main religious positions in the kingdom.[16] The main content of the promise is absolutely specific and has to do with a judicious piece of budgetary advice:

stop raising an internal tax and impoverishing the oasis; launch into wars of conquest which, though dressed in the colours of Islam, correspond to banal imperatives of economic survival.

The alliance was a success. In the space of thirty years, the Saudis conquered Lower and Central Najd. In 1788 Qatar and part of the east coast fell to them, and in 1789 Jabal Shammar. In 1791 they launched raids against Oman, and by 1795 they were at the Hijaz frontier, by the following year at the gates of Yemen, and by 1798 in Iraq and Syria. In 1800 they invaded Bahrain and Oman, and two years later Karbala in Iraq and Taif in Hijaz. They entered Mecca in 1803; Medina surrendered in 1805; Hijaz was subjugated in 1806. In 1808, the apogee of Saudi expansion, the armies of Muhammad ibn Saud's grandson, Saud bin Abdelaziz, laid siege to Sanaa in Yemen, occupied Hodeida on the Red Sea, ravaged the outskirts of Aleppo in Syria and occupied part of Palestine: that is to say, the Saudi armies controlled a front with a length of 4,000 kilometres.

Born in Diriya, one of the smallest and least prosperous of the Lower Najd oases, Saudi power seemed to know no bounds. In fact, Diriya had an empire more extensive than present-day Saudi Arabia, although after 1810 its expansion was halted by the British assault to the south and east, and after 1811 it was broken by the Egyptian invasion of the Peninsula from the west. Following a siege of several months, Diriya itself fell to the Egyptians in September 1818.[17]

How were the Saudis able to notch up such successes? How could the shrunken Diriya become in a few decades the wealthy capital of a prosperous empire? The nineteenth-century Najd historian Uthman bin Bishr describes it as follows:

> When I saw Diriya at the time of Saud bin Abdelaziz (may God's mercy be upon him), I observed great wealth, large numbers of people, incomparable weapons decorated with gold and silver, thoroughbred horses and Omani dromedaries, magnificent clothes and signs of prosperity beyond all description and all numbering.... The power of that city, the grandeur of its buildings, the energy of its people, the size of its population and the extent of its wealth are beyond all description. He who knows cannot encompass everything in his knowledge. If I had tried to count the people hurrying from one end of the city to the other, the thoroughbred

horses, the dromedaries of Yemeni stock and the luxuries of every
kind that the inhabitants and strangers bought there, my book
would not have sufficed to take in everything. I saw many wonders
there. Whoever enters the seasonal fair will certainly see people
of diverse origins – Yemen, Tihama, Hijaz, Oman, Bahrain, Syria,
Egypt – from various capitals and the whole world. It would take
too long to list them all. Some were arriving, others leaving, and
yet others were settling for good in the city.[18]

How did it attain such prosperity? The first explanation, as we have
seen, is budgetary and economic. By abolishing fiscal pressure on
the agricultural produce of the Diriya emirate and making the state
finances dependent upon conquest, Abd al-Wahhab broke the vicious
circle of a subsistence economy doomed to produce no more than
it consumed, or to invest any meagre surplus in the upkeep of
an already fairly well-off ruling class. (The Sauds, far from being
the 'Bedouins' they are sometimes reputed to be, were originally
landowners, tradesmen and camel hirers – central Arabia's equivalent
of the Gulf coast merchants.) For the inhabitants of Diriya, war
policy and the end of taxes signalled a new alliance with their
prince; for the other oases and the Bedouin tribes, the war of
conquest caused terror and submission before luring them with
unheard-of profits; and for Arabia as a whole it was tantamount to
an economic revolution, since in a few decades Najd passed from
a system involving constant movement of goods among tribes and
oases (whether through trade or plunder) to the accumulation of
goods on behalf of a political centre and a ruling family: 'Earlier
a ghazu had been merely a valiant raid; now it became a seizure
of the property of "polytheists" and its transfer to the hands of
"genuine Muslims".'[19]

It is not surprising that, under such conditions, the religious
reform swiftly took hold in Arabia, and that the Najdis 'captured
Mecca without facing any resistance from the citizens'.[20] Abd al-
Wahhab ushered in a virtuous circle whereby war permitted capital
accumulation and conquest made roads safer; capital and security
brought about an unprecedented blossoming of trade; Diriya grew
rich and was able, in return, to assure its rule through the distribution of wealth and its vassals' hope of making their fortune.

What jihad *said* was struggle against people who did not bow to reformed Islam, but what jihad *produced* was a prosperity which, though relative, marked a decisive advance. The fight against unjust taxes and the ban on usury shared this same objective: to produce earnings, to free productive craftsmen and farmers from the yoke imposed on them by the rulers and the moneyed classes. Economic revolution thus went together with social revolution: the down-trodden classes that transformed matter or cultivated it, the craftsmen and farmers who ranked lowest in the caste system of traditional Arabia, were released from the symbolic or institutional fetters on their activity. Furthermore, the prospective gains from conquest knitted together all the social categories around the political-religious leadership; and, for the first time, it grouped the sedentary and Bedouin population around the same objective. In short, 'Wahhabism became the ideological weapon of the movement for centralization in the Arabian Peninsula',[21] the theoretical and theological expression of its social unification and political-economic centralization.

In political terms, the reform initiated by Muhammad ibn Abd al-Wahhab effectively established the rule of one family over all other families in the Peninsula. Far from merely providing the future Al Sauds ('those from the Saud family') with religious legitimacy, it also invested them with a historical mission: to achieve the unity of the peoples of the Peninsula, just as Abd al-Wahhab had achieved divine unity in thought and guarded it against any polytheist or idolatrous attack. As a reform movement that produced a revolution, Wahhabism permitted Arabia's forcible entry into history. Assigning a new origin to the march of time, Abd al-Wahhab's movement distinguished its own course from the ignorance (*jahiliya*) that had gone before – ignorance of religion, ignorance of God, and a concomitant ig-norance of history and the course of time. Does not Abd al-Wahhab, in one amazing page of the *Kitab al-Tawhid*, quote these words of the Prophet: 'Do not curse time, for God himself is time'?[22]

What Abd al-Wahhab founded was not only a novel politics, a strengthened economy and a unified society, but also a new science: the historiography that blossomed to an extraordinary extent in the eighteenth and nineteenth centuries. Uthman bin Bishr sketched the principles and the self-understanding of this new history:

I know that people from Najd and their ulema, both ancient and
modern, had no inclination for their history, for its great men,
for its events, causes and consequences, so that it was only rarely
that certain ulema wrote it down. To denote a particular year they
would say 'it was the year of the death of so-and-so's son', and
they remembered neither his name nor the cause of his death. And
to denote the year of a death or an accident they would say: that
was the year of so-and-so's fall, and they remembered neither how
nor where it had happened. As for us, we know that there have
been many deaths from the time of Adam to our own day, but we
wish to know the truth and the cause, that which is strange and surprising
in a death, and all that is missing in the way they write history.[23]

To put it in another way: Muhammad ibn Abd al-Wahhab set out
the elements of the future Arab and Saudi self-consciousness, one
lived in the mode of symbolic autonomy, material independence and
a regained sense of historical presence. It is certainly this – and not
the events following his arrival in Diriya – which constitutes his
main contribution to the construction of Saudi identity. With Abd
al-Wahhab, something like an endogenous history became possible
– not only possible but thinkable and real.

Saudis do not call themselves 'Wahhabis'

What actually happened between the Wahhabism of the eighteenth
century, bearer of reform and revolution, and the contemporary
Wahhabism that is described as violent, murderous and threatening? How did self-affirmation turn into the denial of others? How
is it that Saudi Islam, whose early successes held out the promise
of reform and progress, ceased to modernize and turned into the
reactionary force about which there is so much talk today?

The originality of the reformation led by Abd al-Wahhab was
that, unlike the Muslim reform movements of the nineteenth and
twentieth centuries, it was not a reaction to foreign cultural invasion
or an expression of resentment towards European imperialism but
an endogenous movement in its own right:

A radical difference can be glimpsed between reactions of a
nationalist kind, provoked by foreign occupation, and movements

in untouched sectors – of a Mahdist or Wahhabist kind – which, along psychological lines little affected by modern times, awaken an originality *whose guarantees are asked of the self*.[24]

Of course, the Saudi movement asserted itself when the Ottoman Empire and the nascent British Empire were beginning to surround the Peninsula with a ring of economic, political and military constraints – a coincidence that eventually hastened the fall of the first Saudi kingdom, whose capital, Diriya, capitulated on 11 September 1818 to Egyptian troops. However, the threat exacerbated the discourse of Najd reform only when the Saudis were directly confronted – in Iraq, Hijaz and Oman – with the foreign domination of the Ottomans and British. In 1806 Jean Raymond, a French officer in the service of the pasha of Baghdad, reported to Champagny (Napoleon's minister of foreign relations) the following words of one Saudi: 'The time is approaching when we shall see an Arab on the throne of the Caliphs; we have languished for long enough under the yoke of a usurper.'[25]

Economic, military and religious self-assertion is separated by a certain distance from Arab nationalist resentment with prophetic overtones, just as there is a distance between purely endogenous reform or revolution and a reaction to exogenous (Ottoman or British) influences, or between conquering opening-up and potentially violent closure. It is a historical distance created through the irruption of external forces into Arabia – a distance between Arabia's bursting into history and history's bursting into Arabia. It is the latter that we must examine, because it laid the foundations for our contemporary Western reading of Saudi Islam – beginning with the very name 'Wahhabism', which, as we shall see, was invented and applied from outside the reform movement itself.

Like the term 'Mohammedan' – now fortunately abandoned by the West in favour of 'Muslim', the theologically more accurate term of Arabic origin – 'Wahhabism' does not correspond to any theological reality and has never been used by ordinary Saudis. This terminological discrepancy may appear to be of only anecdotal interest, but that would be to minimize the misunderstanding to which it has given rise. One French journalist could write, for example: 'To carry through their worldwide campaign, the Saudis

know that they must shake off a "Wahhabi" label that is geographically much too limited. In the Sunni world, they prefer to present
themselves as Salafists'[26] – as if the label 'Wahhabi' were a natural
given that Saudis hush up for tactical reasons, as if the identity they
invoke were no more than a strategic variable at the discretion of
the regime in Riyadh.

In reality, the name that Saudis give themselves corresponds to a
strong sense of identity, though one that has been broken up and put
together again at various times in history. To overlook the scale and
significance of the terminological discrepancy, to make unguarded
use of the adjective 'Wahhabi' or the noun 'Wahhabism', is to slip
in a certain understanding of Saudi Islam which, with its exogenous
terms, is not the understanding that Saudis have of themselves and
is quite capable of leading astray an outside observer.

Why do Saudis not call themselves 'Wahhabis'? It is above all for
theological reasons. Since its defining feature is the worship of one
God, Saudi Islam objects to any idea of an intermediary between
God and believer, be he the Prophet Mohammed himself, not to
speak of Muhammad ibn Abd al-Wahhab. All worship is due to God
alone, and so the term 'Wahhabi' is as illegitimate as 'Mohammedan'.
No more than the Prophet himself could Muhammad ibn Abd al-
Wahhab enjoy a position that Muslims demand should be kept for
exclusive use.

Saudis present themselves as *salafiyun* – that is, as successors of
the holy ancestors (*salaf*) who were the Prophet's companions – and
therefore as 'reformers', since a return to original Islam involves a
purifying reform. Some, who wish to lay greater emphasis on God's
oneness (the first article of faith for a Muslim), describe themselves
as *muwahhidun*, zealots of God's oneness, 'unitarians'. Others are fond
of the term *ahl al-Sunna wa-l-jama'a*: that is, people of the Sunna and
the community of believers, respectful of the deeds and words of the
Prophet written down in the hadiths that set believers the example of
how an ordinary human being should live. In most cases, however,
Saudis dismiss with a wave of the hand all such terminological
refinement and present themselves simply as Muslims.

The multiplicity of terms therefore expresses something like the
impossibility of giving a name to the belief in one God. What is

surprising about that? In Islam, God himself is mainly invoked negatively, by reference to what he is not, for God in his oneness is hard to name. Hence the Muslim profession of faith: 'There is no god but God', *la ilah illa Allah*.

Wahhabism: a theologically false and diplomatically overdetermined concept

Saudis do not use it and sometimes take violent objection to it: for example, in 1998, in a festival speech marking the centenary of the refoundation of Arabia, Prince Salman bin Abdelaziz, governor of Riyadh province, scathingly referred to 'those who call us Wahhabis'. Where, then, does the term 'Wahhabism' come from?

It was coined at the end of the eighteenth century by the reformer's own brother, Sulayman ibn Abd al-Wahhab, with the intention of compromising the movement of which he was the first opponent;[27] it was then soon exported, at a time when Arabia was entering world history and people abroad were naming the intruder after the man with whom it identified itself: Muhammad ibn Abd al-Wahhab. First used as an insult by Arabs from Najd, Hijaz and Egypt, who feared Saudi expansion, the term 'Wahhabism' was taken up by European diplomats on the lookout for any force that might counter the power of the Ottoman Empire. For Britain (which in 1798 sent its first resident to the Arabian–Persian Gulf, a man called Brydges) and for France (whose armies were fighting in Egypt in the same year), the traditional Ottoman and tsarist empires represented an obsolete form of domination, now threatened by the economic and ideological imperialism that would reach its peak in nineteenth-century colonialism. The dual British and French threat to these empires was therefore compounded by the Saudi threat, so that Istanbul and St Petersburg, Paris and London all took a lively interest in the conquests of the Sauds, either to deplore or to rejoice at them.

In 1803 Italinski, the Russian consul in Istanbul, wrote:

> In its present situation, the Porte fears only France's intentions and the rebel movement of some Arab tribes, called Wahhabis, who

account for nearly 60,000 effectives. They plan to seize the wealth
of the Mecca and Medina shrines and undertake to found a mono-
theist religion, defying Muhammadanism. To convert the [inhabit-
ants] to the worship of the Quran, an ulama ['alim] has been sent
there who is an expert in the sacred books. Other measures have
been taken too: an army has been formed to attack them from the
line that runs from Basra to al-Arish, while the sharif of Medina
will attack them from Hijaz.[28]

In the same year Italinski sent a more urgent letter to St Petersburg:

> Should Abd al-Wahhab capture Damascus, his importance and
> might will eventually reach a degree that may prompt him to
> declare the sultan a usurper of the caliph's throne and restore the
> caliphate of the Umayyads, whose descendants were ever con-
> sidered the holders of the exclusive right as heirs to the spiritual
> guidance of the Muhammadan community; even in this capital,
> there are many of his supporters.[29]

Here is one of the first mentions, if not the very first, of the
term 'Wahhabism' in the literature of European diplomacy. Soon it
was all the rage: in 1806, as we have seen, Jean Raymond wrote
a Mémoire sur l'origine des Wahabys for the French minister of external
relations; in 1809 Jean-Baptiste Rousseau, a Frenchman residing
in Iraq, composed a Note historique sur les Wahhabis for the use of his
civil service;[30] and, in the same year, Louis Alexandre de Corancez,
French consul in Aleppo, published a Histoire des Wahhabis.[31] Not for
nothing did Italinski note 'the intentions of France'. And, indeed, in
1806 Napoleon instructed a Spaniard, Badia y Leblich, to offer his
services to the Saudi emir for the construction of a reverse alliance
against the Ottomans – although this never bore fruit, because the
emissary did not manage to get as far as Diriya.[32]

The term 'Wahhabism', then, was coined outside Arabia as a category
in the diplomatic and military discourse of European powers concerning
the Middle East: 'An army has been formed to attack the Wahhabis
from the line that runs from Basra to al-Arish', wrote Italinski – and
so 'Wahhabism' became not a descriptive term but the exact theoretical corollary and operational concept of the military force that was
to crush the Saudis. We should further note that Italinski refers to

Abd al-Wahhab as the general of the Wahhabis – whereas, in fact, Muhammad ibn Abd al-Wahhab had died in 1792 and withdrawn from state affairs in 1773, after the conquest of central Najd, and could therefore not have been leading the Saudi armies to Damascus in 1803. That had anyway never been his role.

'Wahhabi' is therefore equivalent to the term 'Bonapartist' in nineteenth-century French political life or to 'Gaullist' in the France of today: it designates the political supporters of a (dead or living) statesman. The vocabulary is always the strategic one of political action, but it has value only if the supporters of the great man actually adopt it – and, as we have seen, Saudis do not call themselves and never have called themselves 'Wahhabis'.

Let us finally note that, in opening an interpretive era that has still not closed, Italinski made of Wahhabism a sect 'defying Muhammadanism', whereas late-eighteenth century Egyptian theologians – followed by Algerian and Iraqi theologians – declared that they could find nothing heretical in 'Wahhabi' teachings.[33] Nor did Italinski himself persist in his error of perspective: his subsequent letters presented the Saudis as orthodox Muslims, so orthodox that they even aimed to overthrow the Ottoman usurper and to hand over to Arabs the leadership of the Muslim empire. All the more astonishing is the durability of the troubled picture that he painted from Istanbul of a political and religious movement in distant Arabia. When we think of Saudi Islam today, it is still in the *external, diplomatic* and even *military* terms that he first suggested.

What we call by the name of 'Wahhabism' is the first European perception, from above and afar, of the Arabian Peninsula and the religion that served as a standard for the most turbulent of its peoples. More than the theological, political or social reality of the reform initiated by Muhammad ibn Abd al-Wahhab and Muhammad bin Saud, the term 'Wahhabism' therefore mainly refers to Arabia's real or imaginary influence abroad, and even to the threats that it posed in the Middle East by splintering the homogenous edifice of the Ottoman Empire.

Theologically false and diplomatically overdetermined, 'Wahhabism' designates more the external unease or curiosity aroused by this 'fanatical sect' than the historical reality or real identity of a political and religious movement. If 'the name of the Wahabis has become sufficiently familiar in Europe', it is because 'these Arabs appear to be called upon to play a great part in history; *should they fulfil this expectation*, it is all the more important for them to become known as it is in its beginnings that the greatness of a nation is to be found.'[34] 'Wahhabism' is indeed much more of an 'expectation', a hope or a fear, than the perception that the Saudis of yesterday or today have of the religious movement launched by Abd al-Wahhab. Still less does it denote the real movement of reform that sprang up in the heart of Najd.

The historically determinate political-military concept of 'Wahhabism' does not and cannot express an eternal essence of Saudi Arabia, as we sometimes catch writers believing. Its careless use today suggests that the power to express or designate does not belong to Saudis themselves but to the powers surrounding the Middle East. Like the very terms 'Middle East', 'Near East' or 'Islamism',[35] 'Wahhabism' basically tells us of the symbolic and identity dependence of the Arab East, the political, symbolic and military 'power vacuum' being revealed there; it does not tell us of any global 'threat' concealed there. As Mamoun Fandy has written,

> our intellectual production is taking place within a political econ-
> omy of writing in which scholarship is tied more to political pro-
> grams than to research programs. The current established discourse
> on Saudi Arabia is frequently tied to specific political agendas, and
> what is funded and published tends to support the ideas and ap-
> proaches sponsors of research wish to propagate. Publications even
> tend to predict outcomes that specific groups would like to see.[36]

The term 'Wahhabism' is a perfect example of such distortion: it involves a *passion* rather than a description, denotes an external fantasy rather than an actual reality, is part of a political strategy rather than a scientific approach.

National identity and insurrection

What does the term 'Wahhabism' mean today, as it is used in the European or American press, taken up by experts and researchers, and sometimes even deployed by Saudis in exoteric texts for a Western readership or in critiques of the religious establishment? Let us first concede the reference to political nationalism that it introduces. For Europeans in the early nineteenth century, 'Wahhabism' was mainly an oppositional political-military movement within the Ottoman Empire, and they were right about that. When Saudi expansion ran up against hugely superior foreign forces, when it so vexed the Ottoman Empire in Hijaz, Iraq and Syria that the sharif of Mecca, Ghaleb, made contact in 1798 with the British and French, when the annexation of Hijaz to Najd in 1806 led the newly enthroned Sultan Mustapha IV to make the recapture of the holy places his only political programme, and when the Saudis aroused the ire of the British in 1809 in the Arabian–Persian Gulf, the Najd revolution changed from a social-economic to a national revolution.

For a Saudi today, the first Saudi state thus represents the first and consummate expression of Arab nationalism, not modelled on European nationalism but entirely derived from Islam. In other words, Islam is inseparable from Saudi consciousness and national pride, not only because Arabia houses the holy places of Mecca and Medina, but also because it was the centre of the first endogenous Arab–Muslim resistance to foreign domination. Even for the youngest Saudis, therefore, Islam is 'the key to their self-perception'[37] and their affirmation of national sentiment.[38]

If Islam is inseparable from Saudi national pride, it is also inseparable from the opposition to the outside world that characterized the permanent insurrection of the first Saudi state. From that restless ancestor, the present Saudi state – indeed, Saudi national consciousness – has preserved an oppositional state of mind that is expressed in Islamic terms. As Mamoun Fandy puts it: 'Saudi Arabia is unusual in that the state usually presents itself as the defender of the faith in the face of a cultural and religious onslaught from the West. Thus, in macropolitical or global terms, the state presents itself as an inherently oppositional entity.'[39]

The same may be said of Saudis in general, for whom the primary meaning of religion is not 'submission to the Riyadh regime' but 'opposition to the way of the world', 'permanent insurrection'. This insurrectional identity is expressed in various ways – from unbuttoned anti-Zionism to religious opposition to the regime in place. Here it is religion which says that God, the one God, is greater than the prince – and the prince can be influenced, even criticized, *ad maiorem Dei gloriam*. It is religion which says that an autonomous civil society is possible, and this provides a basis for the contemporary social-political modernization that is at once purely Saudi and strictly Islamic.[40]

In a way, then, 'Wahhabism' may be thought of as an insurrectional national identity. But, at the same time, it indissolubly links all religious forms to the interpretation of Islam given by the Saudi state, so that for an outside observer it mainly denotes the permeation of society, from top to bottom, by an ideology in which submission to the ruling power is justified in the name of religion. So great is the ruler's monopoly of religious expression that it is difficult to conceive of a *religious* opposition. The term 'Wahhabism' – and this is its first contemporary meaning, quite different from the one it had for Corancez, Raymond or Italinski – postulates the identity of official Islam and societal Islam, the Islam of the elites and the Islam of the people, state Islam and oppositional Islam.

Curiously enough, outside observers use the term uncritically and without reservation, thereby reflecting the long claim of the Saudi regime to be the architect of the oneness of Islam. To see officially imposed 'Wahhabism' as the alpha and omega of Saudi Islam is thus to accept, if not the terminology, then the discourse that the Saudi regime has developed over a number of decades, and to deny that, beyond the will to power of the Sauds, Islam can express the wishes and aspirations of Saudi society. It is to deny that Islam can constitute an autonomous force in society.

Religion does not explain everything

The term 'Wahhabism' inscribes in a single word the supposed essence of Saudi society and politics; it conflates religion with tradition, and tradition with the violence of 'a nation that wages war out of religious principle'.[41] This masks the fact that, as we saw in the first chapter, Saudi identities are much more complex than something simply imposed from above by an ideology. Rather than an accurate description of Saudi ideology, 'Wahhabism' is an imported concept that has been stuck on to a reality much less univocal than it would appear.

First, to use the term today is to make a false assumption that religion is all there is to the Saudi tradition. But, although religious tradition should not be confused with Bedouin or tribal tradition, it is not certain that religion and tradition peacefully coexist with each other. In fact, the opposite is highly likely, and since its refoundation in the twentieth century the Saudi state has invoked the unity of the Muslim nation to overcome tribal reflexes that stand in the way of a 'unified' and 'homogenous' society. Similarly, when contemporary Saudi Islamists use a religious argument to combat family or tribal tradition, they do not think they are breaking with Islam or shutting themselves up in the narrow confines of a sect. Use of the term 'Wahhabism' therefore indicates a persistent conflation of religion with tradition, in which 'Wahhabism' is seen as belonging to the past and should either be embraced as such (in the name of an endogenous 'Arabian' reaction) or rejected en bloc (on behalf of a necessarily exogenous 'progress' stemming from the West). It is the need to choose between these two options that seems to us open to dispute.

Second, the conception in which 'Wahhabism' has remained immobile ever since the pact of 1744 between Muhammad ibn Saud and Muhammad ibn Abd al-Wahhab means that Saudi culture and politics can be seen as an ahistorical essence involving an alliance between the temporal and the spiritual power, sabre and turban, throne and minaret – as if the grand mufti and theologians (ulema) were able to dictate how the royal family should act, in return for surrounding the House of Saud with an Islamic aura in Arabia and the Muslim world. The truth is that, although the word 'alliance' may accurately describe the pact between Muhammad ibn Saud and Muhammad ibn Abd al-Wahhab, it does little justice to the complex relations that have actually taken shape in the twentieth century between the royal family and the major religious figures in Saudi Arabia. Indeed, one of the Islamist criticisms of the regime is precisely that relations between the temporal and the spiritual power are based more on subjugation, or instrumentalization, than on reciprocal courtesies and favours.[42]

Third, by foregrounding a Muslim doctrine that is supposed to have daily application in the kingdom, one avoids the trouble of a precise analysis of Saudi culture and society, as well as of the relations uniting society with the political regime and the religion. It is too easy, for example, to derive directly from some pure concept of 'Wahhabism' the actual content of religious teaching, the place of women in Saudi society or the persecution of the Shiites. Such an abstract deduction would at the very least have to be supplemented with an account of how education functions, how women fit into society or how Shiites are treated – and that is what is often cruelly lacking in recent works on Saudi Arabia.

The corollary of an exclusive emphasis on the religious origins of Saudi culture and customs is that many writers fail to address other sources of identity that govern the construction of society and the political system. In the complex edifice of the Saudi cultural heritage (turath), the Salafi Islam of Najd is joined not only by tribal and regional cultures but also by the other Saudi Islams (Shiah, Sunni and Sufi), imported Western modernism, references from Arab nationalism, Arab socialism, Communism, and so on.[43] The term 'Wahhabism' flattens the multiple Saudi identities into one univocal identity, which gains in false obviousness what it loses in explanatory power.

Unlike a contextual reading geared to historical circumstance, any analysis that relies on the term 'Wahhabism' has already decided in advance that Saudi Islam can only be reactionary or medieval and that those who claim to represent it can only be fanatics, whether they are in power or belong to the opposition. A single cultural essence serves to swallow up a social and political evolution, although here, as elsewhere, we have no reason to think that the society or polity has actually escaped the complexities of history. Not only is it objectively incorrect to write that 'Muhammad ibn Abd al-Wahhab is the originating source for the ideological current bearing his name, Wahhabism';[44] this assertion surreptitiously fastens two conceptual yokes so tightly together that they become extremely difficult to loosen again. The first of these inseparably links together political authority and theological authority, whereas the real history of Saudi Arabia consists of debates and sometimes conflicts between those authorities. The second conflates Islam and tradition, whereas Islam has presented itself – and continues to present itself – as an instrument with which to purify, rationalize and reform traditions.

We may conclude that a Wahhabism-centred approach blurs our understanding both of Saudi Arabia's influence beyond its frontiers and of Saudi religion, politics and society.

What globalization of Saudi Islam?

The globalization of Saudi Islam – that is, its Saudi-funded expansion to the rest of the Muslim world and the West – has become a truism of the kind of literature that sees in it the root of all violence in the name of Islam (acts of violence committed by Saudi 'Islamists' against Muslim peoples and now turned against the West), as well as the root of the backwardness of the Muslim world and the terrorism it 'naturally' produces.

A good example of this view was expressed in a contribution to debate that appeared in early 2003 in the French daily *Libération*:

> All over the world, imams trained in the Wahhabi school preach hatred and violence in mosques paid for with Saudi funding. This ideology has ravaged entire countries, such as Afghanistan yesterday and Algeria still today. It poses a threat to the Muslim world, constantly holding back its march towards modernity. It is the underpinning of Islamist terrorism. It is the real obstacle to a peaceful settlement of the Israel–Palestine conflict. Its wild anti-feminism, apocalyptic sectarianism and medieval puritanism also make it strangely close to the Christian far right in the United States.[45]

A 'school' sending feelers all over the world, 'funding' for anything remotely connected with violent Islamism, an 'ideology' that springs from Saudi soil and contaminates, decimates and kills: 'Wahhabism' is seen as a hydra sprouting heads in all climes, decapitated in Afghanistan but renascent in Indonesia, vanquished in America but still stirring in Europe. A kind of extirpatory literature thus calls upon Western and especially American leaders to join battle with the source of all evil: 'Should the regime be spared, on the pretext that it could only be replaced with something worse? But this

supposedly lesser evil has presided over all the humiliations that
Saudis have inflicted on the region and the world.'[46] A cooler look
at reality shows, however, that the image of a 'Wahhabi' tumour
implanting worldwide 'metastases'[47] contains not only an odious
appeal to hatred but a profound error of perspective.

If the globalization of Saudi Islam is a question of ideological
expansion, we can say that this 'Wahhabi' expansion is altogether a
thing of the past. In the late eighteenth century – contrary to the
widespread image of an Arabia turned in on itself – Saudi Islam did
export itself to India, where two reform movements (created by Hajji
Chariat Allah and Ahmad Barelwi), in accordance with Saudi political
and social orientations of the time, called for 'struggle against the
British and a rebellion of the disadvantaged social classes'.[48] Linked
to Sufism, not in opposition to it, the 'unitarian' branch of Indian
Muslim reformism was described as 'Wahhabi' by its reformist ad-
versaries, in a spiralling of insults born of political competition
among movements on the same religious 'market'. Beyond India, the
padri movement spread the ideas of Abd al-Wahhab to Indonesia, while
Baghdad saw the flowering of a legal and theological school close to
Saudi Islam and staunchly opposed to the Shiites of Mesopotamia.[49]
In the nineteenth century, however, the centre of gravity of Muslim
reformism shifted from the heart of the Peninsula to the Egypt of
the Nahdha (renaissance).

The caravans of traders and pilgrims crossing Arabia (especially
Najd, its central region) meant that already in the eighteenth century
the Peninsula was by no means a closed area, but the opening to
outside influences greatly accelerated in the twentieth century. On
the one hand, the worldwide transport revolution meant that the
number of pilgrims never ceased to grow in the course of the
century, accentuating the cultural and religious porosity of Hijaz
and enabling the Saudis to spread their brand of reformism (but
also to absorb influences from highly divergent readings of Islam).
On the other hand, and more important still, the capture of the
holy cities of Mecca and Medina by the third Saudi state in 1926
opened Najd to new external influences. The conquest of Hijaz thus
marked a profound change in Saudi Islam – a change of direction
that may be described as a shift from a purely 'inland' Islam to

a more eclectic one. In 1926 Rashid Ridha, an Egyptian reformist disciple of Muhammad Abduh, made himself the champion of the Saudis and of the Islam they were promoting.[50]

Beginning in the 1960s, a new historical factor intensified this opening of Saudi Islam to Egyptian reformism: namely, the open rivalry between Arabia and Egypt for moral and political leadership of the whole Arab world. At the same time, Nasserite and Baathist repression of the Muslim Brotherhood, in Egypt and Syria respectively, triggered large-scale migration to Arabia, where members of the Brotherhood (most notably Muhammad Qutb, brother of its main theoretician, Sayyid Qutb) swelled the ranks of university teachers and theologians. There would be a lasting impact, both on Saudi official Islam and on the Islamic opposition to the Sauds that grew in the 1980s out of the successful grafting of Egyptian reformism twenty years before.

These important events marked a reconciliation between 'inland' Saudi Islam and Egyptian 'Mediterranean' Islam, between one branch of Muslim reformism stemming from eighteenth-century opposition to the Ottomans and the other major branch produced from the nineteenth-century encounter of Islam with European ideas, between a Saudi reformism of 'affirmation' and an Egyptian reformism of 'resentment'.

Ali al-Umaym, a Saudi liberal intellectual, describes as follows this two-way exchange:

> From the point of view of its political regime, Saudi Arabia could not escape the intellectual edifice built by the Muslim Brotherhood, which, in comparison with its own Salafi religious thought, represented a complete and total system. Salafi religious thought has a number of huge gaps and is marked by considerable weaknesses with regard to the multidimensional challenges of modern life. The important task of filling the gaps and weaknesses in the local Salafi system therefore fell to the thought of the Muslim Brotherhood. For it is an up-to-date Muslim thought, which concerns itself with communism, socialism, nationalism, liberalism and all the currents from the West in grammar, literature, culture, art, philosophy, sociology, economics, and so on. Ideologically and intellectually, it involved a conservative Islamic reaction to the Egyptian-style Westernization and secularization of the 1920s,

whereas the local Salafi system, during the same period, was
intellectually outdated and lived in and for the past. In the 1970s,
considering the contiguity, cohabitation, coexistence and two-
way exchange between the two systems of thought – that of the
Muslim Brotherhood and that of the Salafis – Salafi thought gained
new momentum through the thought of the Brotherhood and the
role of its social, cultural and educational activism in Arabia, which
was not confined to the mosques, religious worship, theology and
preaching.[51]

Whereas the original Salafi Islam of Saudi Arabia is structurally
centripetal – that is, it seeks to put Muslims on the right path by means
of preaching – the reform championed by the Muslim Brotherhood
is structurally *centrifugal*: that is, it combats Westernization with the
effective and less pietistic weapons of social action and education.
In the 1970s and 1980s, the Muslim Brotherhood was particularly
significant as the force behind a deep reform and modernization
of the Saudi educational system; they also gave the Saudi judicial
apparatus the means to extricate itself from a dead-end clash with
Western legal norms.[52] In a Saudi society that has been open to the
West since the 1950s, and increasingly receptive since the oil boom
of 1973, the encounter between the Islam of the Muslim Brotherhood
and the Salafi Islam of the Saudis gave the latter the strength to
modernize itself and to compete effectively with Westernization (that
is, with deracination) in social and political terms.

Thus, the fact that two Islams have met up on Saudi soil and
fused into an original reformism has profoundly altered the landscape of Saudi Islam and led to the birth of an Islamist opposition
to the regime in Riyadh. This historic encounter – together with
the communications revolution, the geographical mobility of Saudis
and their frequent presence at Western universities and in European
and Arab capitals – has helped to shape a complex and multiform
Saudi Islam, alive with multiple references and sometimes shaken
by doctrinal and political tensions.

As Olivier Carré has written, 'Wahhabism properly so called no
longer exists';[53] it has been replaced by a 'Muslim ecumenism' open
to the principal modern tendencies of Islam, inclined by geography
to embrace Shafeite, Malikite, Hanafite and Sufi influences from Hijaz

– it is not unusual today to meet Saudis practising Sufi rites, even in Riyadh – but also, especially since the agreements of 1993 and 2003, Shiite influences from Hasa, Hijaz or Asir. The policy of reconciliation with the Shiite minority, which the regime has pursued since the 1980s, points towards its greater integration into Saudi society. And recent joint declarations by Shiite and Sunni intellectuals, arguing for democratic reforms under the aegis of Islam, bear further testimony to this spectacular recomposition of Saudi Islam.[54]

It is therefore a mistake to speak of the 'globalization of Wahhabism' or to see the spread of Saudi Islam as the force behind the recent development of radical Islamist currents – many of which have nothing to do with it and make no claim to be acting on its behalf. The actual spread of Saudi Islam came to an end in the nineteenth century, in the face of competition from the successful Egyptian reformism of the *Nahdha*. Today's recent developments in the kingdom, and related developments in the Arab world and the West, should therefore be attributed not to a 'Saudiization of global Islam' but to a 'globalization' of Saudi Islam – by which we do not mean the expansion of an ever pure 'Wahhabi' Islam, but rather the rise of a 'worldly' Saudi Islam as a result of the many influences from which it has benefited. This globalization, or rather 'terrestrialization', is obscured and rendered untheorizable by the term 'Wahhabism'. But it is the key to contemporary Saudi Islam, to its official and popular, political and social expressions, and to the religious opposition to the regime in Riyadh.

PART II

Powers and oppositions

3

Genesis and structure of the modern state,

1902–1973

Power requires an army, money and ways of
communicating with absent people. The prince
therefore needs people capable of helping him in
the affairs of the sword, the pen and money.

Ibn Khaldun

What are the keys to the present-day political reality in Saudi
Arabia? How can we avoid those traps, sometimes conventional,
sometimes based on self-interest, which govern our perception of
Saudi politics?

Islam and oil: two weak explanatory keys

Seen from outside, Saudi political life appears to be the product of
two causalities: one Islamic and one oil-related. In this optic the
Islamic causality contradicts the oil causality, since Islam is assumed
to be resistant to the West and oil extraction is the chief source
of modernization and alignment with the international market.
But the two causalities do not conflict only with each other: they
are also paradoxical in themselves. Islam is both an instrument of
legitimation for the Saud family and the backdrop for opposition to
its regime; while oil both drives the submission of society to the
state and undermines the monarchy by placing Arabia under the

economic and military domination of the United States, its main customer and supplier.

This explains the hackneyed image of a kingdom prey to the contradiction between Islamic tradition and Western modernity. It also explains the two rhetorical figures often used to describe Saudi political space: the 'double-edged weapon' of Islam and the 'protected dictatorship' of the United States. The Saudi ethnologist Madawi al-Rasheed, for instance, writes about King Faisal's policy in the 1960s: 'His Islamic policy was a double-edged sword. It enhanced Saudi Arabia's position internally and internationally, but also invited criticism whenever the Islamic ideal was perceived to have been violated.'[1] Serving both to legitimize the state and to criticize it, Islam here becomes a mere instrument – or weapon – that the Riyadh government and the opposition use in their different ways. But it is not certain that the instrumental metaphor fully accounts for the nature of Saudi political Islam, whether mobilized by the regime or the opposition.[2]

Oil is supposed to mean that the regime holds limitless sway over society by purchasing its submission, but also that the regime itself has been subject to American pressure ever since the famous meeting of 14 February 1945 between King Abdelaziz and President Roosevelt on board the *Quincey*. In the time-honoured version of events, the young Saudi Arabia and the powerful United States contracted a marriage of convenience, whereby Riyadh opened its oil fields to Washington and Washington undertook to protect Riyadh from any external or internal attack; Arabia became a dictatorship that repressed all opposition, all discontent, all deviation – but a *protected* dictatorship or 'American protectorate', based on the principle: 'I protect, you pay.'[3]

Saudi Arabia would thus appear to be prisoner of a vicious circle: either the regime gambles on Islam, at the risk of giving the opposition free rein and arousing the ire of the United States; or it banks on oil and the alliance with the United States, but incurs the wrath of its opponents without necessarily finding a disinterested partner in the American administration. In either case, Saudi Arabia seems inevitably exposed to multiple contradictions. From *A House Built on Sand* to *The Rise, Corruption and Coming Fall of the House of Saud*,[4] a whole

Western literature does indeed tirelessly seek to demonstrate that the Saudi state is on the brink of collapse, as if the worst predictions had not already failed to come true and perhaps testified less to the fragility of the regime than to the inadequacy of the instruments trained upon it.

In fact, it is by no means clear that Islam or oil provides us with the right gateway into Saudi politics. The 'Islamic nature of the regime' and its 'rentier economy' are convenient essences involving spectacular causality, but neither tells us how the state was built, how it maintains itself and how it manages to mobilize the population. In other words, neither Islam nor oil can account for current Saudi politics, just as French political and institutional life cannot be deduced from such abstractions as 'secularism' or 'post-industrial economy'. Rather than on external contradictions and paradoxes, our analysis should focus on the specific negotiations, internal perceptions and real power games at work in the recent political history of Arabia. And, to us, the question 'Why this remarkable stability?' seems more fruitful than 'When will Arabia fall?'

Najd: the Prussia of the Peninsula

On three occasions in modern history, Najd was the base from which the Sauds moved out to conquer the Arabian Peninsula. The first Saudi state, as we have seen, was annihilated by the Egyptians at Diriya in 1818. Between 1843 and 1865, the second Saudi state was an abortive enterprise that never extended outside Najd and Hasa, both because of dissension within the Saud family and because an Ottoman-backed tribal power – the Al Rashid emirate at Hail, capital of Jabal Shammar – emerged in northern Najd. Finally, the third Saudi state came into being in 1926 and has been known as the Kingdom of Saudi Arabia since 1932. So, although the three successive kingdoms have few structural links with one another, the Saudi political memory goes back further than the twentieth century: the space in which it is deployed is an orientated space, from the political and cultural centre in Najd to the distant edges of the Peninsula, Yemeni Tihama, the Omani coastal plain and the borders of Mesopotamian Jazira.

Like an Arabian Prussia, Najd has for three centuries been the driving force of a *Drang nach dem See*, which has inexorably led the inhabitants of Najd to incorporate neighbouring peoples, to open their economy to the seas and long-distance trade, and to extend their spiritual and cultural dominance to the huge quadrilateral separating Asia from Africa. Following the reforms of Abd al-Wahhab and the ensuing social revolution, the horizons of Najd opened wider as a result of trade, conquest and pacification of the desert.

The first sign of this opening was the trade that brought new goods, capital, customs and lifestyles to the heart of central Arabia. As one Najd historian put it in the nineteenth century:

> Trade is a special occupation of the Najd people. Many of them are traders and travel to the lands of Rum [western Asia and Anatolia] and different parts of the Arabian Peninsula. They do not come to the Rum's lands with their own Najdi goods; they come with money and bring silk, copper, iron or lead from Aleppo or Damascus, depending on the conditions. They sell thoroughbred horses, which are in great demand in the Rum lands. Besides, they sell many camels in Aleppo and Damascus. Some people told me that they had seen merchants from Najd, particularly from Qasim, who sold dates from their regions in Damascus; perhaps they went even to Egypt. They buy only arms and coral. They trade with other Arab lands too. They go there with money. They bring much coffee, storax and incense from Yemen.... I know also that some goods from India, like sugar, cardamom, cloves, cinnamon, pepper and curcuma, are in demand in Najd. Most of them are brought from Yemeni ports. Some goods come from the ports of the Omani littoral. Many goods are brought there from the al-Qatif and Bahrain ports. The Najdis' customs allow them to leave their motherland for twenty years or more, even for China. Many Najdi merchants live in Aleppo and Damascus, as well as Egypt.[5]

Muhammad ibn Abd al-Wahhab was therefore not an isolated case, and Najdis travelled throughout the Middle East with the benefit of the political calm that the first Saudi state had brought to the Peninsula. As we saw in the previous chapter, trade enriched the towns of central Arabia, especially Diriya; the origins of the first Saudi state lay not in the shapeless desert wastes but in the urban oases of Najd, linked to one another and the outside world by a network of trade routes, pilgrim itineraries and camel tracks. Irrigated by winter wadis and surface groundwater, the Najd oases formed a territory in their own right as early as the eighteenth century, with their own commercial links and intellectual influences. This was the canvas on which the whole history of Al Saud rule in the Arabian Pensinsula would be drawn, as the conquest of the fertile expanses of Qasim, al-Kharj and Hasa, together with annexation of the east-coast ports of Arabia and Hijaz, turned the Saudi state from a military-religious to an agrarian and commercial power. In place of the desert's domination over the towns, and of nomadic tribes over sedentary tribes, the Sauds substituted the domination of town over desert, trade over pillage, commerce over prehension, and orientated history over the cyclical time of the Bedouin epics and eclogues.

The next two Saudi states partly reproduced these basic features of the first: concentration of wealth in the hands of urban merchants; centralization of a huge territory; commercial opening to the outside world. These structural traits were expressed politically in a monarchy whose prince was first warrior, first believer and first merchant, and ideologically in the Tawhid doctrine and its flexible application to profane cases.

Beginning with these elements, we may say that the construction of the first Saudi state was an endogenous affair based on a strict Najdi reading of the world, whereas foreign domination and an internal momentum intersected in the second and third Saudi states. This means that, although Saudi Arabia is one of the most ancient states in the Middle East, it is not a totally vernacular construct.

Was Arabia colonized?

Arabia, at the confluence of Asia and Africa, was the last commercial bastion on the Indian trade routes and a rebellious outlying province of the Ottoman Empire, as well as a potential prey for European empires in and after the eighteenth century. Eager to demonstrate the purely 'traditional' and endogenous character of Saudi Arabia, experts in 'Saudiology' have often sought to downplay this foreign influence – a tendency which, consciously or unconsciously, has served the wishes of the House of Saud but also masked a whole swathe of Saudi history and, above all, Saudi consciousness and identity. From Jacques Benoist-Méchin through Helen Lackner[6] to Nazih Ayubi,[7] the verdict comes out the same: while recognizing the influence of foreign powers in Arabia, these authors systematically refuse to describe it as colonial. Political analysis of the Saudi kingdom therefore often begins with a paradox: 'The Saudi entity [is] no longer fully autonomous, although of course the country was never formally colonized.'[8]

It is this curious concessive clause that needs to be questioned.[9] Between 1745 and 1818, as we have seen, the expansion of the first Saudi state greatly disturbed the sultan of Istanbul, and the bad reputation of the 'Wahhabis' reached Europe, marking the irruption of the Saudis into world history. From 1788 to 1798, when they conquered a large part of the Peninsula and pressed on into Mesopotamia and Syria, the Mameluk pasha of Baghdad, vassal of the sultan of Istanbul, became sufficiently concerned about the skirmishes to launch an expedition in 1799 against the Diriya forces. From 1802, the year in which the Saudis sacked the holy Shiite city of Karbala in Iraq and, more than 3,000 kilometres away, captured the town of al-Taif in Hijaz (a province protected by the sultan of Istanbul), the pasha of Baghdad and the sharif of Mecca asked their suzerain to intervene. The Saudi occupation of the holy cities, Mecca in 1803 then Medina in 1805, was the starting point for a major expansion: by 1808 the Saudis were everywhere, their arrogance was proving intolerable, and their greed was exasperating the kinglets who ruled on behalf of the Ottoman Empire.

When the counter-offensive came in 1809, however, it was the British who recaptured points on the east coast, as the imprudent Saudis were threatening the naval and commercial monopoly that London was trying to establish in the Indian Ocean. In the same year, Sultan Mahmud II urged Mohammed Ali, viceroy of Egypt, to intervene in Hijaz. The Egyptian expedition moved off in 1811. In 1812 Mohammed Ali's son, Tusun Pasha, retook Medina; in 1813 he reached Jeddah and then Mecca. A number of incidents ensued (including a Saudi victory under the command of a woman, Ghaliya, at the Battle of Turaba in 1814) before the Egyptians broke through to

Najd. After a siege lasting several months, Diriya fell to Mohammed Ali's second son, Ibrahim Pasha, on 11 September 1818. Abdallah ibn Saud, whose reign had begun in 1814, was taken into captivity in Istanbul and beheaded.

The date 11 of September 1818 therefore marked the beginning of the occupation of the Arabian interior. Until 1843 Cairo exercised direct influence there: it posted garrisons, negotiated treaties with the tribes, took Saudi princes into captivity or reinstalled them as puppets on the throne, and generally conducted a real power politics, officially on behalf of the sultan but in reality for the glory of Mohammed Ali. The Egyptian occupation came to an end in 1840, when the threat from the French and the British led Mohammed Ali to withdraw his troops from Najd, Hasa and Yemen. In 1843, however, it was with help from the Egyptians that Faisal Al Saud, grandfather of King Abdelaziz, regained Riyadh after passing through Jabal Shammar (where he received the provisional allegiance of Prince Al Rashid). This was the beginning of the second Saudi state.

Meanwhile, the advancing British negotiated a truce in 1819 with the emirs on the eastern coast of Arabia, supported the emirs of Bahrain against the Saudis, demanded that the Egyptians stop intervening in Najd, and finally, in 1839, occupied the port of Aden. After the death of Mohammed Ali, the British and Ottomans were left in control of the Arab game and, from their coastal positions, pursued a classical policy combining carrot and stick, subsidy and gunboat. The British bombarded Jeddah in 1858, as well as the Saudi possessions of Dammam (1861), Ajman (1865), al-Qatif (1866) and again Dammam (1866). Few countries 'which have never been colonized' were pounded as heavily by a colonial power as the second Saudi kingdom, and the disappearance of the Saudi state in 1818 and its disorganization after 1843 were direct consequences of Egyptian, Ottoman and British policies in the Arabian Peninsula. In 1887 the fall of Riyadh, the last bastion of the second Saudi state, was caused by the forward thrust of the Najdi emirate of Hail, which was subordinate to Istanbul. Abd al-Rahman Al Saud, emir of Riyadh, fled to Kuwait in 1891.

In 1893 the British government revised its Arab policy. Lord Lansdowne, then chancellor of the exchequer, declared in May to the House of Lords: 'We should regard the establishment of a naval base, or a fortified port in the Persian Gulf by any other Power as a very grave menace to British interests, and we should certainly resist it with all means at our disposal.'[10] By then, after years of sparing Istanbul, nothing prevented the British from attacking the Ottoman Empire, and in less than ten years the Saudi state was restored. In 1902 Abdelaziz bin Abd al-Rahman Al Saud retook Riyadh with the help of the same British who, for some fifty years, had harassed the Saudis wherever their rule threatened the seas.

British patronage of the third Saudi state took concrete shape on 26 December 1915 at Darain (Isle of Tarut, facing Dammam), when Abdelaziz and Gulf resident Sir Percy Cox signed a treaty proclaiming a protectorate. This was dissolved twelve years later, on 20 May 1927, at Jeddah, when Abdelaziz and the British representative Sir Gilbert Clayton signed a 'treaty of friendship and good intentions', which, though recognizing the 'complete and absolute independence' of the Saudi possessions, did not prevent the British from intervening militarily on several occasions in central Arabia. 'The vast and sparsely populated Arabian kingdom was surrounded by British colonies, protectorates and dependencies. Even if it remained independent, Britain felt that the kingdom would be unable to hurt British interests.'[11]

From Ottoman domination to the British demiurge

It might be objected that Egyptian or Ottoman domination was not the same as colonization, since it was conducted by Muslim peoples against other Muslim peoples; that the protectorate treaty linking Britain and the Najd emirate was signed in a time of world war and revoked just twelve years later; that a protectorate should anyway not be confused with the legal expression of genuine colonization; and that the British did not create an administration in Riyadh or invest men and capital in central Arabia. In short, Arabia was a formal and provisional protectorate, which should not be confused with a real colony.

The first of these arguments seems unacceptable, given that Egyptian and Ottoman pressure in central Arabia was sufficiently great to overthrow an empire, raze its capital city and maintain dominance over all or part of Najd until as late as 1914 (when the princes of Hail were still receiving material and military support from Istanbul). Abdelaziz Al Saud himself had to declare allegiance to the sultan of Istanbul in 1904 – the year in which the Ottomans, alarmed by the new Saudi conquests and the capture of Qasim, sent a force of 5,000 men to Najd. The evacuation of these troops began in 1906, after they had become exhausted by two and a half years of garrison life in Najd, *bint al-jahannam*, the 'daughter of Hell'. In 1910, however, Abdelaziz again accepted the sultan's suzerainty and paid him tribute.

Nor does the 'Islamic' nature of the Ottoman Empire or its status as an independent power stand up for long to close scrutiny. From the 1840s to the 1860s, the Tanzimat reform movement led to de-Islamization of the judicial and educational systems and the armed forces, as Islam became a private affair and the Ottoman Empire evolved into a multi-denominational state. At the same time, these reforms opened the Ottoman economy to European capitalism, helping to weaken the political authority of the sultans, especially in the western part of the empire.[12]

The counter-reforms that Sultan Abdul Hamid introduced in the 1870s led to a reawakening of interest in the eastern part of the empire, especially as the British had established forward positions all around the Arabian Peninsula, in Yemen, Hijaz and the eastern coast (known as the Trucial Coast since the treaty of 1819).

During the period of its slow disintegration, the Ottoman Empire conducted a colonial policy through interventions both direct (as in 1904) and indirect (as in the support for Al Rashid of Hail), through the declaration of Hijaz as an Ottoman province, the appointment of the sharifs of Mecca,[13] the opening of the Damascus–Medina railway line in 1908 with support from the Second German Reich, and so on. As far as Arabia was concerned, this policy was directed not only at Hijaz (where it involved elements of modernization) but also at Najd; the aim was to keep central Arabia in a state of permanent war, thereby warding off any new Saudi push towards the holy cities of Mecca and Medina.

Ottoman rule was hesitant, disorderly and destructuring because of the rivalry with the British Empire. But what of the system of

British protection? Was it comparable to a genuine colonization? It is true that Britain did not establish a colonial administration in Najd, but nor did it fail to pursue a veritable gunboat policy in the Gulf and the Red Sea, against the Saudis and the Hijaz Arabs. It is true that the British Empire abstained from political intervention in Najd – mostly to avoid displeasing the Porte – but it did lend its support, via Prince Mubarrak Al Sabah of Kuwait, to the attempts of the young Abdelaziz Al Saud to recapture Riyadh and secure the Saudi throne. Movements and counter-movements, indirect aid and hidden subsidies would seem to suggest that the British were more involved in a 'small game' in Arabia than in direct colonization. But such a view underestimates the strategic importance of Arabia in the early twentieth century and the interest it aroused during the First World War. It also neglects the profound changes that British intervention precipitated in central Arabia.

In the late nineteenth century, as an ally of Imperial Germany, the Ottoman Empire earned its stripes as an enemy of the Western powers, and in the early twentieth century its borderlands became economic and military fronts in the great contest that eventually erupted in the 1914–18 war. In March 1914, after two attempts to fix the limits of their respective zones of influence, London and Istanbul divided up the Arabian Peninsula along a line running approximately from the straits of Bab al-Mandab (between Arabia and Africa) to the Qatar peninsula, so that the South fell to the British and the North (excluding Kuwait but including Najd) to the Ottomans. This division of the Arab cake followed almost twenty years of indirect rivalry, in which Arab princes had served as intermediaries. In the front rank, Abdelaziz Al Saud ran from legation to legation in the years after 1902, meeting Russian consuls, British representatives and Ottoman colonels with a view to shoring up the revival of Saudi rule in Najd.

Until the First World War, British policy in the Peninsula largely imitated Ottoman policy by setting princes against one another and against Ottoman rule. But it also involved a considerable degree of incoherence: the Indian Office in Bombay was in charge of Najd affairs (mainly through Harry St John Philby, Abdelaziz's future adviser), while the Arab Office in Cairo, acting through Thomas

Edward Lawrence, negotiated with Sharif Hussein of Mecca the finer points of the 'Arab revolt' that was supposed to attack the Ottoman Empire from the rear. The outbreak of the First World War triggered a sudden 'globalization' and a hardening of the latent conflict that had hitherto opposed the British and the Ottomans in Arabia. Evidence of this is the direct strategic, military and financial assistance that the British gave to Abdelaziz against the Shammars, as well as the signing of the protectorate treaty in 1915.

It was necessary to act fast. As early as 1914 Abdelaziz asked the sharif of Mecca, the prince of Hail and Prince Mubarrak of Kuwait to stay out of the European conflict and to conclude an agreement whereby the belligerent powers would guarantee the self-determination of the Arab peoples. Although Sharif Hussein shared Abdelaziz's national sentiment, the prince of Hail made known his pro-Ottoman sympathies and Mubarrak advised Abdelaziz to negotiate with the British as his suzerains. So far as the British were concerned, the point was to gain ground from the Ottomans, and so the central location of Najd, combined with Abdelaziz's irresolution and his distance from the 'Arab revolt', made him the obvious person to go for. On Christmas Day 1915, Abdelaziz received a thousand rifles and £20,000 sterling from the government in Bombay, and the following day he signed the Treaty of Darain. As early as 1915, then, the treaty linking Abdelaziz to the British meant that T.E. Lawrence's activities would never be more than a sideshow in comparison with the serious action in the east that involved support for the emirate of Najd.

On 16 May 1919 Lord Milner, the British colonial minister, stated that it was necessary to create an 'independent' Arabia that would be within the Crown's sphere of influence and immune from the political intrigues of the other European powers. The promise that the British had given Sharif Hussein before the First World War would eventually be kept on 18 September 1932, with the foundation of the Arabian kingdom. But this 'Saudi Arabian Kingdom'[14] was not Hashemite and covered only four-fifths of the Arabian Peninsula, not the whole of the region.

British aid to the Saudis did not merely facilitate the creation of an independent Arabian kingdom; it also had a lasting influence on

its structure. Although the sums in question (£5,000 a month from
November 1916, £100,000 a year from March 1921, plus occasional
supplies of sub-machine guns, rifles and financial liquidities) were
derisory in comparison with Britain's financial strength, they were
enormous in terms of the budget of the new Saudi state and played
a huge role in winning the allegiance of the tribes.

As we can see, the structure of a *rentier state* funded and supported
from abroad (in this case by a European power) already existed by
1916. It testified to the globalization of Arabia – a corollary of the
formation in Najd of a second front between the Allies and the Central
Powers. Thus, the sudden rush of oil wealth after the Second World
War did not create, but was inserted into, an alienating budgetary
system that had been further strengthened on 18 July 1943, when
President Roosevelt included Arabia in the lend-lease[15] scheme to
counter 'the rapidly increasing British influence in Saudi Arabia'
and to ensure that 'the reserve of oil in Saudi Arabia will remain
under the control of Americans'.[16] This provision, which allowed
the Americans to supply money and weapons directly to Riyadh,
immediately drew expressions of mocking surprise from certain US
political circles: 'I don't know how this decision will be explained
to members of Congress,' wrote Harry Hopkins to Jesse Jones, 'nor
how they will be persuaded that Arabia is a democracy suffering
fascist aggression.'[17]

In other words, oil did not alone bring about Saudi Arabia's
subjugation to the West. Nor was it the only factor in the US–Saudi
pact, which would mainly serve to cement a military alliance against
the German enemy and, in the postwar period, against the Soviet
bloc. The current dependence of the Saudi economy and polity – a
dependence that the oil boom of 1973 made quite formidable – is
therefore a distant effect of British imperial policy in the Peninsula
at the turn of the twentieth century.

As early as the First World War, it was thanks especially to the
manna from London that the Saud family was able to establish its
pre-eminence over the other regimes in the Peninsula. Once it had
gained this position, mostly by force of arms, the newly founded
Kingdom of Saudi Arabia was able to gain relative autonomy from
the European powers, and to carry out an unprecedented political,

social and economic strategy. In fact, three strategies governed the foundation of modern Arabia: politically, the consolidation of a family whose contours closely followed those of the kingdom; socially, the removal of 'Bedouinism' as a significant reality; and economically, the constitution of a class of technocrats and merchants dependent upon the royal family.

Taking power through women

One of the regular items in the list used to argue that Saudi Arabia is not a genuine state is its supposedly tribal character, as if it were the property of one family to the exclusion of all others. This analysis is often illustrated by the story of the Riyadh man in the street who puns that the royal family (*al-'usra al-malakiya*) is the property-owning family (*al-'usra al-malika*).

Now, far from confirming the tribal character of the third Saudi state, the pre-eminence of the Saud family was based precisely upon the most intense opposition to tribalism. When the official ideology dismisses tribal affiliations in favour of allegiance to God or the reigning family, this should not be seen as a stock formula or as proof that Arabs from the Peninsula have readily bowed to a religious ideology. Rather than an expression of tribalism or religious domination, the equation between the Saud family and the Saudi state is the result of a long historical process stretching over three-quarters of a century, which even today is subject to numerous reservations and forward or backward steps. The royal family is present at all levels of power – naturally at the head of the state and in the Council of Ministers (where in 2003 it held four of the twenty-four portfolios[18]), but also on the boards of large companies and everywhere in the senior civil service. It has had to assert its power in a delicate context where many rival independent tribes have jealously claimed the liberty to choose and change their alliances, switching from support for the Sauds to support for the sharif of Mecca or Prince Al Rashid of Hail, or offering their services to the Ottomans or the British as the circumstances dictated.

At the turn of the twentieth century, three political systems were operational in Arabia: one based on the assertion of power with sacred origins but also foreign support (such as that of the sharifs of Mecca, who were appointed by the sultan of Istanbul); one based on the assertion of tribal and Bedouin power, with financial support from an empire (e.g. Al Rashid of Hail's reliance both on the powerful Shammar tribal federation and on Istanbul); and the more 'democratic' rule of merchant oligarchies, supported or not supported by a foreign power (e.g. the British-backed regime of the Sabahs in Kuwait, or the Najd merchant oligarchies of Qasim who formed temporary alliances with the Rashids, the Ottomans or the Sauds).

When Abdelaziz returned to Riyadh in 1902, none of these three options was on offer: as he was neither a descendant of the Prophet nor the ally of a powerful Bedouin tribe nor the representative of a merchant oligarchy, he had to create a political regime that had no precedent. British strategic support would prove invaluable, since it enabled him to purchase tribal support through a mechanism that persists today in the general tendency of the Saudi state to buy off opposition instead of repressing it.[19] At the same time, since British aid was not large enough to guarantee the definitive submission of tribes, it led to a situation of constant warfare in which tribal support had to be ensured through the prospect of more and more gains from conquest.

It was at this level that Abdelaziz's first, matrimonial strategy operated. The impressive number of wives of Arabia's first king has always been the occasion for stories, commentaries and legends. Philby, the British adviser to the Sauds, reports that Abdelaziz married 135 virgins and 100 other women, choosing them from the great Bedouin tribes, the tribal reigning families, the family of the descendants of Abd al-Wahhab, the great sedentary families of Najd or, more prosaically, families of popular stock or even the slave population. In this way, Abdelaziz fathered as many as forty-three sons and more than fifty daughters.[20]

These unheard-of extremes of polygamy enabled Abdelaziz to create his own dynasty and to extend it to all the tribes, all the great families and all the regions of Arabia, with the aim not so much of forging alliances – what lasting alliance can result from an easily terminable marriage with a wife likely to be humiliated and replaced by another? – as of subordinating 'the Arabian population through a systematic appropriation of its most cherished and valued members, women'.[21] Abdelaziz's matrimonial strategy should therefore not be seen in a tribal framework, since its aim was precisely to violate (literally as well as figuratively) the honour of the great families and tribes of the kingdom. It should be understood, rather, as the assertion of *supratribal* power and the constitution of a privileged *class* that now numbers more than 12,000 male and female members.

Any form of rule by the Sauds was unthinkable in tribal terms, given that the Abdelaziz family was sedentary and lacked any claim to nobility. It was therefore absolutely necessary for the Sauds to find a way of asserting their pre-eminence over the Arabian tribes that broke with the usual tribal syntax and made Abdelaziz both the virtual and the real centre of power. If there is such a thing as paternalism in Saudi Arabia, it is anchored in the strategy of taking power through women, much more than in mere distribution of the proceeds of oil. As we have seen, the structures of power predate the discovery of oil and cannot be said to stem from it: the key to the success of the Sauds was that, in taking the helm, they knew how to break out of their natural family group and traditional region. Perhaps as much as their choice of foreign ally, this was the difference between the Rashids and the Sauds: the strict tribalism of the Shammar allies of the Ottomans was matched, and superseded, by the unprecedented supratribalism of the Saud allies of the British.[22]

Until recently, this supratribal affirmation of the Saud family lay behind its extraordinary *political representativeness*. Appropriating tribal political mechanisms for their own use, the Sauds could guarantee to every member of a Bedouin tribe or a sedentary oligarchy that his grievances would find an attentive ear in high places. The princes' majlis, existing not only for the affirmation of royal prestige but also for the airing of requests through specially authorized individuals, is an informal assembly where the 'court' of a member of the royal family comes together; it has been, and to some extent still is, one of the centres of power in Arabia. If we consider that one or two hundred friends, employees and assorted parasites gravitate around even the youngest and least powerful prince, that the total number of male princes is in excess of six thousand, and that, through the

complex system of *wasta* (intermediaries or 'connections'), everyone is entitled to have access to the summit of the state, then we
can see that this adds up to a significant form of organic political
representation.

In the late 1980s, the system functioned more or less as follows:

> The king is, in principle, accessible to all his subjects, in accordance
> with ancient tribal and Islamic traditions. In practice, the king
> delegates that accessibility too, for example to Prince Salman, the
> governor of Riyadh, and the latter in turn to his *wakil* [represent-
> ative]. But nothing prevents anyone from appealing to the higher
> level if he does not achieve his aim at the lower one. The higher
> one goes, however, the more formidable the obstacles encountered.
> It is relatively simple to get to see the prefect of Afif. Anyone want-
> ing the ear of the *wakil* in Riyadh can count on days of waiting:
> the Cerberuses around the desk have an infallible instinct for their
> master's priorities and whoever can and cannot lay claim, in all
> reasonableness, to a few seconds of his time.... The average Saudi,
> however, engages an intermediary [*wasta*], someone who regularly
> mixes in exalted circles and whom he tries to persuade, if necessary
> via other intermediaries, to smooth his path to the satrap.[23]

There should be no illusions about this 'Saudi democracy', however. Reserved for members of the most influential tribes and 'clients'
of the great sedentary families, it is closed to most members of the
middle classes and consolidates the oligarchic character of the regime
more than it opens it to popular aspirations. In 1992, facing a social
revolution associated with intensive modernization and the rise of
deracinated middle layers sometimes lacking any tribal reference, the
royal family was finally compelled to reconstitute the Consultative
Assembly (Majlis al-Shura) as a new mechanism of representation
that would try to respond to pressure from the opposition and the
'new Saudis'.[24]

Twilight of the Bedouins

Abdelaziz's second anti-tribal strategy is the one that has made the
most ink flow; it still elicits heated comment and the tracing of
sometimes imaginary genealogies. We are referring to the formation

of an armed body of religiously indoctrinated men of Bedouin origin, the Ikhwan or 'Brotherhood', for the purpose of conquering huge expanses of land. Some have seen this 'army of God' as the bloody ancestor of today's Islamists, a spectre whose successive apparitions have been Juhaiman al-Utaibi (organizer of the seizure of the great mosque of Mecca in 1979) and Osama bin Laden. But what such analyses have failed to note is the distance separating contemporary Saudi Islamism (an urban and globalized phenomenon) from the last great manifestation of the 'Bedouin spirit' in Arabia. Besides, for many Saudis of Bedouin origin, the whole story of the Ikhwan is still today a source of martial pride.

From 1912 to 1929, this episode without precedent in Arabia made it possible for the royal family to assert itself symbolically and militarily as the holder of all authority. The creation of a Bedouin army allowed Abdelaziz not only to fulfil his declared objective of conquering the Arabian Peninsula but also to enrol Bedouins in the very enterprise of destroying Bedouin economy and society. The idea for the Ikhwan, which was put together by three sedentary ulema (two qadhi or judges, Abdallah Al al-Shaikh from Riyadh and Shaikh Issa from Hasa, and Abd al-Karim al-Maghrebi), involved first and foremost the sedentarization of the Bedouin tribes.

The first settlement (hijra) was founded by Mutair Bedouins in January 1913, at al-Artawiya, halfway between Qasim and Kuwait. Based on agriculture, it soon expanded into central Arabia. There were 52 hijra by 1920, 62 by 1923 and 120 by 1929. With the help of a lot of preaching, sometimes violent pressure and the disbursement of subsidies from Riyadh, Bedouins were called upon to follow the example of the Prophet's Hegira (hijra) from Mecca to Medina by accomplishing a modern Hegira from unbelief to belief, insubordination to subordination, ignorance (jahiliya) to knowledge: that is, 'to abandon forever the city of polytheism for the city of Islam',[25] in the words of the manual written a century and a half earlier by Muhammad ibn Abd al-Wahhab, which served as the theological basis for the movement (and which appears to have been printed and published by the British in Bombay).[26]

The idea of the Ikhwan was similar to the idea that had led a century and a half before to the creation of the first Saudi state;

the religious vocabulary of 'holy war' served to express a will to conquer, to centralize huge territories around Najd and to convert the Bedouins to a settled way of life. Abdelaziz made his first use then of the Islamic lexicon, but as an instrument for sedentary Saudis to take power away from the Bedouins by making them dependent upon subsidies from Riyadh, whether tied to a plot of land or dispatched all over the Peninsula to bear the good news of the Saudi conquests.

Their armies terrorized central Arabia in the regions of Hijaz and Jabal Shammar. In May 1919, their crushing victory over the troops of the sharif of Mecca at Turaba spread their fame as far as the West, where the press echoed the bombastic and frightened tones in which European diplomats had reported the 'Wahhabi' victories more than a century earlier. When threatened by the British resident in Jeddah, however, Abdelaziz felt compelled to withdraw his troops – just as, a few months before, also under British pressure, he had had to withdraw the Ikhwan from Hail. Yet the British allowed the Ikhwan to capture Hail on 1 November 1921, and gave the green light for their conquest of Hijaz in the summer of 1924. On 5 September the Ikhwan took al-Taif amid a bloodbath; on 15 October Mecca surrendered without a fight; on 6 December 1925 Medina laid down arms and on 22 December Jeddah opened its gates after a year-long siege. On 11 December 1925, the Hijaz ulema and nobility proclaimed Abdelaziz king of Hijaz.

The submission of Abdelaziz to the British led the Ikhwan to remonstrate for the first time with their prince, when they gathered in late 1918 at Shaqra, between Riyadh and Qasim. It was probably Faisal al-Duwish, sheikh of the Mutair Bedouin and the brains behind the rebellion, who actually spoke these sharp words to him:

> We demand a fight against the enemies of the faith! Is that not why you recruited, instructed and trained us? You have only to say the word, O Abdelaziz, and we will follow you to the death, provided that it is against sharif Hussein, who is prostituting the holy cities! Otherwise, *you should know that we will never obey orders from abroad.* In speaking thus, I express the feelings of each one of your soldiers![27]

From that date the writing was on the wall for the Ikhwan – even if Abdelaziz made full use of their fighting capacities, particularly during the conquest of Hijaz. The agreements fixing the frontiers of central Arabia, signed on 2 December 1922 at al-Uqair, on the Arabian–Persian Gulf, helped to seal the fate of the Bedouin army. The open space of steppe and pastureland was delimited for the first time in the history of Arabia, by virtue of the British mandates in Transjordania and Iraq.[28] For the first time, too, Bedouins had a nationality attached to them: Iraqi in the case of the Muntafiq, Zafir and Amarat; Najdi in that of the Shammar and Aniza. The British recognized the legal existence of the Saudi state, which was now officially known as the Emirate of Najd and its dependencies (*Imarat Najd wa Mulhaqatiha*).

Checked in the north by the new international frontiers, the movement of conquest marked time on the edge of Transjordania. In August 1923, following the traditional northward flow of the summer migration, the Ikhwan managed to penetrate Transjordania and Iraq, but they were captured by British forces and twelve of their number were executed in Amman. In August 1924 the Ikhwan again entered Transjordania through the Wadi Sirhan, only to be driven back by the British air force. In late 1926, Ikhwan leaders presented Abdelaziz with a seven-point statement, in which they protested against the centralization of the Saudi state, the contempt shown for Bedouin tribal territories, and the British influence in what had been a protectorate since 1915.

On 6 December 1928, the Ikhwan repeated their injunctions to Abdelaziz, who promised to negotiate with the British and won the acclaim of the sedentary notables of Najd. 'The tribal army's demands were couched in the language of religion, but as expressed at the Riyadh Conference in 1928, they were clearly a reaction to what had become of nomadic life during their few years of service in the Saudi army.'[29] These demands were ignored, and a confrontation became inevitable. On 31 March 1929, Abdelaziz defeated the Ikhwan at the Battle of Sibila; the Ajman Bedouins, who had resumed their traditional way of life in 1928, were hunted down and their sheikh was killed. But in July 1929 the Ajman cut the road from Riyadh to the Arabian–Persian Gulf, while the Utban cut the Hijaz road;

central Arabia was entering into turmoil. The last Ikhwan were finally overcome in December 1929, when they were pushed south by British machine guns and encircled by British forces and the troops of Abdelaziz. Their leaders were seized and taken in captivity to Riyadh.

The Ikhwan movement, reactionary as much as revolutionary,[30] allowed the nascent state to break the tribal system and to conquer vast stretches of territory. The creation of the Bedouin army was the first and most striking of the anti-Bedouin measures taken by Abdelaziz; it opened the way for a series of reforms to bring the Bedouin tribes under the Saudi state and to favour the sedentary population by creating a state-protected agriculture via the interior ministry. An Agricultural Development Bank was founded in 1964, and a number of decrees on landed property were promulgated between 1957 and 1961.

This process of sedentarization dramatically accelerated after 1968, when a new law on collective ownership forced Bedouins to emigrate to urban areas as paupers reliant on handouts. For a while groups of Bedouins had tried to maintain their way of life, while improving it through the use of motor vehicles and the formation of agricultural and pastoral units copied from the tribe and supported by the welfare state. A few tribes did successfully achieve this changeover, until the state put an end to it through the law of 28 September 1968 on the allotment of collective land, which made illegal the concept of 'customary ownership' underlying the tribal appropriation of land and tied state assistance to criteria defined by various technical and administrative departments. The law therefore 'favoured state employees and shopkeepers more than members of tribes able to brandish historical claims to a territory';[31] it favoured the sedentary population over Bedouins, with the result that, at least since 1968, there has been a 'complete disjuncture between the Saudi state and the Bedouin part of civil society. If there is a government in Arabia, it is not Bedouin; and if there are still Bedouins on this territory, they are excluded from a regime that has always acted to restrict and neutralize them.'[32]

At the same time, the state was at pains to settle intertribal conflicts, which did not end in the 1960s and 1970s when oil revenue began to reach the countryside. Economic and social upheavals led to the gradual disappearance of the Saudi Bedouins, now threatened in their collective existence by the establishment of a modern society and state administration. Far from being Bedouin, then, the Saudi state was actually constituted through the more or less forced sedentarization of the Bedouins. In the 'official' rhetoric of modern city-dwellers, praise for the state that 'pacified' Arabia and 'subdued' the violent tribes has come to occupy an important place. In any event, the nomadic population is now estimated at roughly 2 or 3 per cent of the Saudi total; state policy has borne perfect fruit.

It would appear that, while the modernizing state has especially targeted Bedouins, it has also turned the figure of the Bedouin into a vehicle of Saudi identity – all the more since Bedouins have no longer been a force in opposition to the central state. With his rough edges removed, the Bedouin is here reduced to minor attributes (camel, hospitality) and folklore elements: 'The fact that an artificial figure of the ethereal Bedouin has now appeared in the consciousness of society and tourists is a fairly clear sign of the process that has placed the Bedouin group under the formal domination of the Saudi state.'[33] Appropriation of the Bedouin figure means that everyone can make a claim to it – for example, by saying that the sedentary population is of Bedouin origin, or that all Saudis are of Bedouin origin. This new discourse says little about the real feelings of Saudis – still less about the historical reality – but it speaks volumes about how the state manipulates tradition for political ends, inventing an anodyne folkloristic 'traditionalism' as the basis for national identity.[34] Thus, what we have learned from the crushing of the Ikhwan movement in 1929 is that the Saudi state is not a Bedouin state but a sedentary and urban state.

The second lasting consequence of the Ikhwan phenomenon was the bringing into line of the Najd religious establishment. Having been enlisted as early as 1914 to supervise the religious activities of the Ikhwan and to appeal for greater tolerance on their part, it was subsequently forced to embellish the actions of Abdelaziz with the religious legitimacy that the Bedouin army required. In July 1926, to control the zeal of the Ikhwan in Hajiz, Abdelaziz set up a 'League for the Promotion of Virtue and the Eradication

of Vice' (Ha'iya li-l-'amr bi-l-ma'ruf wa-l-nahy 'an al-Minkar), the famous
Mutawwi'un or 'Mutawas'; and three years later, in July 1929, he
created a Public Morality Board in Riyadh to combat the influence
of the Ikhwan (not, as some Western observers appear to believe,
to 'combat Westernization').

The Mutawwi'un are today the relic of a movement deprived of its
mover, even if the League's reactivation since the Iranian Revolution
has made it an obsession with Westerners living in the kingdom.
In reality, the League is now an autonomous department of the
ministry of religious affairs, and its activists are Saudi state employees.
Representatives of this 'public morality' department appear more and
more rarely in public, but this does not mean that they are any less
feared. We should add that League members should not be confused
with the mosque preachers, also state employees and also called
Mutawwi'un, nor a fortiori with members of the Islamist opposition
against which they are often instructed to fight.

Indirectly, then, the Ikhwan movement led to the Gleichsschaltung
of the Najd clergy. After the capture of Hijaz and the incorporation
of its traditional clergy into the Saudi religious elite, this tendency
would gather new and tremendous momentum.

The founding alliance:
Hijaz merchants and the Sauds

Three errors of perspective, bound up with the fascination that
imaginary Islamic, Bedouin or oil-related causalities hold for the
Western historiography of Saudi Arabia, weigh heavily on our understanding of the genesis of the Saudi state. The first of these errors is
to see Abdelaziz's marriages but not their purpose of going beyond
tribal alliances and arrangements to concentrate political-military
power in the hands of a single family. Many would argue that the
state merges with the Saud family, but the Saud family has also
done everything to merge with the state and to convert itself into
a genuinely supratribal oligarchy.

The second error is to describe the Ikhwan movement as a purely
religious phenomenon, without seeing in it the end of Bedouin

economics and politics, or, in other words, without grasping the paradox that a section of the population (the Bedouins) participated in the destruction of their own way of life and social system (nomadism). The third error is to read the financial muscle of the Saudi state without seeing that it is rooted not only in oil revenue but in the formation of a modern centralized state around an efficient tax service. For, after the capture of Hijaz and before the flow of oil wealth, part of the strategy of the Saudi state was to establish a powerful technocracy.

In line with the usual schema of modernization, Arabia's contemporary political and economic history has been a matter of administrative, fiscal and monetary unification and gradual centralization. The chief impulse behind this rationalization was not religious but had to do with the necessity of accumulating resources and revenue.

In this preoccupation with financial aspects, the third Saudi state – an expansionist state based on a major rallying of the population of Najd, then Hasa and finally Hijaz and Asir – resembles the first Saudi state. The Saudi credo is thus summed up in an administrative order from 1933: 'Following the old method is not an end in itself. Investigate new sources; and find new people who can pay the *zakaat*; and make use of the different tribes as informants to disclose new sources of wealth. These are the instructions of your majesty the King.'[35] The instructions are categorical: the new administration must be inventive and creative; it should refuse to 'follow the old method' and enlist the traditional classes (Bedouins or members of Hijaz corporations) in the collection of information and resources.

Apart from the succession of kings,[36] three alliances with sections of society that were, so to speak, forced to dig their own graves made possible the unification and centralization of a huge territory with varied geography and a far from irenic political history. The regime first allied itself with the tribes, which were then forced to end the tribal system, to show submission through their women and to orchestrate their own demise in the context of the Ikhwan movement.

The second alliance – in the period following the seizure of Hijaz, when Abdelaziz tried to crush the endemic sedition of the Ikhwan – grouped around the Najd political-military oligarchy the corporations of Mecca and Medina. These corporations lived off Hajj (pilgrimage) services and would harvest the mass of taxes and duties that provided the core of state expenditure down to the beginnings of oil exploration in the 1950s; this contribution to the building of a revenue service would eventually be their undoing.

The third alliance, which truly laid the foundations of a modern state administration, brought together the Sauds and the great merchants of Jeddah. As we have seen, the alliance underpinning the Saudi regime was not tribal in nature; nor was it religious, since religious power was conceived as being directly subordinate to royal power. The truly founding alliance, then, was contracted with the merchants of Hijaz, so that it was an urban capitalism and a supratribal oligarchy which, in its original manner, structured the modern Saudi state.

This state was built on the shores of the Red Sea, not in the Najd desert. Moreover, the budgetary apparatus of the nascent state drew on revenue that it raised from trade or the Hajj pilgrimage, making the third state structurally 'maritime' and 'mercantile', not the inland construction that is often described. Unlike the first Saudi state, then, the third is a maritime product – and, unlike the second, it has moved out beyond Najd and lastingly incorporated four-fifths of the Peninsula. In fact, thanks to a remarkable process of 'decentralization', the third Saudi state was constructed entirely in the province of Hijaz, where it could rely upon commercial and administrative know-how inherited from the powerful Ottoman bureaucracy, and upon many centuries of trade with the outside world.

In December 1925 Abdelaziz created, in Jeddah, a department of foreign affairs that would be the precursor of the foreign ministry run by the Syrian Yussuf Yassin, and, in Mecca, a police and security authority and a general health department. At the same time, he set up an education board, and the Hijaz schools dating from Ottoman times were supplemented in 1926 with a dozen schools in Najd. The core of this embryonic administration was created through a modern tax system, which, in 1944, was unified through the suppression of tribal fiscal practices and the rights of the Hijaz corporations over the Hajj pilgrimage area. The creation of the *mudiriya* or Department of *Zakat* and Income Tax (DZIT), under Abdallah al-Sulayman, enshrined both the royal monopoly of taxation and the break from the Islamic fiscal system: 'The reforms linked the *zakat* rate to the changing budgetary needs of the state. *This act contradicted Islamic law* and broke with the established pattern of generating new revenues through levies falling outside the scriptural proscription.'[37]

Birth of a kingdom and a unified state administration

In 1934 the first budget of the kingdom revealed that the main source of state income was taxes raised during the Hajj, followed by the oil concessions of 1933 and mining revenue, and finally the *zakat* and income tax. The new state was recognized by the Soviet Union on 16 February 1926, by the UK, France and Turkey the same year, and by the United States in 1931. The Kingdom of Saudi Arabia was formally constituted on 18 September 1932, in response to a petition by the merchants of Hijaz for the fusion of its various provinces and the establishment of an internal market corresponding to the size of their appetites.

In the 1920s and 1930s, a number of political parties coexisted in Hijaz, including one opposed to its unification with Najd: the Hijaz Liberal Party, led by Tahir and Hussein al-Dabbagh and supported (from Transjordania and Iraq) by the Hashemites. Political life was relatively free at the time: Abdelaziz set up elected municipal councils in Mecca, Medina, Jeddah, Yanbu and al-Taif, which complemented the activity of the Hijaz consultative council (Majlis al-Shura) created by the Hashemites on 6 October 1924, at a time when they were on the brink of collapse. In 1926 a new constitution for Hijaz legalized the power of the elected councils and the co-opted Majlis al-Shura. Elected chambers of commerce in Jeddah, Riyadh and Khobar (on the Gulf coast) functioned both as advisers to the prince and as enforcers of official regulations – a dual role that made them the real sites of economic power down to the 1970s. In July 1928 a royal decree created a joint Majlis al-Shura for Hijaz and Najd, and, although the decree never took effect, the regulations adopted by the Majlis of Hijaz applied in practice throughout the country. In other words, the relative autonomy that the Sauds accorded to

Hijaz made it the political, economic and administrative laboratory of modern Arabia.

In 1930 a foreign ministry was created under the leadership of Faisal ibn Abdelaziz, the future king. This was followed by the creation of a regular army (to replace the defunct Ikhwan militia), a military academy at al-Taif, and a finance ministry that incorporated the powerful DZIT. In 1932 a Hijaz Council of Ministers was inaugurated by Faisal, who now held the three most important offices in the kingdom: de facto prime minister, viceroy of the most modern province and minister of foreign affairs, ahead of his elder brother, Saud, and second only to his father, King Abdelaziz. He learned the ropes as a technocrat in Hijaz and the West, and within a few decades had accumulated solid experience as a top administrator.

At the level of the economy, in response to a demand from the large merchants that was relayed by the British protector, a single commercial code was adopted in 1931 along the lines of the Ottoman code of 1850. By the mid-1930s, then, the state administration was in place and the Saudi market was unified. With the conditions present for a lasting alliance between the Sauds and the Hijaz merchants, it was possible to eliminate those who opposed political and economic unification in order to maintain their privileges: that is to say, the Hajj corporations and the political parties of Hijaz. The parties were outlawed in June 1932, and the most active oppositionists were repressed with British help.

However, in keeping with a tradition that went back to early stages of the conquest of the kingdom in the first decade of the twentieth century, the oppositionists were subsequently reintegrated into one of the circles of power and forced to submit to the king's authority. It was in this way that Tahir al-Dabbagh became Hijaz education minister in 1935. The great merchant families, for their part, took advantage of the new trade outlets opened up by market unification and government price controls. Based in turn on political and administrative unification, the new commercial and fiscal unification went together with monetary unification. A Saudi Arabian Monetary Agency (SAMA) was created in 1952, and a new national currency – the rial – replaced the thalers, sovereigns, Egyptian pounds and Indian rupees that had been in use until then.

The construction of the Saudi state therefore merged with the stabilization of revenue, commercial regulation and trade. This did not proceed without rough patches and conflicts, the most important of which opposed the Najd military oligarchy to the two heterogenous social groups forming the Hijaz merchant oligarchy: the corporations of the two holy cities and the merchant families of Jeddah.

While the power of the corporations was gradually eroded by fiscal rationalization and market unification (which deprived them of their monopoly over Hajj services), the opposition of the great merchants was broken down through a 'contract' with the royal family whereby the merchant oligarchy exchanged its political autonomy for fiscal allegiance to the new state – and the enrichment that would accompany access to a single national market. In 1938, as a sign of this loss of autonomy, the Majlis al-Shura was coupled with another body, the Council of Representatives (Majlis al-Wukala), which was more tightly subject to the royal administration. The Jeddah Chamber of Commerce was annexed in turn by the royal regime, and in March 1954 it became the ministry of commerce. In the same year, a national administrative court was created on the model of an old Persian institution, the Diwan al-Mazhalim. In October 1963 a new administrative map demarcated four regions, and in 1974 a new division into eighteen provinces (thirteen directly under interior ministry control) would confirm the strengthening of royal power. The other side of the wholesale state-led modernization, then, was the state's gradual absorption of all social and economic forces through the constitution of a powerful administration.

Hijaz 'civil society', with its impressive parties, associations and press, was itself eventually swallowed up by the state administration. In 1938 the daily paper *Al-Madina al-Munawwara* was created in Medina, and in 1939 the weekly *Sawt al-Hijaz* (Voice of Hijaz) became *Al-Bilad al-Sa'udiya* (The Saudi Land). It was not long before an intellectual apparatus also came into being: the first religious university, the university of Umm al-Qura ('Mother of Cities', one of the nicknames for the holy city), was founded in 1949 in Mecca; the first lay university opened at Riyadh in 1957, and the first college of engineering in 1960. In the same year, against the advice of the religious establishment, the future King Faisal set up a Female

Education Board, and the first university for young women logically saw the light of day a few years later, in 1968. Education was free, and higher education was largely subsidized through a generous system of grants.[38]

Of course, the development of a genuine welfare state, based on the rationalization of public finances, did not follow a straight and uninterrupted course; there would be many retreats in the 1950s. After Arabia joined the International Monetary Fund in 1957, budgetary matters were at the heart of a power struggle between King Saud and Crown Prince Faisal that lasted from 1958 to 1964. Saud was a 'traditionalist', who relied on Bedouin layers of the population and toyed with a fairground nationalism: he tried to have Nasser assassinated in March 1958, but shortly afterwards, when he was himself removed from power, he joined forces with Egyptian nationalism and accused Faisal on Radio Cairo of being 'an agent of imperialism and ally of colonialism against his Arab brethren'.[39] Faisal, on the other hand, may be thought of as a modernizing technocrat concerned to put public finances on a sounder footing and to struggle against corruption. The two men's open rivalry expressed itself in spectacular resignations, sudden disappearances abroad, contradictory positions, bragging and threats, until Faisal finally won out and was proclaimed king in 1964.

Meanwhile a second front had opened in the royal family, between Faisal the 'liberal' and his brother Talal the 'socialist', a 'free prince' who supported the idea of a constitutional monarchy that Saud had associated with the regime in 1960 to counter Faisal's plotting. In 1958 Faisal, then prime minister, had curbed public expenditure, devalued the rial, introduced import restrictions, forbidden the princes to engage in business and reduced their annual allowances. Prince Talal, who was appointed finance minister in the famous government of 2 December 1960, created a planning committee and a system of tribunals to settle disputes in the state administration; he also called for nationalization of large swathes of the economy and aroused the ire of business circles. The merchants, the bourgeoisie and the 'liberal' branch of the royal family chose Faisal against Talal, while King Saud was pushed out by the most influential princes. After going into voluntary exile in Cairo, Talal maintained that socialism was the fundamental principle of Islam and – at a press conference in Beirut – said that his aim was 'to establish a constitutional democracy within the framework of a monarchy'.[40] He returned to Arabia in the 1970s and continued, more discreetly, to campaign for an opening up of the political system. Talal ibn Abdelaziz is today one of the royal family's most fervent apostles of reform.

'We are progressives by virtue of our Islam'

In 1973, on the eve of the oil boom, the Kingdom of Saudi Arabia was a relatively strong state, based on an alliance with the business bourgeoisie and a powerful fiscal administration that brought in revenue and information about the national economy. It was a protectionist state, which taxed labour, capital and foreign goods and in 1960 imposed a system of 'sponsoring'.[41] It was an interventionist state committed to planning, which assigned to Petromin (the General Petroleum and Mineral Organization) the task of creating a public industrial sector.[42] It was a welfare state, which in 1963 founded a General Social Security Organization and provided free and subsidized national education. It was a liberal state, which favoured the interests of the Hijaz merchants and the Aramco-connected bourgeoisie that had sprung up in the Eastern Province.[43] And it was an authoritarian state, scalded by the civil strife and palace revolutions of the 1950s and 1960s and terrified by the rise of a nationalist and socialist opposition.[44] The economic boom of 1973–83 resulting from the sharp rise in oil revenues then tore this state apart and plunged it back into the past, so that the tax administration became superfluous and social security came to be seen as mollycoddling.

Was it an Islamic state? Formally yes, but substantively no. Formally, the administrative modernization and social-economic progress were spoken of in the language of Islam. After the ulema opposition of the 1920s and 1930s, which had emerged in response to the sudden importing of 'progress' from the West in a context of religious rivalry between Najd and Hijaz, the royal regime was careful to justify any political or social change by reference to the revealed text. But, with a schema very similar to the account of progress given by Auguste

Comte, the French pope of positivism, progress was conceived along the lines of natural plant growth, as the *harmonious* development of potentialities present from the beginning. A third-grade sociology manual, published in 1978, accordingly found the key to social progress in acclimatization (*imtizaj hadhari*, gradual adaptation to the dominant Western social model).

More a modernization of Islam than an Islamization of modernity, the official ideological tendency is neatly summed up in a slogan that marries Islam and progress, religious thought and social planning: 'We are progressives [*taqaddumiyun*] by virtue of our Islam.'[45] So far as religion is concerned, this trend may be seen in the considerable liberties that the royal regime has allowed itself. Already in 1924, for the elaboration of Islamic law (*sharia*), it authorized the ulema to use comparative reasoning (*qiyas*) as well as concepts of a general interest (*maslahat 'amma*) and a prince's interest dependent on circumstances (*masalih mursala*), neither of which had been recognized by the Hanbalite school. Islamic legal thought itself therefore allowed a lot of scope for 'profane' political considerations, while serving the economic and social 'developmentalism' of the state.

Substantively, however, the modernization schemas were borrowed from the West, particularly from the Egyptian example of the application of British and French norms. Saudi public law is very largely of French inspiration, and the Institute of Public Administration was founded in 1960 along the lines of the École nationale d'administration. The ideologies guiding the economic and social reforms of the 1950s and 1960s – from Anglo-American liberalism in the case of Faisal's reforms to a watered-down version of Arab socialism in the case of those drafted by Talal – were imported en bloc.

Modernization succeeded because, in the 1960s, state revenues doubled, economic activity increased and an endogenous industry gradually took shape around the production of consumer goods and construction materials. The impact of oil was marginal, endangering neither the development of a productive economy nor the redistributive structure of the state apparatus. Until the 1970s this economic and social growth was the main source of legitimacy for the state and the royal family.

In this context, Islamic legitimacy was only one link in the chain of reasons – from 'people's welfare' to 'harmonious social progress' – which was supposed to convince Saudis that their state belonged to the best of all possible worlds. Modernization could be and was spoken of in the language of religion. Nevertheless, allegiance to the royal family was at first bound up more with modernization of the economy and society: economic centralization and unification for the bourgeoisie, public service and redistribution for the emergent middle classes. Until the 1970s the Sauds presented themselves above all as the benefactors of society, embodied in the tutelary figure of King Faisal, the 'reformer' of school manuals and of the popular imagery of the regime. Paradoxically, it was the oil boom of 1973 that put an end to this relative equilibrium.

4

Bellicose Islamism?

1973–2003

> The world cannot do without the Arabian Peninsula,
> but the Arabian Peninsula can do without the rest of
> the world.
>
> *Salman al-Auda*

Islamist movements are regularly suspected of threatening modernity
and liberty, and in the West they are often read through the lens
of the religion to which they pin their discourse and the violence
they employ against 'infidels' (*kuffar*). Saudi Islamism is no exception
to this general schema. Did its most famous representative, Osama
bin Laden, not say that he was acting *ad maiorem Dei gloriam* and for
the victory of Muslim peoples over the impious West?[1] Did those
behind the attacks of 1995, 1996 and 2003, in Riyadh, Khobar and
again Riyadh, not have their sights trained on the American and
Christian 'occupier'?

The pitfalls of religious culturalism
and economic determinism

If the Western media take literally the religious rhetoric of the Islamist
movements – regularly trying to show, with quotations from the
Koran, that the Text either legitimizes or repudiates violence – it is

striking to note how in Saudi Arabia, and generally in the southern Mediterranean, the perception of Islamist movements is radically different from our own.

Wahib bin Zagr, a businessman, economist and liberal editorial writer from Jeddah, said one day: 'We don't have a religious movement in Saudi Arabia or the Arab world: the Islamist movements are political not religious.'[2] As a political movement striving for power and based upon a broad social mobilization, Islamism is known in Arabic as *islam siyassi* – that is, precisely, 'political Islam'. This term is sufficient to distinguish it from ritualistic and formalistic private practices, from 'the question of ablutions, childbirth and foot-cleaning in the absence of water',[3] to which Arab regimes – Saudi Arabia being no exception – have sought to reduce Islam. Yet Saudi Islamists themselves object to the term *islam siyassi* and prefer to describe themselves as *salafiyun* (Salafists).

From 'political Islam' or 'Salafism' to 'Islamism' (an old word for Islam that entered the Western vocabulary in the nineteenth century), from 'unitarian' Saudi Islam to 'Wahhabism', the recurrent terminological contortions show how difficult it has been for the West to conceptualize these movements which challenge its own semantic and political ascendancy. The first analytic move that refrains from denunciation and cries of fear will therefore consist of discarding hasty appellations and restoring the explanatory role of the multiple instruments of social science. This means to refrain from reducing contemporary Islamist movements to their religious and cultural dimension or, in other words, from 'overemphasizing the *lexicon* of Islamist actors in comparison with the substance of their *behaviour*'.[4] It is necessary to renounce the essentialist claim that the roots of Islamism lie in its ideology or references to the sacred texts, but also to keep economic determinism within bounds, to accept that 'we cannot simply describe the Islamist as a marginal actor driven to revolt by unemployment and frustration',[5] and to put explanations in terms of poverty and exclusion back into the broader framework of political and social analysis.

Saudi Arabia is of interest to the study of Islamism precisely because it shows the limited relevance of the twin essentialisms of purely religious or purely economic analysis. Although it is already an Islamic country, an Islamized society, Saudi Arabia has seen the emergence of political oppositions which, as elsewhere in the Muslim world, express their revolt in religious terms. And, although it is a wealthy country, marked by high oil revenues and average living standards equivalent to those of Western Europe, Arabia has seen the rise of an opposition that recruits from the official intelligentsia as well as from the denser ranks of student youth.

Hence the following two paradoxes. First, it would appear that Saudi Islamism espouses Islam not to counter a secular nationalist or socialist ideology – as in Egypt or Algeria – but to attack a state on the very ground from which it draws part of its legitimacy. Second, rather than being an expression of shortage or extreme need, Saudi Islamism appears to be a revolt born of the affluence that followed the oil boom of 1973.

Yet although, on an initial analysis, the reality of Saudi Islamism already calls into question the instruments usually applied to Islamist movements, the dominant perceptions also illustrate the resonance of those vague fears of terrorism which too often serve as a guide to understanding, and whose hold unfortunately tends to divert political analysis into the short-cuts and simplifications of a police manhunt.[6] After all, is Saudi Arabia not the homeland of bin Laden and fifteen of the nineteen kamikazes of 11 September 2001? Has it not been hit several times on its own soil – in 1995, 1996 and, most recently, 2003?

How should we think of Saudi Islamism, once it is agreed that the usual analytic frameworks – the religious lexicon and economic determinism – have to be seriously qualified? Is it reducible to terrorist violence alone? And, perhaps most important of all, given its ramifications in international organizations such as al-Qaida, how far are we even justified in speaking of *Saudi* Islamism? In the land of the two holy mosques, cradle of Islam and focal point of the Muslim world, what is the relationship between Islamism and nationalism?[7]

From 1973 to 2003 – from the creation of a Shiite Islamist movement in the Eastern Province through the seizure of the Great Mosque in Mecca in 1979 and the reforms of 1992 to the coalition of liberal and Islamist intellectuals around Crown Prince Abdullah

– contemporary Saudi history coincides with the growing strength of an Islamic opposition to the regime of the Sauds. Why is it that the 1970s and 1980s, decades of oil prosperity and a massive flow of petrodollars into the Arabian Peninsula, were the very time when a powerful opposition, highly structured in its discourse as well as its means of action, took root in broad layers of the population? Why did this surprising 'revolt of affluence' express itself in the language of religion, and not in the politically tested idiom of Arab nationalism or socialism, or even trade unionism or communism?

The 1970s were a period of intense politicization of Saudi society, thanks to more frequent exchanges with the West as well as the successful educational policy pursued by the state a generation earlier. In 1975, for example, a Saudi Communist Party was founded. Its limited lifespan and weak roots in society precisely raise the question as to why Islamist movements have proven so much more lasting – from the Shiite Reform Movement (also founded in 1975) to the Jama'a al-Thibat (Constancy Group), Ahl al-Da'wa ('Preaching People') and Munazzama al-thawra al-islamiyya (Organization of the Islamic Revolution). Why is it possible to say today that, unlike secular political ideologies, Islamism in Saudia Arabia and the rest of the Muslim world has given an expression to previously silent layers of society?

The deadly boom of 1973

The appearance of Islamism in Saudi Arabia should be traced back to the oil boom of 1973, which, in the collective memory of Saudis and the administrative memory of the state, was the founding moment of the new 'age of abundance' (*'asr al-tafra*). In October 1973 Egyptian troops crossed the Suez Canal and, without meeting any resistance, recaptured those parts of their territory that had been occupied by Israel since 1967. On 17 October, under pressure from King Faisal and with the aim of supporting Sadat, the Organization of Arab Petroleum Exporting Countries (OAPEC)[8] met in Kuwait and agreed to impose an embargo on oil exports to certain Western countries.

This decision did not interfere with Saudi Arabia's growing output of oil and actually enabled Aramco (which was nationalized only in 1988) to increase its prices and thereby encourage American energy independence.[9] Thus, while Saudi oil revenues skyrocketed from $4.3 billion in 1973 to $33.5 billion in 1976 and $116.2 billion in 1981,[10] the image of the kingdom in the West suffered sharply from the sudden rise in oil prices that the 'modest and ineffective'[11] embargo helped to bring about.

Why did the Islamist challenge blossom precisely at the time when oil revenues were soaring in Arabia, when easy money should have made it possible for the state to buy off any budding revolt and to trade social prosperity for the tranquillity of the royal family? Why, in defiance of all political expressions of the theory of the rentier state, did the principle 'no taxation, no representation' here seem inoperative,[12] since the demand for political participation emerged at the very moment when the state thought its sudden rush of wealth would dispel all political worries?

When oil prices rose in 1973, the Saudi state really did see the new abundance through the prism of tax exemption and economic liberalization, drawing a clear and seemingly definitive line under the patient construction of a highly statized but diversifying national market. In economic and institutional terms, the boom of 1973 would remove Saudi Arabia from the path of development and condemn it to *purchase* growth.

This new conjuncture enabled the Saudi state to kill off its recently acquired administrative rationality and to stop tuning its (administrative and economic) instruments for knowledge and regulation of the national economy. Most taxes and duties were abolished as early as 1974. The powerful DZIT, backbone of the state's administrative and economic rationality and its main instrument for knowledge and regulation of the national economy, became a pale shadow of its former self, so that, whereas in the 1960s 'almost every village had had a DZIT representative, only seven offices were left by mid-1970s'.[13]

The rise in oil revenues did not spell the disappearance of the Saudi state administration, however, but rather its exponential growth, as every Saudi was now eligible in principle for a post in the civil service. This terrible paradox is one of the roots of the economic crisis that has followed the fall of oil prices since the early 1980s. At the very time when the cognitive and regulative functions of the state administration were withering away, the administrative apparatus was swelling in a way never seen before. The task of distributing the oil rent called for an administration in touch with the real economic situation and the needs of the country, but the state had been stripped of the feelers that linked it to the economic actors and the whole of society, from the heart of the big cities to the smallest agricultural settlements. In short, after 1973 the Saudi state administration became a bureaucracy.

Modernization checked

The end of economic modernization was expressed in a shift from redistribution of the (mainly fiscal) resources collected by the state − with all that these implied for knowledge of the needs and mechanisms of the national economy − to distribution of the rent bestowed on the royal family by the only partly nationalized Aramco. In fact, this distribution acquired the force of a tidal wave; the sums injected into the economy in the form of subsidies for real estate investment, industry and agriculture kept growing and growing, from 16 million rials in 1970 to 28.6 billion rials in 1982.[14] Furthermore, the oil opulence produced derivative sources of revenue that were encouraged by the state. Between 1973 and 1978, a whole set of decrees strengthened the legislation requiring foreign companies to use the good offices of a Saudi sponsor and agent and to pay commissions sometimes as high as 40 per cent of the value of a contract.

Once the fiscal instruments for knowledge and regulation of the economy had been dismantled, nothing stood in the way of the formation of a bloated and myopic bureaucracy. The administrative requirement of all-round growth conflicted with distributive justice as well as economic rationality itself. In defiance of all reason, the great beneficiary of the years of abundance, in agriculture as in other sectors of the economy, was the new bourgeoisie of Najd.

Between subsidies and the proceeds of sponsorship, comfortable fortunes could be built up in the space of a few years. And, as the regulative functions of the state administration had gone by the board, the distribution of wealth coming in from elsewhere now took place in uncoordinated but perfectly legal ways. The royal family broke off its founding alliance with the Hijaz bourgeoisie and relocated the ruling functions of the kingdom in Najd; ministries, civil service departments and embassies packed up and moved from Jeddah to Riyadh. The state administration was 'Najdized' from the late 1960s on, three out of five senior civil servants then originating in central Arabia.

After 1973, a whole class of Saudi entrepreneurs was created *ex nihilo* on the basis of state subsidies and scarcely transparent contracts that gave it a right to tidy commissions. Linked by family or tribal connections to the bureaucratic source of opportunities and sinecures, this new middle class was essentially urban and concentrated in Najd, whereas the big bourgeoisie of Hijaz had to make do with the much less desirable purgatory of oil-related growth. Paradoxically, then, the 'Najdization' of politics and economics resulted in an extraordinary social regression, bringing back into favour 'tribal' practices that had lapsed since the constitution of a modern supratribal state in the 1920s and 1930s.

The 'corruption' of the royal family has to be understood in relation to this emergence of a new unproductive yet wealthy bourgoisie. The defence minister, Prince Sultan, was nicknamed 'Prince Five Per Cent' because of the commissions he took on arms contracts, but the ·practice was legal and general[15] – within the limits imposed by the networks linking the new bourgeoisie to the bureaucracy and the state administration. Once 'corruption' had found its way into economic and juridical customs, it became just one instrument among others for the distribution of oil money. In any event, the quickest amassing of fortunes took place around subsidized investment (especially in real estate and industry) rather than in the sponsoring of foreign companies.

More serious than corruption, and less well known, was the emergence of major inequalities between Najd and other provinces, as well as between the urban and rural populations. In 1981 the province of Najd held no more than 26 per cent of the total Saudi population, yet it concentrated nearly half of the highest incomes in the kingdom (above 100,000 rials a year). Conversely, 40 per cent of Saudi households had an income below 5,000 rials a year (in 1980), and these were mainly concentrated in the outlying provinces.[16] Moreover, the need to import unskilled labour from Yemen, Egypt and Asia (Pakistan, India, Thailand and Philippines) led to a deep and lasting gulf between Saudi nationals and the immigrant population.

In a way, then, poverty made its appearance together with the oil boom of the 1970s[17] – not in absolute terms but in contrast to the formidable growth of subsidized or officially favoured activity, and also in contrast to the major accumulation of capital in the hands of a new Najdi (and mainly urban) bourgeoisie. Whereas, from the founding of the kingdom in 1932 until the early 1970s, the state had taken up the wager of modernization and unification by building a powerful and well-informed bureaucracy and by enforcing monetary and fiscal regulation of the internal market, the years following the oil boom of 1973 saw modernization rapidly recede into the background.

However much the growth-obsessed state spoke apologetically of economic and social progress (and especially infrastructural development[18]) as a great achievement of the royal family, the increased dependence of the economy on exogenous monetary flows, the dismantling of the administrative apparatus of knowledge and regulation and the rise of major inequalities meant that such 'progress' was little more than a façade for public display. The destruction of the state's regulatory and planning instruments did not really make itself felt in the 1970s, but after the collapse of oil prices in 1981 it resulted in short-term economic regulation (in the absence of the kind of long-term predictive knowledge that had previously been available). The modernization of Saudi Arabia was thus blocked by the effects of the oil boom. The flame of modernity, now fallen to the ground, had only to be taken up by new hands. But, in any event, it could no longer provide the state and the royal family with their chief source of legitimacy. A page in the administrative and economic history of the country had turned.

Retrograde Islamism?

It was precisely in the late 1970s that the first two signs of an Islamist opposition occurred. On 20 November 1979, during the annual Hajj pilgrimage and on the eve of the fifteenth century in the Hegira calendar, a group led by Juhaiman al-Utaibi and Muhammad al-Qahtani calling itself the 'People of the Hadith' (*Ahl al-hadith*) seized the main mosque in Mecca and resisted a two-week siege. The action was eventually terminated only with the help of a French rapid deployment force (the GIGN), and some sixty of the rebels were subsequently executed (in addition to those killed during the GIGN assault).

This first 'Islamist' uprising was revealing in two ways. First, the People of the Hadith employed a mainly political and economic discourse, accusing the royal family of materialism, corruption and subservience to the West. Juhaiman also demanded greater autonomy for the ulema and denounced their subordination to the government. After this spectacular public airing, these same issues were raised in most of the later demonstrations organized by the Islamist opposition.

Second, the fact that two members of influential (though peripheral) Bedouin tribes had instigated the capture of the mosque was evidence of a tribal resurgence and made it possible to nickname the People of the Hadith the 'new Ikhwan'.[19] This was also the analysis of the Yemeni sheikh Muqbil al-Wadii, who was jailed in the 1970s in Saudi Arabia for his links with Juhaiman's movement, which he read in terms of 'traditional vengeance rather than political or religious reform'.[20] It seems to have been possible to mobilize this 'tradition' precisely because the state, having abandoned its goal of social modernization, made tribal and family ties the cornerstone of its relationship with society. In a way, the state may be said to have got the opposition it deserved; Julaiman's archaic tribalism was a response to the artificial 'traditionalism' of the Saudi state itself.

In 1979 and 1980, in the wake of the Iranian Revolution and as a protest against Riyadh's contempt for tribal and religious minorities (further intensified by the 'Najdization' of economics and politics), Shiites in the Eastern Province rose up in rebellion. On 27 November

1979 they publicly celebrated the Ashura,[21] and early the following year they organized demonstrations and strikes involving oilfield workers and students from the well-run modern university of petro-leum and mineral studies at Dammam. Though harshly repressed by the National Guard, this 'Eastern Province Intifada' subsequently induced the regime to concern itself more with the social and economic situation of the Shiite minority, and to promise reforms and other measures, which ten years later, in 1993, would help to bring about a genuine Sunni–Shia rapprochement.

The seizure of the Great Mosque and the Eastern Province Intifada – the first two public signs of the Islamist opposition – were revolts of the periphery against an arrogant centre (Najd) that had become the blind spot of Saudi society. Beginning in 1980, the state responded to the warning shot across the bows by further 'Islamizing' the now chaotic and sharply unequal modernization process, the most notable result being that women had their rights curtailed and, for the first time, were forbidden to study abroad or to appear on television.[22] Crown Prince Fahd also undertook to adopt a Basic Law and to set up a consultative assembly in place of the Hijaz assembly, which had played only a very marginal role since the 1960s; while Prince Nayef, the interior minister, actually established a committee to draft an Islamic constitution. Nevertheless, the promised reforms got under way only in 1992, under the impact of a new upsurge of Islamist opposition. Twice before, the Saudi state had appealed to a religious legitimacy – to counter the Ikhwan revolt and then the leadership of Nasser's Egypt in the Arab and non-aligned world. After 1979 the Riyadh regime again mobilized its ulema, but without any great success; the Islamist sedition spread to Najd in the 1980s and divided the ulema themselves over the attitude they should take to the government.

In 1987 a young intellectual from Asir, Said al-Ghamdi, created a sensation by publishing his research on the Saudi modernist move-ment (*Harakat al-hadatha*), in the form of tape-recorded lectures that circulated in millions of copies and became one of the main talking points in the kingdom. A book by Sheikh Awad al-Qarni, *Al-hadatha fi mizan al-islam* (Modernity by the Yardstick of Islam) had the same objective: to accuse 'modernist' intellectuals of compromising with a state whose priority was no longer modernization, and to warn the public of an ideological seizure of power (in the press and the literary scene) by a minority of Western-trained intellectuals who had been co-opted by the government. The movement had its source in mosque discussion forums, animated by a rising generation of sheikhs trained in the schools of Saudi Islam and the Muslim Brotherhood.[23] A number of them would become famous after the second Gulf War – most notably Salman al-Auda and Safar al-Hawali.

The split between 'liberal' and 'Islamist' intellectuals was now complete, and Saudi dailies lined up with those advocating one or the other cause. Above all, through the readership it provided for Said al-Ghamdi's work, Saudi society disowned the 'Western-style' modernization that had given the Riyadh regime most of its legitimacy until the 1960s. As the discursive emphasis on moderniz-ation, growth and progressive 'achievements' coincided with the appearance of major inequalities and the ending of the voluntarist policies of the 1950s and 1960s, the first public manifestation of Najdi Islamism (not just tribal or Shiite Islamism, as in 1979) was a challenge to the ideological options of the government. The main charge was that the government supported intellectuals who, while keeping quiet about what the state had really done (centralization of wealth, abandonment of social and economic progress), spoke up to suggest qualities that the state did not have (by glorifying the 'modernism' of the Sauds).

Islamists from the Movement for Islamic Reform in Arabia (MIRA) – a movement created in 1996 around Saad al-Faqih, then in exile in London – described very well the political and social contra-diction resulting from the chaotic 'modernization' of the 1970s and 1980s:

> The Islamic movement replaced all imported secular ideologies, such as nationalism and socialism. This has been admitted by representatives of the secular groups themselves, who began to recognize in public their defeat in the face of Islamic competition. One well-known secular intel-lectual explained that secularists had ignored the social dimension after the late 1970s and entirely depended on the regime and the media.... The intellectual and moral predominance of the Islamist movement went hand in hand with its almost total absence from the media and decision-making

positions. This curious combination is at the root of the rulers' alienation from the nation. This split between society and the state led to grave tensions, which were only waiting for an opportunity to appear in the open. The Gulf crisis was the spark that lighted the timber: that cultural shock, that historic event impelled the forces and tensions constituting society to manifest themselves politically in the light of day.[24]

Rather than being fundamentally reactionary, the Saudi Islamist movement initially engaged in a complex and restless debate with modernity and its self-proclaimed heralds. Indeed, the fame of this movement stemmed precisely from the lively debate in which it opposed modernism and Western influence, and from the public display of contradictions that it saw in the modernism flaunted by the state and official intellectuals. 'Islamize modernity' or 'modernize Islam': the Islamists saw this hackneyed alternative as characteristic of the government's shift from modernization–Westernization of Islam in the 1960s to Islamization of Western modernity in the 1980s. For the Islamists – and this is the core of their debate with modernist intellectuals – Islam and modernity can be counterposed to each other only if one assumes that modernity is necessarily Western, that social justice and economic development need to be instilled from outside and cannot derive from the categories of Islamic endogenous culture: 'The modernist movement active in certain intellectual circles *did not really champion modernization but sought to combat Islam in the name of modernization.*'[25]

Political, social and economic modernity can be effectively expressed only in the vocabulary of Islam: this conviction, already expressed in the mid-1980s, accounts for the huge popular success of the Islamist positions, since it underlines the gap between a resolutely Muslim society concerned about social justice and an intellectual-technocratic community fascinated by the West and caring little about social and economic progress. François Burgat wrote in connection with the Egyptian and North African Islamist movements: 'The "law of God" is here primarily endogenous rather than celestial.'[26] The same is true in Saudi Arabia, as the strategies of both the government and the opposition movements strikingly demonstrate.

Before we examine the consequences of the second Gulf War, and assess the identification of Islam with modernity that is the spearhead of the Islamist mobilization, we should look for a moment at what distinguishes the Islamist movement from the nationalist and socialist oppositions to the Saudi regime.

History of dissent

The struggle against modernization imported from the West provides the key to the Saudi Islamist movements. But what exactly is their *differentia specifica*?

Sociologically, there is little in common between the uprising of the Ikhwan, a rural Bedouin militia, and the contemporary opposition of urban, sedentary Islamists. Moreover, whereas the Ikhwan denounced the very construction of the state and the centralization of powers in the hands of the Saud aristocracy, the great majority of Islamists accept the 'Saudi' character of the Arabian kingdom and campaign for reforms within the framework of the existing state, not for its revolutionary destruction. The contemporary Islamist opposition is therefore closer, structurally and politically, to the second wave of protests that culminated in the Aramco strikes and student demonstrations of the 1950s.

Between 1945 and 1956 – that is, between the first Aramco strike and the suppression of the general strike – a trade-union movement managed to establish itself in the Gulf oilfields. Workers' committees not only demanded various social benefits (wage rises, fixed working hours, an end to discrimination between Arabs and Westerners) but forged an alliance with the population of the Eastern Province around frankly political demands. In 1953, strikers and inhabitants of the Gulf coast towns demonstrated against the American military and economic presence in the area. And in 1956 King Saud was greeted in Dammam by a mass demonstration, when workers and local people shouted anti-American slogans, attacked the US consulate and demanded the closure of the US military base at Dhahran.[27] On 17 July 1956, when the vote was taken for a general strike, the Central Committee of Arabian Workers demanded a constitution, trade-union legislation and the recognition of political parties.

As it has often done, the Saudi government first responded with conciliatory gestures, then shifted to a tougher line, and finally opened talks again. Although Aramco accepted the workers' demands in 1945 and 1953, and although the government adopted an Egyptian-style labour code in 1947, the tone hardened in 1953 with the banning of strikes and trade unions. In 1956, Aramco workers were officially denied the right to strike and demonstrate, and a general strike in the summer was violently repressed. Fresh strikes in 1963 and 1965 were treated more gently, and in 1969 a new labour code incorporated the workers' principal demands: a forty-hour week, four weeks of paid holidays, sickness insurance, and so on.

The great Aramco strikes made it possible for a structured political movement to appear for the first time. In 1953, in the image of the nationalist movement that had seized power in Egypt the previous year, young officers, civil servants and Aramco workers created a Front of National Reforms around an anti-imperialist, constitutionalist, pro-Arab and socialist platform. Though banned in the 1956 wave of repression, the Front continued its activities in Egypt, Syria and Lebanon, especially around the emblematic figure of Nasser al-Said, a former Aramco worker, author of a *Rissala ila al-malik Sa'ud* (Letter to King Saud) and creator (in 1962 in Cairo) of a Federation of the Sons of the Arabian Peninsula, which later moved to Sanaa and became the Union of the Peoples of the Arabian Peninsula. As to the nationalist party in exile, which in 1958 renamed itself the 'National Front for the Liberation of Saudi Arabia', it became a piece in the intricate game that opposed King Saud to his half-brother Faisal in the 1960s.

Members of the royal family made their own the issues of the labour and nationalist movement: the 'free princes' around Prince Talal embodied, not only for the Saudi liberal bourgeoisie but also in Western eyes, the constitutionalist and nationalist wing of the royal family. Thus, on 25 May 1960 Prince Nawaf ibn Abdelaziz, one of Talal's supporters, stated to the Egyptian daily *Al-Jumhuriya* (The Republic): 'There is a trend towards convening a constituent assembly for the first time in Saudi Arabia, drafting the first constitution of the state and setting up a supreme court and a supreme planning commission. The problem is how to accomplish this experiment.'[28]

The experiment would not be conclusive, as Faisal and Saud rejected the proposals of the free princes. But Talal's supporters joined the government in December and provided 'liberal' backing for Faisal's reforms; both their espousal of the nationalist protests and the repression of political dissent enabled the royal family to limit the influence of the dissident movements in Saudi society.

Nevertheless, in the 1950s the protest movement was not confined to the Eastern Province (which, thanks to Aramco's activity, was modernizing more rapidly than Najd); in Qasim, student unions were formed in 1956 at Unaiza, Buraida, Shaqra and al-Rass. The students called for dissolution of the League for the Promotion of Virtue and the Eradication of Vice, arguing that it was a 'source of putrefaction and danger for young people seeking to educate themselves', and demanded that curricula should be brought into line with those of Egypt and Syria. The government responded in two phases: first, by quite harshly repressing the movement, which King Saud accused of crypto-communism; and, the next year, by creating a secular university along Egyptian lines: the King Saud University. The student revolt was brought under control. Once again, after an initially violent reaction, the regime had given in to popular demands.

During the 1960s, the main hotbed of protest was considerably closer to the centre of power, since the boundary between the regime and the opposition ran through the royal family itself: first dividing Saud and Faisal, then opposing Talal and Saud to Faisal. Moreover, against the backdrop of rising nationalism in the Arab world, the army showed signs of revolt in the decade preceding the oil boom. In 1962 a Saudi air force pilot took refuge in Egypt and disclosed the existence of a revolutionary organization in the army; in 1969 a military coup was forestalled, probably with CIA help, and hundreds of officers, workers and civil servants were arrested. Three more attempted coups were uncovered in the space of a year. Faced with this rebelliousness in the armed forces, the royal family pursued a dual strategy of increasing the material privileges of army officers and strengthening the National Guard; in 1962 it gave command of the latter to the current Crown Prince Abdullah, with the task of protecting the royalty from disturbances in the army.

The protest movements of the 1950s and 1960s were therefore defused through a dual policy of repression and redistribution, threats and conciliation, which alternated between blanket rejection and attempts to preserve a social consensus around the royal family. In 1985, a Saudi Communist Party official explained the decline of militancy in the 1960s not only by government repression but also by the many concessions that the workers had won before they were marginalized by the flow of oil wealth: 'The main event was the emergence of a society of consumption. Fortune smiled on Saudi workers.'[29] The dual royal strategy was therefore evidence of the malleability of Saudi institutions, and of the rulers' constant wish to integrate opponents and to overcome contradictions. 'For me everything is a means, even obstacles',[30] Abdelaziz said in his twilight years – and these words could be the motto of the Saud family and the entire state.

From the nationalist and socialist oppositions of the 1950s and 1960s through to the Islamist protest movements of the 1980s, an evident continuity may be seen in their (sometimes violent) dynamic of opposition to the regime, as well as in their denunciation of US military bases in the kingdom and US corporate tutelage over Aramco (and hence indirectly over the royal family) until its nationalization in 1988. Where the nationalist and Islamist oppositions diverge is visible in the manner in which the government responded to them. Whereas the 'secular' movements of the 1950s and 1960s were partly integrated through the redistribution of national wealth (more extensive workers' rights, greater prioritization of public services), it was not possible to solve the problem of Islamism by means of economic prosperity, since it was precisely a revolt against the skewed distribution of oil wealth. Beginning in the 1980s, the government therefore attempted to spruce up its Islamic image and thereby – with no great success – to occupy the public space mobilized by the anti-modernist rhetoric of the religious movements.

A second, more important divergence is that the Islamist movements express themselves in the very language used by the regime after 1980 to justify its pre-eminence in society – a fact which makes negotiations possible and even lays the basis for a *shared* government. The main divergence therefore has to do with the great dignity that Islamism attaches to Muslim symbolic referents, rather than the Western ideological paraphernalia wielded by nationalist, socialist or communist movements or trade unions. The dignity of Islam rings out as a signal for the regaining of an endogenous cultural and ideological framework and the sidelining of imported categories such as 'modernization', 'secularism' or 'progress'. In Western ears it echoes as the signal for radicalization with terrorist propensities, but in essence it is only the expression – sometimes the extreme and dangerous expression – of a quite ordinary yearning for autonomy.

Re-Islamization of an already Islamized space?

The strength of Saudi Islamism – as of the Egyptian Islamist movements, for example – is that it builds on the intuitive categories that constitute society in its relationship to itself and the wider world. What, then, of the paradox that we identified earlier? Unlike its Egyptian, Syrian, Tunisian or Algerian counterparts, Saudi Islamism appears as the end product of the re-Islamization of an already Islamized space. This paradox, interpreted as a competitive upbidding, allows an outside observer to reduce Saudi Islamist movements to their most visible and most internationalized fringe, in keeping with the enlarged image of the kingdom: if the Sauds are fanatics, just imagine their Islamist opposition!

This paradox is not really peculiar to Saudi Arabia. In Egypt, Syria, Tunisia and Algeria, Islamism might also perfectly well appear as 'God's revenge' on a secularized political system. But that would be to obscure the fact that, in those countries, society has never strictly speaking been de-Islamized, that the state itself has used Islam as a justification:

> In Algeria and Tunisia, a long time after Morocco, councils of *ulema* were hastily set up to give religious backing to public policies. After it had been largely shorn of its prerogatives, the help of the University of Al-Azhar and the Mufti of the Republic of Egypt was solicited in order to endow the regime of Nasser and his successors with religious legitimacy.[31]

This uneven picture therefore forces us to draw a distinction between social practices and the political discourses that reflect – or, more often, do not reflect – them.

In most Arab countries – Egypt or Tunisia, for example, where independence brought to power elites trained in the school of the West – official political discourse is a discourse of modernization and Westernization. Sometimes it strenuously insists on categories such as democracy and human rights, which are known to please American or European backers, but a lack of interest in any expression of them at the level of political reality means that elite discourse is often more a skilful veneer for publicity purposes than an actual programme of government. The Saudi elites are no exception in this respect, although their rallying to Western values came later and has been more limited. Did one 'liberal' prince not declare in 2002: 'Of course we are supporters of democracy. But what would happen if we let Saudis vote? Wouldn't they bring the Islamists to power?'[32] While the government 'communications strategy' in Egypt or Algeria is geared to the 'defence of democracy' against 'fundamentalist extremists', the external discourse of the royal family in Saudi Arabia sometimes takes up the same theme, although here it becomes a matter of 'protecting the stability' of the Saudi economic site in the face of 'terrorist threats' from Islamist movements.

At the same time, from the Mitidja plain through Upper Egypt and the Nile Delta to Lower Najd, social practices have not ceased to refer to the normative framework of Islam, so that there is less difference, for example, between the peasantry of Middle Egypt and the farmers of Qasim or the new city-dwellers of Riyadh and Jeddah than there is between the latter and the bourgeois circles close to the regime, whose US-educated sons are by now steeped in liberal conceptions. In Arabia as elsewhere – witness the success of Said al-Ghamdi's theses – Islamism consists mainly in a semantic recentring around cultural and political themes battered by Westernization. As a *movement of cultural preservation and political opposition*, Saudi Islamism sets itself the aim of ending the cultural 'schizophrenia' of the bourgeoisie and the regime, the impossible attempt (much commented on in the European media) to combine Western references with an Islamic cultural and ideological framework.

The previously mentioned paradox is therefore only apparent: although Saudi Islamism has emerged in an already Islamized social space, its oppositional challenge relates to a political space monopolized by the royal family and the Najd bourgeoisie – a space which makes only superficial reference to religion. Rather than 'God's revenge', Islamism therefore appears as a *revenge of society*: it is a means for society to bring social practices and political discourse into line with each other, to say loud and clear what it actually does from day to day, to end the schizophrenia characteristic of political regimes with weak symbolic independence that find themselves torn between reference to Islam and fascination with the West.

Is this cultural 'preservation' itself the source of dangerous deformations, or at least of an ideological withdrawal of Saudi society into itself? In other words, is it to be feared that Saudi Islamism will close the doors and windows of society and cut it off from the world behind the high walls of the sharia; that the dynamic of opposition to an imported modernity and government strategies will prevail over the affirmation of a social and political future; that the strategy of *protest* will gain the upper hand over the dynamic of *reform*?

As we have seen, reference to the sharia does not preclude all innovation,[33] and it saves for the legislature a *political field of interpretation* in which a diversity of references is inevitable. In the case of Saudi Arabia, this is what has happened with concepts deriving from Ottoman commercial law, Egyptian labour law and French administrative law. Although the hermeneutic strategy of the Islamists rejects any ideological intrusion into the circle of interpretation of the Koran and Sunna, it must still face the requirement of keeping interpretations up to date, as must the government itself and the official ulema.

This updating is ambivalent and sometimes contradictory, expressing itself in symbolic gains (reference to basic rights) or, on the contrary, in ideological retreats (the 'Takfirist' excommunicatory deviation of part of the Saudi Islamist movement). The updating is therefore not exempt from climb-downs and defeats, but the essential point is that it lays claim to symbolic independence and cultural autonomy. It is based on a movement of memory, preservation or recollection – three translations of the term *dhikr*, which, according to Jacques Berque, is 'reference to that which is memorable'. ('It is a question not so much of the past as of a return to one's roots in something that one wishes to bring back. In these "forgotten hard lakes" of which Mallarmé speaks, the Arabs think that the future will spring forth.'[34])

The preservation of Islamic values is therefore not only evidence of society's support for the Islamists; it does not express only opposition to the government, nor only rejection of the West's ideological imperialism. It also tells us that, for Arab peoples today as for European peoples yesterday, the path of development and progress is to be sought in a cultural renaissance, a return to oneself pregnant with future novelties. In much the same way as the Egyptian or Tunisian Islamist movements, Saudi Islamism should be read in terms of this balance between 'reaction' and 'action', memory and projection, ideological return to one's roots and conquest of new territory. Although a (sometimes violent) withdrawal remains a possibility, it is not the only one. Nor, above all, is such a withdrawal the monopoly of Islamist movements or the automatic result of a return to the sacred texts. As we shall see, recourse to violence is much more conditional and circumstantial than a quasi-genetic code written into the ideological structure of Islamism.

Islamism, nationalism and anti-imperialism

In the 1970s and 1980s, Saudi Islamists sharpened their ideological weapons and limited their activity to the formation of religious non-governmental organizations – unprecedented in Saudi Arabia – and the launching of a debate within society against the modernists. Having first appeared on the margins of society, in Hijaz and the Eastern Province, the movement began to sink deep roots in Najd in the early 1980s. The second Gulf War, in 1991, and the violent trauma it inflicted on Saudi society[35] provided the Islamists with the opportunity to make their entrance onto the stage of politics itself.

The second Gulf War was a political, economic and social turning point as important as the oil boom of 1973, bringing the irruption of the outside world into Saudi society and a violent questioning of the government's actions. Although, since the 1960s and especially the 1970s, the elites had been in constant intellectual intercourse with the West and fully participated in the globalization of trade and information, the vast majority of Saudis remained cut off from the outside world because of the censorship and narrow focus of the media. In 1991, the horizon suddenly opened up and exposed the government's tactics: in the eyes of Saudi society, King Fahd's prostration at the announcement of the Iraqi invasion of Kuwait (which the official media took a long time to report), then the King's appeal for US and European troops to intervene to protect the kingdom from an Iraqi push south – all this seemed unworthy of the enlightened rule that the Sauds claimed to exercise.

For the intellectual elites, both religious and liberal, the allied military intervention was a slap in the face for the alliance that the Sauds had pursued with the United States since the Second World War. The issue was not so much the 'infidel' occupation of the land of Islam's two holy sites as the contradiction between a supposedly preventive Saudi–US alliance and the need for the kingdom to call in US troops to protect the country. Paradoxically, the massive arms purchases and colossal military expenditure, amounting to $275 billion between 1975 and 1990 (or roughly a third of GDP for the years 1987–90[36]), had not prevented the government from appealing for outside intervention. The US response to the Iraqi invasion ended in the military occupation of Arabia – an occupation which, most unusually, was funded by the occupied country itself, since it is estimated that the Saudis had to foot a bill of $70 billion after the Gulf War, both for 'Desert Storm' and for arms orders once the war was over.

If, for intellectuals, the US intervention flew in the face of the alliance dating back to 1945, it was because the aim of that alliance had been to provide the Saudi armed forces with real autonomy and real strength. The Islamists did not fail to underline the bankruptcy of government military policy, and to propose a profound reform of the army partly inspired by the Israeli model.[37] In this connection, as in the areas of foreign policy and the economy, an Islamist presents himself primarily as an expert in modernization and reform.

As Mamoun Fandy wrote about Safar al-Hawali, a sheikh born in 1950 at al-Baha, between Hijaz and Asar, and one of the leaders of the movement in 1991–92: 'Safar Hawali's religious discourse gives way to a discourse of national security and geopolitics. Religion may be behind it, but the critique is certainly based on a different language.... It is clear ... that Hawali is writing as a strategic thinker rather than a theologian.'[38] The same Islamist intellectuals also consider that the United States is waging an unjust policy in the Middle East, intervening to protect the Kuwaiti oil wells but abandoning to its fate a Palestine that is also occupied by a foreign country.

For the Saudi intelligentsia, then, the imperialist character of US policy is perfectly obvious – and, in the autumn of 1990, Islamists and liberals did not fail to point it out at public and semi-public meetings in the universities and mosques. This marked a veritable revolution, since debates previously held in private were now being aired in public spaces. In September 1990 Safar al-Hawali distributed two lectures on cassette: 'You Will Remember What I Say to You' and 'The Divine Escape Clause'. In the same period Salman al-Auda, a sheikh born in 1995 near Buraida, in Qasim, released a tape-recorded sermon, 'Why Do States Disintegrate?', in which he painted in broad strokes the picture of a national, constitutional and liberal Islamic state, even quoting Western states as an example:

> We differ from these [Western states] in the frame of reference. They think that the nation is the source of all authority and legislation, and we think that Shari'a is the source. Nonetheless, we share with them respect for the individual. We differ with the pharaonic model [of the Shah of Iran, Khomeini or Nasser] and the Communist model, because of their contempt for the individual.[39]

While al-Hawali meticulously dissected the reasons for the US intervention in the Peninsula, analysing it as a thinly disguised manifestation of imperialism, al-Auda laid the basis for an Islamic theory of the modern state, quoting both Ibn Khaldun and Ayatollah Khomeini, Ibn Taymiyah and Nasser. Between al-Hawali's anti-imperialism and al-Auda's Islamic nationalism, the broad lines of the Islamist mobilization of the 1990s took shape: the Islamists would demand the political, economic, diplomatic and military independence of Saudi Arabia, as well as a constitutional formalization of the relations between state and society.

In January 1991, the Islamist movement was stirred up by an official ulema fatwa conferring Islamic legitimacy on the allied intervention in Iraq and the Western military presence in the kingdom. This fatwa was the signal for revolt among the generation of young sheikhs trained in intellectual debate in the 1990s. In order to air their disagreement with government policy, and to counter official charges that the young sheikhs were traitors to Islam or theologians as blinkered as the worst official ulema or as intolerant as the religious police, a group of fifty-two Islamists around Safar al-Hawali, Salman al-Auda and Nasser al-Umar addressed in May 1991 a 'Letter of Demands' (*Khitab al-matalib*[40]) to King Fahd, also bearing the signature of the Grand Mufti himself, Sheikh Abdelaziz ibn Baz.

1992: reforms and repression

Already before the publication of the 'Letter of Demands', a group of forty-three secular intellectuals had sent a similar petition to King Fahd with a list of ten reforms, including creation of a consultative assembly, reopening of the municipal councils, modernization of the judicial system, guarantees of greater media freedom, reform of the religious police and 'greater participation of women in public life, within the scope of the sharia'.[41]

The 'Letter of Demands' contained many of the same points. The Islamists demanded – also in a context of respect for the sharia – a consultative assembly (Majlis al-Shura) 'independent of any pressure that might affect its real responsibility';[42] a government of experts and technocrats; equal rights and respect for dignity of the individual; responsibility of the rulers; a more just distribution of the oil revenues; reform of the army; reform of the media (freedom of expression within the scope of the sharia); reform of foreign policy; autonomy of religious institutions; and independence of the judicial apparatus.

Less than a year later, the government responded to the popular agitation, demonstrations, petitions and public criticism with a dual policy reminiscent of its strategy in the 1950s and 1960s. With one hand, the government granted significant structural reforms that involved a 'Basic Law for the Kingdom' and a statute for the provinces (now reduced from eighteen to fourteen), as well as a consultative assembly consisting of sixty royal-appointed members and chaired by the former justice minister, Sheikh Muhammad ibn Jubair. With the other hand, it strengthened the police apparatus of the interior ministry and placed the mosques (the locus of free debate) under close surveillance. Between 1992 and 1994, according to interior ministry figures (MIRA figures are ten times higher), 110 Islamist militants were arrested and detained for periods ranging from a few weeks to a few years.

In response to the government reforms, which they saw as intended only to strengthen royal control, the Islamists, grouped since April 1992 in a University Reform and Advisory Committee, published in September an 'Advisory Memorandum' (*Muzhakkarat al-Nasiha*) that repeated the 'Letter of Demands' and added some further proposals for administrative, economic and social reforms. This memorandum was the basis on which a Committee for the Defence of Legitimate Rights (*Lajnat al-difa' 'an al-huquq al-shar'iya*) was founded on 3 May 1993 by Abdallah al-Masaari, Abdallah al-Tuwayjri, Abdallah ibn Jibrin, Hamad al-Sulayfih and Abdallah al-Hamid; the movement was managed by Muhsin al-'Awaji, Abdelaziz al-Qassim and Saad al-Faqih, among others.

This Committee immediately became known in the West via the BBC, but it was just as quickly banned in Saudi Arabia and, in April 1994, its office moved to London under the auspices of Muhammad al-Masaari and Saad al-Faqih. In 1996 Saad al-Faqih founded a movement of his own, the Movement for Islamic Reform in Saudi Arabia (MIRA: *al-Harakat al-islamiyya li-l-islah*). In exile the Saudi Islamist movements lost their socially representative character, but the unusual weight and prominence they gained in the international media allowed them to criticize the royal family without pulling any punches. The export of Islamism, here as elsewhere in the Arab world, went together with a radicalization of its theoretical positions.[43]

Inside Saudi Arabia, the government rejected any *infitah* (opening up), although it was proving hard to stem the public debate that had begun in 1990 in the mosques and religious universities. The hardening of the government position also impelled the Islamists 'of the interior' towards greater radicalism. In 1994 the arrest of Salman al-Auda brought the students of Qasim onto the streets – a 'Buraida intifada' similar to the student revolt of 1956, except that Islamic discourse was now the driving force instead of communism and socialism.

Repression of the intifada in Buraida, together with the government strategy of closure, drove a minority of the Islamist movement to take violent and desperate action. Another minority, having returned from the 1980s war against the Soviet enemy in Afghanistan, also went underground and turned to violence. The two bomb attacks of 1995 and 1996, against US military installations in Riyadh and Khobar, were doubtless an expression of the political frustration of this extremist fringe; they were certainly not a direct consequence of the legalist and constitutionalist demands of the majority current within Saudi Islamism. In Arabia, as elsewhere, 'Islamist' violence is more often a 'secondary' violence, triggered by repression or the ending of negotiations, rather than a 'primary' violence intrinsic to Islamist mobilization.[44]

Islam against traditions

From 1990 to 2003, *infitah* (opening up) went hand in hand with *sahwa islamiyya* (Islamic awakening), each enabling the other and being fleshed out by it in return. The historical birth and spread of Saudi Islamism was not a continuous movement, even if, in retrospect, its unity appears strong and corresponds to the growing dissatisfaction that marked the period from the breakdown of the welfare state to the recession, from the military intervention of 1991 to the sheikhs' activism of 1992 and 1993. As we have seen, the tendency first appeared in a class eminently linked to the state and living on state incomes and subsidies – the class of men of religion, intellectuals and academics owing much to the introduction of Muslim Brotherhood thinking into the educational system in the 1960s.[45] It is this which makes Saudi Islamism a composite ideological object, one that cannot be regarded simply as a revolt of the poor.

In a sense, therefore, it is a movement within the state apparatus – which is not so surprising if we consider the central position of civil servants within Saudi society and the fact that, since 1973, the royal family has never ceased to assert its hold over the state administration. Did not Islamists turn in 1991 to Prince Salman, governor of Riyadh, to support their demands and pass them on to higher places? This natural proximity to power is part of the ambivalence of Saudi Islamism, a movement co-opted by the state after the state had tried to stifle it. This also explains the relatively low level of repression, in comparison with the methods of the Egyptian or the Syrian government. Here there has been no wholesale massacre, few life sentences on political grounds: the repression itself is one element in the endless process of negotiation between the royal family and society. In the end, its proximity to power is the strength of Saudi Islamism, giving it some representation at top levels of the state and enabling it – since 2002 – to participate openly in the reform process initiated by Crown Prince Abdullah[46] (de facto regent since King Fahd's embolism in 1996).

The Islamists drew closer to the regime in the late 1990s, first using the columns of daily papers and then politically committing themselves more and more to the crown prince's reform project. This rapprochement drew a shifting line of divide between the two major tendencies: *al-Sahwa al-islamiyya*, sometimes called the 'Saudi Muslim Brotherhood', which 'had the lion's share, both among Islamists and in society';[47] and the jihadist Salafists or 'neo-Salafists' (*al-salafiyun al-judud*), who oscillated between systematic excommunication (*takfir*) of the rulers and liberals and a rapprochement with moderate Islamists.

The 'top down' strategy of the Sahwa Islamists should not obscure the vigour of the support they received 'from below'. As we have seen, this dual approach was the original feature of Saudi Islamist mobilizations and distinguished them from the more 'elitist' and media-oriented activity of the liberals. It was on the basis of society's own system of references that the Islamists intended to renew Saudi society and politics, and this creative preservation enabled them to *take up the flame of modernity* that the state had abandoned since the mid-1970s. Usually, this modernity did not speak its name but

claimed to be an Islamic 'reform' (islah) of society and the state
– but the reform was the stage for a *radical critique of tradition* just as
much as for a return to absolute divine law. Islam was at once a
heritage and a *critical instrument* targeting the way in which society and
the regime functioned.[48]

In our view, the modernizing force of the Saudi Islamist project
lies in this strategy of critical preservation, which goes beyond
opposition to modernity imported from the West. MIRA members
make this quite clear:

> The Sahwa project set out not only to embarrass the government
> and to open channels for the expression of popular demands,
> but also – more profoundly – to *break the tradition which, in the guise
> of religious law, actually contradicted the sharia.* The aim was to criticize
> the rampant secularism that had been gaining ground in public
> opinion and even been given religious legitimacy – a secularism
> that expressed the maxim 'Render unto Caesar that which is
> Caesar's and to God that which is God's' in a pseudo-Islamic
> language, whereas Islam does not recognize such a dichotomy.[49]

In other words, the dichotomy criticized by the Islamists was the
one through which the government avoided all criticism and all
responsibility:

> One of the ideas with which King Abdelaziz managed to infect
> people's minds was that 'governments know best what is good
> for the nation'. This idea is particularly dangerous because of its
> elasticity and unlimited applications. It could be taken to a point
> where it overturned explicit and recognized Islamic command-
> ments in the Koran and the Sunna, on the pretext that problems
> of the general interest remained at the ruler's discretion. Another
> major problem was that, when combined with the principle of
> compulsory obedience to the ruler, it presupposed that the govern-
> ment's opinion would be supported by the nation. As time passed,
> the idea that 'governments know best' took deep root in people's
> minds and proved detrimental to *the idea of a social norm or convention*.[50]

The state no longer takes responsibility for modernization. Against
this background, the Islamist movements have sprung from the
demand of Saudi society for a new modernity, no longer copied from
European models (welfare state, French-style public administration,

state socialism, etc.) but expressed in a language that affirms Arabia's symbolic and real independence by referring to a norm which, though revealed, is endogenous and not borrowed. As Salman al-Auda put it in one of his tape-recorded sermons: 'The world cannot do without the Arabian Peninsula, but the Arabian Peninsula can do without the rest of the world.'[51]

With a normative yardstick transcending the politics of the royal family, the Islamists began in the 1980s to criticize the chaotic modernization of Arabia. In the late 1990s they associated themselves with the reform project of the crown prince. Thus, Saudi Islamism should be seen not as an upsurge of obscurantism but as a *revolt of reason*. From the creation of the first Islamist movement in 1975 through the reforms of 1992 to the present-day recomposition of the political and intellectual field around an alliance of Islamists and liberals, it is the emergence of an endogenous rationality irreducible to any Western input which has made it possible to say that the main aim of Saudi Islamism – as Nilüfer Göle put it in a Turkish context – is to 'put an end to the identification of civilized existence with Western existence'.[52]

This means that, with regard to recomposition of the political and ideological field, *Saudi Arabia is not an exception* within the Arab and Muslim world. It too is part of the movement of resistance in the South to the economic, ideological and political influence of a North that more and more sees its relations with the Arab and Muslim world in terms of strategy, security and even police action. In Saudi Arabia as elsewhere, perhaps more than elsewhere, this movement of resistance takes the form of 'preservation' and speaks a religious language that draws some of its force precisely from the West's inability to understand it – a religious language that is *the language of independence*.

PART III

Economy and society

5

From the era of opulence

to the age of need

They have no covered and crowded bazaars.... Their
market is open, without a roof. The road that crosses
the market is very broad; loaded caravans can pass
through it.
Anonymous Najd writer, nineteenth century

From an economic point of view, Saudi Arabia is doubly curious. First,
the main indicators appear satisfactory: since 1990 annual growth has
averaged 1.5 to 2 per cent; gross domestic product (GDP) reached
$185 billion in 2002, or $11,000 per capita; the rate of inflation
is low (1 per cent in 2003); the trade balance and the balance of
payments are positive; and the budget deficit is reasonable enough
(3.6 per cent of GDP). Everything seems to be going well – with
the exception of the public debt (estimated in 2002 at 350 per cent
of GDP, or 107 per cent of GDP in the case of the external debt),
unemployment figures (variously estimated at 15 to 25 per cent of
the active population) and the acute dependence of the economy
on the oil sector.[1]

In fact, oil revenues are equivalent to 90 per cent of exports,
roughly 70 per cent of state revenue and more than a third of
GDP.[2] The Saudi economy is still based largely upon monoculture
of an abundant resource (Saudi Arabia's proven oil reserves are a
quarter of the world total), whose extraction is cheap ($2 a barrel,

compared with $10 a barrel for North Sea oil) and which in 2002 fetched a world market price of approximately $24 a barrel. Oil dependence is therefore a long-term economic problem, whereas high unemployment is a medium-term social problem.

Second, despite the colossal oil wealth, the Saudi economy never really seems to have taken off. Its results are poor in comparison with some developing countries that lack natural resources of their own, as if the oil wealth had slowed down development instead of speeding it up. Comfortably well off, blessed by nature but relatively neglected by growth, Saudi Arabia offers the strange picture of what one Riyadh intellectual called 'a society testing development' rather than a conventional 'developing country'.

This doubly paradoxical situation, in which oil seems more a burden than a trump card and traditional indicators conceal an at least uneven economic and social reality, requires us to develop a historical perspective, an analysis of the current macroeconomic policies of the Saudi state, and some assessment of prospects for the near future. The paradoxical situation we have just outlined is characteristic of a rentier state: that is, a state living essentially on income from sources outside the national economy.[3] This structural imbalance or original alienation of the economy may well be Saudi Arabia's principal handicap.

The recent history of the Saudi economy may be represented in three major cycles:

- constitution of a unified national market through state intervention (1925–73);
- imported growth following the 1973 oil boom, together with economic deregulation (1973–83);
- slowdown following the fall in oil prices, with the state powerless to stem the decline.

The Saudi state is thus faced with two major economic problems: to restore its authority over the national economy; and to diversify the economy and free it from dependence on the oil rent.

What oil miracle?

On 7 May 1938, Well no. 7 in the Dammam oilfield began to deliver a continuous flow of oil, thereby confirming the existence of major deposits in Saudi Arabia. The oil was present in extractable quantities and was cheap to produce: for Standard Oil of California (the future Aramco) it was a historic day. One year later, on 1 May 1939, the first Saudi oil tanker left Ras Rannura, amid festivities along the coast that would continue for several days.

Since the end of the First World War, the American oil corporations had been hoping to profit from the huge oil market that the break-up of the Ottoman Empire had brought into being. Sidelined by British and French companies at the San Remo conference (1920), spurred on at home by a newly emerging oil lobby that waved the spectre of the depletion of domestic oil reserves, US corporations took advantage of Britain's haughty lack of interest in the Eastern Province of Saudi Arabia and moved into it themselves. In 1933 King Abdelaziz awarded Standard Oil of California a sixty-year concession covering more than a half of Saudi territory.

In the troubled inter-war years that followed the crisis of 1929, whose effects were felt until the Second World War, fierce competition between a rising United States and a declining Europe led Washington to launch a policy of conquest in the Middle East as explicit as that which European powers had conducted in the previous century, and with a similar pursuit of the energy resources necessary to economic growth, defence and the national interest. Neocolonial domination was still obscured by the noisy decline of colonialism, but after the Second World War the hold of industrial America over the Middle East constantly asserted itself beneath the successive masks of the 'anti-colonial struggle', the 'struggle against communism' and the 'struggle against terrorism'. Today the United States controls the whole of the Middle East – from the running of Iraqi affairs to military surveillance of the Arabian–Persian Peninsula, and from supervision of the Israel–Palestine peace process to massive support for the faltering economies of the region. The history of this prehensile relationship began in the east of Saudi Arabia.

The historic date of 7 May 1938 pointed ahead to fifty years of uninterrupted growth of the world economy, thanks to a plentiful source of cheap energy and under the triumphal aegis of the United States. But, in terms of the Saudi economy itself, the real revolution was both older and more recent. In any event, it is better to speak here of two revolutions.

The first took place when the subsidies paid to the Najd emirate, by the Ottoman Empire and then the British Empire, broke the fragile structure of the central Arabian economy, transforming social relations into dependence upon the prince and political relations into dependence of the embryonic state upon a powerful foreign power. The Ottomans deployed this system of subsidized relations not only in Najd but also, as we have seen, in Jabal Shammar, Hijaz and the Eastern Province. Beginning in the early twentieth century, the British took over the whole procedure and systematically extended it, allocating a monthly sum to Abdelaziz for loyal services and subsequently establishing a protectorate in due form. The oil royalties that came on stream in the 1930s were the sequel at the level of a whole subcontinent to this system of military pay.

We should note that, despite the Ottoman and British imperial subsidies and then the oil revenues, the social-economic situation changed only very gradually for the mass of the population, whose lives remained subject to the rhythm of drought and epidemics until the 1950s. The secure source of external revenue meant that the economy changed its form but not its content, with its alternation of rains and drought, its poor harvests and seasonal migration, its effervescence at the time of the pilgrimage and its port and caravan trade.

The second economic revolution dates from the 1960s and 1970s, when oil revenues rose sharply and made up the largest share of state revenue and GDP. From 45 per cent of GDP in 1968 to 79 per cent in 1973, oil became the principal driving force of the economy and almost the only source of growth.[4] Oil now finally benefited the whole population, so that within a few years Saudis passed from an age of penury to an age of plenty, from social and economic conservation to progress and modernization.[5]

As we have seen,[6] political and administrative modernization got underway in the 1920s and manifested itself first of all in the constitution of a national economy. The building of a strong tax authority, the dismantling of tariff barriers and the monopolies exercised by Hijaz merchants' and artisans' corporations, the introduction in 1952 of a single currency: all these were expressions of the same political strategy. To strengthen their military rule over four-fifths of the Arabian Peninsula, the Sauds cemented together the newly formed nation and won the support and cooperation of the big merchants of Hijaz by opening up a large domestic market. The political subservience of Hijad was therefore obtained through economic and fiscal integration of the Saudi possessions; the modern Saudi state was constructed on this alliance between the Sauds and the big Hijaz merchants.

Based on trade, pilgrimage and oil revenues, the economy then experienced a period of continual growth. In the 1960s the state also fostered a process of industrialization that gave the lie to the idea, popular with theorists of a rentier state, that the oil rent is sufficient explanation for a failure to industrialize.[7] In the end, the regulatory power of public policies rested upon the existence of a relatively efficient tax authority, whose work in collecting income tax, *zakat* and customs duties as well as precise and extensive information about economic trends enabled the state to steer the economy through various conjunctures.

This relative harmony was nevertheless based on the coexistence of two contradictory structures. The first, going back to the age of Ottoman and British colonization, led to the dependence of the national economy on an external source of revenue. The second, which first appeared in the 1920s, corresponded to the administrative attempt to replace external with internal revenues. The imbalance was therefore structural: on the one hand, an economy fundamentally turned outward; on the other, public policies through which resources were turned inward. From the 1920s down to the present day, through all the twists and turns of the economic conjuncture, this imbalance has remained at the root of a crisis of Saudi economic policies: in the 1950s it could be seen in a series of budget deficits;

in the 1960s it governed King Faisal's austerity and liberalization policies; and in the 1970s it was only temporarily obscured by the huge inflow of oil revenues, before emerging once again with the passing of the oil affluence.

Imported growth and stagnation

Following the 1973 boom and the massive rise in state oil revenues, the Saudi economy experienced a decade of phenomenal growth. At the same time, the state relaxed its fiscal vigilance and deregulated the economy, thereby sharply increasing its dependence on external revenues. With the fall in oil prices (1981) and the first post-boom budget deficit (1983), the economy then entered a zone of turbulence. Conjunctural crises succeeded brief upturns, and a state rendered impotent by ten years of deregulation was itself buffeted by private interests and sharp turnarounds.

Yet, although the 1973 boom marked a hiatus by virtue of the sharp rise in oil revenues – the difference of degree became a difference of nature, sweeping away fifty years of public policies – it also revealed a strong structural continuity. Growth remained fundamentally imported, since it was based on external contributions to the national economy and in turn bolstered a dual dependence on the outside: dependence on goods produced in the West, which Saudi Arabia imported at high cost and in large quantities; and dependence on immigrant labour from the Arab world and South Asia. Through a cumulative mechanism characteristic of rentier states, dependence on the oil rent actually became more intense and expressed itself in constantly rising imports of industrial and agricultural materials, finished products and manpower. The more oil Arabia exported, the more goods and labour it imported: this vicious circle was the basis for the importing of growth.

The fiscal authority was dismantled after 1973, at the time when oil wealth was flooding into the state coffers. Taxes were now considered superfluous and eliminated one after the other, while customs duties were significantly lowered, with the result that the state deprived itself both of knowledge about the economy and of instruments to act upon it. The 1973 boom therefore led to deregulation of the economy, and to removal of the instruments of economic knowledge and control at the very moment when they were most needed. The inflow of wealth became a source of imbalances between sectors and regions rather than a source of development. Combined with deregulation, imported growth also meant *imported disorder*.

The 1973 boom thus produced a highly paradoxical situation, in which the state became at once ubiquitous and powerless, super-wealthy and impotent, dirigiste and free-market. It was dirigiste because more than half of GDP (peaking at 79 per cent in 1973) came from oil and the whole development strategy had to pass through the mediation of the public sector. And it was free-market because, at the same moment, the state ceased to intervene in the economy through the classical channels of taxation and tariff regulation or through the informal channel of the alliance between the Sauds and the big Hijaz merchants. In creating *ex nihilo* a new capitalist class – the Najd entrepreneurs – the state asserted its power to create or destroy social classes. At the same time, however, the Najd entre-preneurs subjected the state to the play of tribal and family strategies and urged it to hand out subsidies without rhyme or reason. This means that, at the same time and altogether paradoxically, the state asserted its control by shaping the economy and society, while the economy and society asserted their own power by subordinating the state to their particular strategies.

The state gave too much and no longer took anything. At once blind and omnipotent, it committed economic errors after 1974 whose consequences became especially worrying when oil prices fell and the economy entered a period of decline. Suffering from the 'Dutch disease' – a massive inflow of wealth combined with a lack of reliable economic information – the state dished out subsidies left, right and centre, not to increase productive capacity but simply *to distribute the oil rent*. Commercial licences, agricultural and industrial subsidies, land grants, free loans on real estate: none of these items of public expenditure was balanced by profitable production or tax revenue.

Over the ten years from 1974 to 1983, the total value of free loans and subsidies granted by the Saudi Industrial Development Fund, the Real Estate Development Fund, the Saudi Agricultural Bank, the Saudi Credit Bank and the Saudi Contractors Fund increased twenty times over, from 1.4 billion rials to 28 billion rials.[8] The paradox is that the state developed the private sector *without receiving any equivalent in return*, since its revenue did not depend on wealth produced within the economy. Private-sector development therefore strongly resembled the outcome of a politics of pure prestige, a disorderly politics based on lavish expenditure.

The example of agricultural subsidies says a lot about the planning capacities of the state administration. Someone travelling by road from Riyadh to Abha would be surprised to pass lorries carrying *loads of hay* from desert or semi-desert regions of Najd, while similar lorries went back empty towards the desert: in other words, Najd was actually *exporting* agricultural produce to the agricultural province of Asir. Whereas, in 1960, 80 per cent of Saudi arable land was concentrated in Asir and 10 per cent of cultivated land in Najd, by the late 1970s the situation had been completely reversed, so that Asir now accounted for 15 per cent of cultivated land and Najd for 65 per cent.[9]

The situation was unjust, because 82 per cent of arable land was owned by 16 per cent of the population; and it was absurd if we consider the geography, climate and water resources that were unused in Asir and wasted in Najd. This resulted from the concentration of administrative power in Najdi hands, which after 1974 tended to hand out subsidies and distribute land as family or tribal ties dictated. Thus, the agricultural sector crystallized all the defects of the distributive policy of the Saudi state: to build a whole new sector around pure expenditure strengthened a lobby whose strategy, heedless of anything but individual rationality, consisted in making an instrument of the state.

After 1981 and the fall in oil prices, these imbalances became truly dramatic: nearly a million construction firms and commercial enterprises went to the wall; real estate prices fell by 30 to 40 per cent, causing the property bubble to burst and ruining thousands of investors; the state began borrowing from abroad (to finance arms spending) and from inside the country (to finance as much as 20 per cent of its budget with so-called development bonds).[10] In 1983 the Saudi budget was in deficit for the first time, and it came back out of the red only in the year 2000, thanks to an unforeseen and temporary increase in oil prices.

In 1986 the volatility of the world oil market, coupled with Arabia's budgetary instability, meant that any forecasting was a risky business, and so King Fahd appeared on television to announce that the state budget would be drawn up on a month-by-month instead of a year-by-year basis. Since then, the actual budgetary results have been markedly different from the forecasts. Public finances have anyway plummeted, and, while the economy has settled into the realm of the short term, government strategy has become a matter of playing it by ear. The stagnation and budgetary instability have been further worsened by massive arms spending, which rose from 26 per cent of the state budget in 1979 to 34–35 per cent between 1988 and 1991,[11] or approximately 25 per cent of GDP in the late 1980s. (By comparison, the military expenditure of France and the United Kingdom is today 1.9 and 2.4 per cent of GDP, respectively.)

In parallel with this economic decline and the failure of public policies, Saudi entrepreneurs – especially the new class created through distribution of the oil rent – took economic power and blocked any attempt at structural reform of the economy. The agricultural, industrial and commercial lobbies expressed their opposition to reforms on a number of occasions, and in 1988, when the government announced a tax on private and public-sector income, the immediate response of business circles forced it to back down in just three days.

Under the pressure of similar attacks, the government also failed to reduce its subsidies to water and electricity companies, agriculture and industry. In 1986, as part of a job-cutting programme in the public sector, the government announced its intention to 'Saudiize' employment – that is, to replace part of the immigrant labour force with Saudi employees – and to involve employers in the funding of social security. But, when business circles launched violent campaigns against the new legislation, the government was once again forced to beat a retreat.[12]

During the 1980s and 1990s, oil price instability expressed itself at the level of the economy in a series of jolts and spasms. Unable to respond effectively to the fall in oil revenues, the state demonstrated a lack of power that the post-1973 wave of deregulation had already started to bring about.

An industrial country?

This gloomy assessment needs to be somewhat modified, however, for two reasons. First, oil prices rose on average after 1990, and the government took advantage of this – and of external and internal borrowing – to improve its finances. A dramatic reduction in the budget deficit, from 12.3 per cent in 1998 to 3.6 per cent in 2002, enabled the state to regain some room for manoeuvre and to look ahead with greater confidence. The oil recovery also allowed the Saudi Monetary Agency and private investors to try to restore the level of their overseas assets (which had fallen from $160 billion in 1982 to $40 billion in 1990 and now stand at $90 billion). Finally, the oil recovery benefited the whole population, since per capita GDP – which had fallen in the mid-1990s to $7,500 – climbed back up to $11,300 by the year 2000.

Second, and more important, the Saudi government has proved capable of diversifying the economy. According to rentier state theory, the single source of revenue for an oil economy means that any diversification of the economy is an illusion, since it is doomed to remain a *welfare economy* based on massive imports of goods and services. It is true that in 1990 imports accounted for 85 per cent of Saudi consumption; and it is true that state monetary policy, with its pegging of the rial to the dollar, helped to boost imports and to reduce the scope for exports. Nevertheless, it is precisely through oil-funded subsidies (and the activity of a particularly dynamic banking sector) that the state has managed to create the basis for a more diverse economy. By 2001 the structure of GDP was considerably more balanced, deriving first from services (43.6 per cent), then from the extraction and refining of oil and gas (34.5 per cent), industry (16.7 per cent) and agriculture (5.2 per cent).

This diversification has been based particularly on the relative success of industrialization policy,[13] since the share of the industrial sector (apart from refining) in GDP rose from 10 per cent in 1990 to 16.7 per cent in 2001. Three industrialization strategies were on offer back in the 1960s: import substitution, with the risks associated with the rial exchange rate and a narrow internal market; international subcontracting along the lines of Southeast Asia, more difficult here because of the shortage and high price of labour; and exploitation of Saudi Arabia's comparative advantage in cheap and plentiful oil and gas to develop a strong petrochemical industry.

The originality of the actually pursued industrialization was that it pragmatically combined these three strategies, with no ideological preference for one or another, to create a strong petrochemical industry. Beginning in 1965, the government established a manufacturing and construction industry, both to replace basic import products (cement, common consumption items) and to perform subcontracted assembly tasks in Saudi Arabia. Buoyed up by real estate fever and public orders for infrastructure, the construction industry and its derivatives experienced high levels of growth.

From 1975 Saudi industry began to diversify and to aim for export markets. The state then adopted the third strategy and took advantage of the national oil resources to launch an impressive petrochemicals programme. With public investment levels reaching $60 billion in ten years, construction, refining and petrochemicals notched up record growth of 12 to 15 per cent a year. The driving force was the Saudi Arabian Basic Industries Consortium (SABIC: *al-mu'assassat al-'arabiya al-sa'udiya li-sina'at al-'assassiya*), founded in 1976 as a public organization and partly privatized in 1985. In launching SABIC, the state won one of the challenges facing a rentier economy: to convert subsidies into investments, unproductive rent into productive capital, external revenues into internal profits, imports into exports. It thereby proved that, beyond and thanks to its oil resources, a rentier state is capable of diversifying its economy. The growth and specialization of Saudi industry after the change in the oil conjuncture demonstrates this with striking force.

From 1986 government industrial strategy began to combine private initiative (33 per cent of SABIC capital) with public invest-ment. The major opening of the economy to imports was one of the greatest brakes on industrialization, and so in 1986 average customs tariffs were put back up from 3 per cent to 12 per cent. The petrochemicals industry diversified into the production of fertilizer, detergents, plastics and glass, while aluminium and steel showed some improvement. Refining capacity, on the other hand, followed the declining curve in oil exports. In the 1990s the recovery of the oil market intensified the growth of industry.

Against all expectations, then, Saudi Arabia is today an industrial country. Thanks to the major comparative advantage in oil and gas, the state has successfully overcome the handicaps to industrialization: the lack of a trained labour force (offset by the importing of labour); the narrowness of the internal market (offset by an export orientation); the protection of Western, especially European, markets (offset by a trade strategy geared to Asia); and speculative trading habits in business circles (offset by a strategy combining private and public-sector initiative). Far from holding back diversification, the oil rent has therefore been the engine driving it. It remains to be seen whether this strategy can serve as a model for the government's macroeconomic policy, and whether it has laid the basis for lasting diversification.

What macroeconomic strategies?

In 2003, at the end of twenty years of economic decline, the government faced two problems: one economic (to diversify its sources of revenue), the other social (to reduce unemployment). As we have seen, the decline of the 1983–2003 period was less conjunctural (bound up with fluctuating oil prices) than structural (bound up with the lack of effective and relevant state regulation). To answer these challenges, the state must therefore restore its authority in the economic sphere: that is, acquire the means to conduct a genuine macroeconomic policy in the face of aggressive and often short-sighted private interests.

If we examine the structure of public spending, we notice that a sterile 71 per cent of the 2003 budget consists of unproductive (or indirectly productive) expenditure; interest payments on the external debt account for 14 per cent of the state budget and public-sector wages and salaries for another 57 per cent – although it should be made clear that some civil servants are seconded to (heavily subsidized) public corporations.[14] As to the breakdown by sections, education represents 27.5 per cent of the state budget, or little more than half the figure for military and 'other' expenditure (48 per cent).

The state therefore has limited scope to reform the economy – which means that it can proceed only by reducing its own expenditure and increasing its income, or by leaving it up to private investors (foreigners, if necessary) to keep the country on a growth course. The government has four instruments at its disposal: regulation of the employment market, fiscal tools, privatization and encouragement of foreign investment. Its simple objectives are to reshape state intervention in the economy and to attract new investment – in short, to make Saudi territory more attractive than it presently is.

Employment policy

In September 2002 the first official statistics on employment estimated the jobless rate at 8.1 per cent of the active population, although the American–Saudi Bank (Samba: al-Bank al-sa'udi al-amiriki) reported a much higher and certainly more realistic rate of 15 to 25 per cent. In the view of Samba analysts, the discrepancy between these two estimates had to do with the fact that the official statistics underestimated the unemployment of young and very young people, especially the group of 15- to 19-year-olds who leave school without a certificate and have the most problems finding a job. In fact, Saudi unemployment is characteristically a phenomenon that affects young people, some 200,000 arriving each year on a labour market that absorbs only a third or so of their number. The rate of participation in labour – an average of 19 per cent (or 32 per cent for men) – is one of the lowest in the world.

We have already seen that in 1986, at the height of the budget crisis, the government launched a major drive to support the employment of Saudi nationals, but that the idea of a quota, designed to allow immigrant workers to be replaced with Saudis, aroused such opposition among business people that it was soon postponed *sine die*.

The main reason for this is that wage differentials between immigrants and Saudi employees are so high that any large-scale replacement would considerably increase the costs of running an enterprise. Thus, according to one planning ministry study, whose results were published in August 2002, Saudis receive average monthly pay of 5,446 rials, in comparison with 1,880 rials for foreigners. Although the 'Saudiization' idea has been regularly wheeled out since 1986, it has clearly failed to bear fruit, and various adjustments (changes in quota numbers and immigrant–Saudi wage differentials, special rules for different sectors, etc.) have not persuaded companies of its wisdom.

The last two waves of 'Saudiization' have had to be cancelled, or anyway renegotiated. Directives for the gold trade, issued in November 2002, were withdrawn after numerous protests from employers, and others issued in October 2002 for taxi drivers (only 10 per cent of whom are Saudis) will certainly have to be revised because of the extra costs they would entail for taxi firms. Paradoxically, then, the Saudiization policy is both *demagogic* (it builds on the contempt that Saudis feel for 'their' immigrants) and *unpopular* (it endangers corporate wealth creation).

Aware of the limitations of this policy, but aware also of its narrow scope for budgetary manoeuvre, the government has decided on a more comprehensive approach to the employment problem, involving immigration quotas and a boost to occupational training. In February 2003 it set a target of bringing the number of immigrants down from 6.14 million, or 27.1 per cent of the total population, to 20 per cent of the population. This will certainly involve further restrictions on the reuniting of families – a policy already implemented in a number of cases. Moreover, since 29 October 2002 all requests for visas and work permits for foreigners have to pass through the offices of the ministry of labour and social affairs, which will enable the state to regulate immigration more effectively.

The promotion of occupational training, for which a special fund of 100 million rials was created in July 2002, is part of a wider reorganization of education. On 11 March 2002, when an accidental fire swept through a girls' school in Mecca, a number of pupils died because the religious police had banned firemen from entering the premises on the grounds that they might see girls in an unveiled state. This incident aroused the ire of journalists and numerous intellectuals, who criticized both the dilapidated condition of the school buildings and the methods of the religious police, accusing them of 'the promotion of vice and the prohibition of virtue'. Following this heated campaign in the press, the religious board for female education (created in 1960) was secularized and incorporated into the education ministry.[15] More generally, attention was drawn to the special orientation of school studies, their main defect being not that they are too religious but that they are too broad for the skills required by the labour market.[16]

Promotion of occupational training and improvement of female education: these are the two axes of the policy that the government adopted in 2003 to capture the employment market from the top (that is, through a natural, market-oriented Saudiization of skilled jobs) and no longer just from below (through authoritarian replacement of immigrants).

Tax reform

Reform of the tax system and the tax authority, which has been encouraged by the International Monetary Fund,[17] is the best means for the state to regain its room for manoeuvre. The only taxes collected in 2003 were *zakat* (which applies only to foreign companies and is set at 2.5 per cent of their profits) and the customs duties affecting all enterprises established in Arabia. As we have seen, the elimination of income tax and other taxes, together with the lowering of customs duties, greatly contributed to the economic deregulation that followed the boom of 1973. In particular, the peculiar combination of dirigisme and free-market policies dates from that early dismantling of the tax authority.

Thirty years on, however, there are no plans to reintroduce income tax and the idea of a value added tax has been put on ice. In 2002 the Consultative Assembly did produce a draft tax code, whose principal new idea was a 10 per cent tax on the income of foreign workers. But on 12 January 2003, facing opposition from business circles, the Assembly decided by 63 votes to 47 to suspend the tax reform – much to the displeasure of certain journalists, who were incensed that they had not been kept properly informed of the ins and outs of the Assembly decision.[18] Businessmen feared a flight of foreign (particularly Western) high-income categories and the extra cost for employers willing to reimburse their employees for the new tax; but they also feared that, once immigrant workers became taxpayers, they would demand at least the same social services as those enjoyed by Saudis who did not pay taxes.

Early in 2003, therefore, reform of the tax system seemed to have reached a dead end. The IMF was advocating a simple tax that did not distinguish between Saudis and immigrants. In fact, the re-establishment of an efficient tax system would allow incomparably more precise knowledge of the economy than the Supreme Planning Commission can acquire; the Commission's forecasts and recommendations are regularly contradicted or ignored, both by the private sector and by the public sector itself. Systematic taxation would also reduce the state's dependence on oil as its main source of revenue, and have the further advantage of causing fewer clashes with business circles than the attempt to create an income tax for immigrants alone. The basis could thus be laid for a new relationship between the state and members of society, who would become *tax payers* rather than state-supported.

Privatization and the promotion of foreign investment

In the year 2000 the private sector accounted for roughly 40 per cent of GDP and employed 89 per cent of the total labour force – but only 5 to 10 per cent of the Saudi national labour force.[19] The privatization of large swathes of the public sector (which mostly employs Saudi nationals) has been encouraged by the IMF, which sees it as a way for the state to reduce its high level of debt. But the IMF directors demand the drawing up of a precise schedule.

In November 2002 the Supreme Economic Council[20] selected some twenty sectors for privatization: telecommunications, mail, seawater desalination, air transport, port and airport services, public construction, municipal services, education, health, motorways, railways, refineries, grain silos, windmills, hotel business, sports clubs and school maintenance.

In December 2002, 30 per cent of the capital of Saudi Telecom was privatized; the public offer, amounting to $4 billion, made it the largest privatization in Saudi Arabia since the partial one of SABIC in 1985. The railways were opened to privatization and foreign investment, and in 2005 work will begin on three new internal links (Riyadh–Jeddah, Jeddah–Mecca–Medina–Yanbu and Dammam–Jubail). Privatization of part of the educational system, especially professional training and adult continuing education (business administration or engineering schools), might answer the main challenge facing the country.

Since March 2000 a government agency has been working to promote foreign investment: the Saudi Arabia General Investment Authority (SAGIA: *al-Mu'assassat al-'amma li-l-istithmar fi-l-mamlaka al-'arabiya al-sa'udiya*). In its first two and a half years, the SAGIA already granted 1,617 licences for a total investment of $13.5 billion, more than half of it devoted to industrial investment. Saudi investment abroad has climbed to $700 billion, while Arabia has attracted no more than $20 billion: a lot therefore still needs to be done to persuade both foreign and Saudi investors to put their money into the local economy. Tourism, female investment (some $27 billion is held by Saudi women), privatization, opening of upstream gas and certain activities of Aramco (the only fully nationalized oil company in OPEC): all recipes are good to make investment more dynamic. On 2 February 2003 the insurance and education sectors were also opened up to foreign investment.

Intellectual circles, the business community and the royal family now agree on the need for deep reforms in the economy, but the nature of these remains a controversial issue, especially when it comes to the most important of all: tax reform. The pace of reform is another cause of anxiety. According to forecasts in early 2003, falling oil prices might cause a 27 per cent drop in state revenue in 2004 and a rise in the budget deficit to 7.1 per cent of GDP; the growth rate is also supposed to rise to 3.1 per cent, thanks to a consumer recovery, gas investment and privatization, while inflation is likely to edge up to 1.5 per cent. If these predictions come true, the Saudi economy will show once again that it crucially depends on fluctuations in the world oil market, and that oil is not an engine of development but a brake on it.

Diversification and regionalization of the economy

This brief economic analysis has led us to three conclusions. First, far from being guilty of authoritarianism or dirigisme, the Saudi state has been distinguished, especially since 1973, by the laxity of its macroeconomic policies. In mid-2003 the trend did not seem about to go into reverse, and this will harm both employers and employees, immigrant workers, unemployed Saudi nationals and foreign investors.

Second, oil dependence is still the principle behind the economy, much to the delight of Western economies, which not only obtain a cheap and plentiful supply of energy but profit from Arabia's huge oil rent to convert Saudi petrodollars into unstructured and often 'unstructuring' imports. Furthermore, Saudi Arabia's supposed hostility to the West does not stand up to scrutiny of its actual oil policy, which has consistently married a low-price strategy with a policy of overproduction, thereby squandering a non-renewable resource whose value increases over time.[21]

Third, the private sector itself remains dependent on oil and on state distribution of the oil rent; it may have grown by 4.2 per cent in 2002 (because of disinflation and low interest rates), but it exports too little and imports too much to stimulate the national economy and, therefore, employment. Despite the development of a relatively strong industrial sector, the economy still seems burdened by its original sin of being a rentier economy.

By exposing the economy to world market turbulence, the oil monoculture has therefore made any macroeconomic policy hazardous or downright impossible. In 2003, more than ever before, diversification remains the first imperative. The fundamental problem is how to transform unproductive rent into productive capital and employment. Of course, thanks to government industrial policy and falling prices for crude, the dependence has markedly declined, so that oil's share of GDP has fallen from 79 per cent in 1973 to 65.5 per cent in 1980 and approximately 33 per cent in the period since 1986. The fact remains, however, that the dependence is still excessive.

Yet Saudi Arabia is the Gulf country most suitable for economic diversification: one third of the population is unemployed, the educational system is undergoing reform, and the infrastructure is of high quality. This considerable potential should therefore induce the government to set two broad objectives: the development of a service economy combining high value-added with high levels of skill; and a relocation of manufacturing and industrial production within the framework of a regional growth strategy.

The Gulf Cooperation Council (GCC), which was created in 1981, could be an excellent instrument of regionalization. On 1 January 2003, after a long period of political impotence due to the fears and divergences separating its six constituent heads of state, the GCC established a free-trade area and a customs union (with tariffs set at 5 per cent); monetary union is scheduled for 2005, a common market for 2007 and a single currency (on the lines of the euro) for 2010. Because of the oil boom of 1973, the GCC went short on economic governance during the years of growth as well as the years of economic decline, being especially powerless to regulate competition among the nascent industries of Saudi Arabia, the Gulf Emirates and Oman. But the constitution of a genuine internal market, not just Saudi but covering the whole Peninsula, requires the existence of efficient states, a properly functioning tax service and – as in Europe – an authority to regulate competition.

The economic strategy of Crown Prince Abdullah includes a number of free-trade agreements (with Lebanon, Syria, Jordan and Egypt – an agreement with Iraq having been under consideration before the outbreak of the third Gulf War). The regionalization of manufacturing and industrial production and of the labour market really could be a solution to the economic stagnation of the Middle East. It is the solution advocated by the IMF and the United States, and the one called for by many Saudi businessmen, including the liberal economist Wahib ibn Zagr, who has repeatedly expressed his outrage in the Saudi press about the inadequate level of economic exchanges among Arab countries. In any event, the strategy of entrepreneurs in Saudi Arabia and the rest of the Peninsula should be to invest in neighbouring countries (in the Middle East, but also in Yemen and the Horn of Africa), to relocate labour-intensive industries and to develop a regional system for the subcontracting and exchange of goods and services.

The team around Crown Prince Abdullah will at least have had the merit of posing the regional question on a number of occasions: most notably, in the context of Prince Abdullah's Israel–Palestine peace initiative in February 2002 and at the signing of the bilateral free-trade agreements in early 2003. Above all, it will have had the courage to outline a strategy for peace through free trade – in the image of what Western Europe achieved after the Second World War by creating the European Coal and Steel Community, then the European Economic Community, and finally the European Union.

Will the team around Prince Abdullah have the time and the means to implement the much-needed reforms that are expected of it? The answer was still open in the autumn of 2003. But it seems to us that Arabia could today be the driving force for the unification and pacification of the region, that it could make of the Middle East what that nineteenth-century Najdi historian called an 'open market, without a roof', a 'very broad' road through which 'loaded caravans can pass'.[22] For, whereas 'a total lack of commerce produces banditry', Montesquieu accurately pointed out that 'the natural effect of commerce is to spread peace'.[23]

6

An ambiguous social modernization

The modernization of Saudi Arabia, begun in the 1920s and speeded up by the oil revolution of 1973, does not concern only the regime for which it is the main source of legitimacy, nor only the economic evolution of which it is both the leaven and the result. Ever since the Sauds' alliance with the upper classes of Hijaz society, it has also been a social modernization, expressed first and foremost in the subordination of traditional social relations (tribalism and family-centred relations, but also corporatism) to the predatory logic of the royal family.

It has been a real modernization, then, as the conflict between the Sauds and the peoples of the Peninsula has given rise to a new urban centralized society for which the economy is no longer a means of subsistence and the state is not only an oppressive apparatus. But it has also been an ambiguous modernization, since social change imposed *from above* often takes changing and contradictory appearances – and rapid, chaotic modernization often produces, for an uninformed observer, impressions of a tradition that should be distinguished from genuine tradition.

Islam and welfare?

In any event, the study of contemporary Saudi society should begin by dispelling two illusions. The first is the religious illusion: that

Islam regulates all social relations and is the cause of all law, all custom and all conduct.

It is true that the five daily prayers set the rhythm of Saudi life – just as they set the rhythm of Egyptian, Syrian, Yemeni or Malaysian life, without necessarily entailing an all-powerful religious causality. It is true that drought is warded off in the mosques, through prayers for rain that are sometimes led by a member of the royal family, although the main battle against drought takes place in the offices of the water ministry that deal with the planning and building of dams. And it is true that – when we consider gender segregation or the strict moral rules governing marriage, family life and kinship relations – Islam seems to shape Saudi society from cradle to grave, from wedding to divorce, from mating to giving birth. Nevertheless, we should be wary here of monocausal explanations. We need to distinguish what is part of Islam from what is part of social modernization or lived tradition – and to distinguish, within that 'lived tradition', what has been recently created from what has ancient peasant or Bedouin roots.

The social causalities, rather like Saudi identities, are multiple and sometimes contradictory. Four main threads form the web of contemporary Saudi society: (1) a vernacular tradition, which sets the general contours of the 'blameworthy' and the 'praiseworthy' and is sometimes of pre-Islamic or extra-Islamic origin (the code of honour, for instance); (2) a reinvented 'national' tradition, serving the propaganda needs of the regime, which sometimes has a whiff of folklore about it (for example, the ethereal figure of the tutelary Bedouin); (3) consequences of economic and social modernization which, though often attributed to Islam or tradition, are in fact novel social structures (the 'status of women', for example[1]); and (4) Islam, which is neither the first cause nor a simple reflection of pre-existing social and economic structures, but is often the *idiom* in which people express tradition or modernity, attachment to the regime or opposition to the royal family, pan-Islamism or Arab nationalism, and so on.

Social phenomena are often the uneven expression of these heterogeneous causalities: for example, while the strict segregation between men and women is formulated in religious terms, it is more the product of a convergence between hurried modernization of society (which impels women to *leave* the family circle) and a code of honour common to the area of Arab and Mediterranean civilization (which forces women to be available only to men within the family).[2] Similarly, although the ban on women drivers is officially formulated in the vocabulary of religion, it really expresses for Saudi men a wish to keep female members of the family 'for themselves', to avoid dissipating a precious and highly coveted social capital. Such rules therefore have little to do with respect for Islamic law but concern the morality of honour and the patrimonial structure of society, updated to mitigate the effects of a modernization that is experienced as aggression.

The second illusion that needs to be dispelled is the hedonist illusion of a society in which economic relations are abstract, wealth is easy to come by and the chore of work is left to non-nationals. When the young hero of Ahmed Abodehman's novel borrows money from his uncle Hizam, who represents the traditional world of the tribe, the old man warns him:

> This money is expensive, very expensive. It cost us terribly dear. It has a moral value, my son. But why does the government give you a hundred rials a month, when you already have shoes to put on your feet, and shelter from the sun or bad weather, without having to make any effort! It's not honest of the government to do that.[3]

That banknotes have a moral value, that ten rials 'are worth ten men', that money is the precise fruit of human effort, that savings contain the hope of satisfying an imperious need: such ideas are turned to dust by the state rent. What is 'not honest of the government' is to detach money from that of which it is the sign, to make it a signifier without a signified – to make money totally abstract. Such dishonesty is comparable to deceit, for something that used to be earned with difficulty is now handed out; nothing is worth its true worth, nothing is of importance any more.

Welfare economics and the society of consumption really have shaped the lives of a whole generation born between 1950 and 1975. A number of consequences follow from this: work is no longer a task necessary to life but a social function commanding widely varying degrees of prestige; wealth is no longer the result of effort but becomes a right; the state no longer rules but buys and protects; the accumulation of capital and property looks less like productive investment than a purely extravagant activity. And yet the hedonist illusion assumes that economic progress and social progress have not gone hand in hand, that wealth has frozen Saudi society in traditional forms that have elsewhere fallen into disuse, that obsolete social phenomena have thereby been able to survive, in keeping with the idea that happy nations have no history.

If these assumptions were true, the petrodollars would have halted the evolution of Saudi society. What they leave out of account is the fact that the inflow of oil wealth constituted an event in its own right, and that the age of abundance ('asr al-tafra) precisely ushered in a new chapter in Saudi history. Contrary to a certain discourse that finds it laudable to flay Saudi indolence, the transmutation of the values attached to wealth and economic activity shows rather well the fanciful nature of the old colonial idea that Arabs are culturally unsuited for work and effort. From a society where wealth was jointly extracted with difficulty from infertile soil and hostile elements, there has been a major shift to a society in which the state undertakes to give everyone a share; the evolutionary progress is undeniable, if only in terms of the new emphasis on the individual that resulted from distribution of the oil rent. In other words, instead of allowing traditional social relations to survive artificially, economic abundance gave rise to a social revolution.

Our hypothesis is that the evolution of Saudi society owes very little to Islam and a great deal to the economic changes that Arabia has undergone since the 1950s. It is therefore a mistake to think that Islam is the cause of Saudi specificities, or that social progress has been seriously out of step with economic progress. Nor is it correct to see 'schizophrenia' in the behaviour of Saudis ('rich bourgeois at once pious and debauched', 'members of a society at once Islamic and centred on oil'). On their own, Islam and oil have not determined history, politics, identities or social relations, and any schizophrenia strikes us as affecting the angle of vision rather than the nature of Saudi society itself. Or perhaps it would be better to say that the schizophrenic split between Islam and the earthly pursuit of prosperity is in the end perfectly ordinary. It is the mode of existence of all societies, torn as they are between saying and doing, code and conduct, ideal norms and real values. A different optic must therefore be adopted if we are to grasp the peculiarities of Saudi society.

An urban civilization

The first entry-point into the functioning of Saudi society is its urbanization, a recent but massive trend resulting both from political-administrative centralization and from the oil revolution. The oil rent, distributed by the state and by Aramco, has permitted three major conurbations to develop along a line of growth from Damman–Dhahran–Khobar in the east through Riyadh to Jeddah in the west, gradually soaking up the great majority of the population.[4]

The urban share of the total population rose from 15.9 per cent in 1950 to 48.7 per cent in 1970, 66.8 per cent in 1982, 77.3 per cent in 1990 and 85 per cent in 2000,[5] making Saudi Arabia one of the most urbanized countries in the Arab world, on a level with Western Europe. At the same time, the population increased very rapidly: from 5 million in 1973 to 13 million in 1990 and 22.67 million today (16.52 million of whom are Saudi nationals). To take just one example, the population of Riyadh has increased one hundred and sixty times over in the space of a century, from approximately 25,000 in 1902 to 600,000 in 1973 and more than 4.5 million today.

'The scale and complexity of urbanized life in Saudi Arabia mean that social relations have changed substantially. A key feature of this change is the distance between the rulers and the ruled.'[6] This distance has been physically reduced, since the government has attracted most of the population around the sites of political and economic power, in a truly formidable flight from the countryside. But the distance has also been symbolically lengthened, in so far as urbanization, demographic growth and economic deregulation have drawn Saudis and their princes further apart while making the former dependent upon the state. This growing gap, apparent in the need to use wastas ('connections') or even wastas of wastas to gain access to the princes, has gone together with an individualization of social and economic strategies. Enlisted into the state service, yet in that very process moved further from the centres of power, society has gained a thoroughly paradoxical autonomy, involving both 'gratitude to rich and generous political patrons'[7] and an urge to get rich by any means available. Here, as elsewhere, urbanization has expressed itself in the atomization of that 'society of cells' evoked by Ahmed Abodehman in one of his editorials.[8]

This tremendous urban growth should not make us forget the ancient roots of city life in Arabia. In Najd, Hijaz and Hasa, there were already trading and agricultural centres in the pre-Islamic era: Mecca and Medina, of course, but also Unaiza in Qasim and al-Qatif and Hufuf in Hasa.[9] The civilization of the Peninsula – with the notable exception of the Bedouin population – is therefore fundamentally and historically urban. Whether the concentration of people around a centre of power was necessary for the cultivation of arid land (the hydraulic civilizations of Najd and Hijaz) or, more prosaically, for defence against the imperialism of Bedouin tribes, the fact remains that the city, rather than the desert, is the main setting for the history and existence of the Peninsular Arabs.

The victory of the city over steppe, mountain and oasis therefore has roots in a long history and a quite specific urban geography. In Najd and Hijaz, in Riyadh and Mecca, the mosque and the souk shared the same space, so that merchants made a living out of their closeness to the mosque, while sheikhs opened their sanctuary wide to trade. A theology student leaving for the great spiritual centres of the Fertile Crescent – Damascus or Baghdad – took the road used by caravans and long-haul traders. Merchants travelling from Aleppo or Jerusalem to Hail or Riyadh brought with them weapons and fabrics, gold and jewellery, but also theology books and religious commentaries. In the holy cities, intense pilgrimage activity still governs this two-way flow between mosque and market, open spaces that can provide a setting for revolt as well as patriotic enthusiasm. The third centre in the urban area of Riyadh and the towns of Najd is therefore the citadel, pointing both outward and inward, pressing against the city walls and separated by a few blocks of houses from the mosque-market. The prince knows that in the end the mosque and the market could prove fatal to him, that 'storytellers flock there, as do caravans', and that 'people ask there for what the public demands'.[10] It is where political assassinations occur – like that of Prince Abdelaziz Al Saud in 1803, who was killed at the height of prayers by a Kurdish dervish – and it is also where palace revolutions are instigated and won, where the people grumbles and stirs. The creation of the Kingdom of Saudi Arabia did not reverse this tendency for the royal space to be set apart; successive palaces, in Riyadh and Jeddah, were built outside the city proper, and even the Consultative Assembly, in a gesture to its origins, is squeezed up against the king's palace, far from the economic centre of Riyadh.

Unlike their counterparts in North Africa, which are lost in a maze of narrow winding streets far from the market, the sacred Saudi mosques have not been frightened by the proximity of commercial space. Nor is there any distinction between the closed space of the city and the surrounding countryside: dwellings and fields, city and oasis, streets and streams extend on either side of the walls, which sometimes also encompass a palm grove, a wadi or a threshing area. The major line of divide runs between the locus of civilization (town-oasis, with its cortege of palm trees) and the open 'wilds' of al-barr (the 'outside'), whose steppe or desert is the realm of unpredictability and nomadic tribes.

Today, when the towns have sprawled out in all directions, the proximity of mosque and market still structures urban space; each modern district of Riyadh clusters around a few concrete minarets and is surrounded by a belt of shops or a couple of shopping malls. The third centre of the city remains: a royal palace lost on the edges of the inhabited area, beside the westward motorway in Riyadh or the Red Sea in Jeddah, a royal palace, however, which the rising tide of property development is fast approaching. Today the city has engulfed the palm groves and gardens, an improbable countryside whose wide green trenches scrape across the tissue of low houses and straight roads. Finally there is the barr, which has lost its capacity to inspire fear in city-dwellers. Taken away from the Bedouins, who now swell the suburbs of the large cities, it has become a place for recreation and holidays wedged between *istirahat* (closed rest areas planted with trees), a place whose motorways, stadiums and amusement parks are lined with hookah cafés, and from which people make sorties in cross-country vehicles to practise *tat'is* (automobile dune-skiing).

Apart from the cardinal points of the city – inside and outside, mosque, market and palace, which are much the same as before – almost everything has changed. In the 1950s real estate development entered a period of unprecedented growth, which became exponential with the boom of 1973. Carried along by the modernization under King Faisal, then by gifts of virgin land as the main way of distributing the rent from rising oil prices, real estate became the most profitable and most prestigious investment in the kingdom. The land surrounding the cities was pre-empted by the state, and the princes gave it as a gift to individuals or sold it to property investment companies, which in turn offered it for sale to the public.[11] The profits were always considerable – estimated to have been as high as 500 per cent at the peak of activity in the market.[12]

The new climate following the boom of 1973 was expressed in a change in the nature of Saudi towns:[13] the country shifted from one system of town planning to another, and thoroughly exogenous urban schemes arrived with the general importing of growth. The city of the 1950s and 1960s naturally continued the broad lines of the traditional fortified town, spreading out in boulevards around the main mosque in accordance with a model borrowed via Egypt from Europe. The city of the 1970–2000 period, however, adopted an American-style grid pattern alongside the old town and its concentric expansion. Most Saudi towns thus came to be split between two centres: the traditional space of the old town and old souk, now abandoned to the poverty-stricken or immigrants, as in the Dira district of Riyadh or the old town in Jeddah; and the business centre in the heart of the new 'American-style' city, an orthogonal system that could be reproduced ad infinitum along the urban motorways.

As in certain former colonies, a second city was quite simply laid beside the first, forming a megalopolis that opposed the homogenous rigour of a mathematical plan to the hierarchical and centripetal character of the traditional space: 'European colonization never ceased to juxtapose to the so-called native cities, especially the Islamic medinas, urban metropolitan forms that supported *different functions and a different population*. In Algiers, as in Tunis and Dakar, it is this which gives the landscape its main structural order.'[14] The same is true in Riyadh, Jeddah or Dammam, except that there the structure becomes a fracture and nothing links the old city to its contemporary outgrowth. The collision between the two worlds can sometimes be dramatic, most notably in the eastern conurbation of Dammam–Dhahran–Khobar, where the 'native' town exists alongside a 'Western' town, the citadel of Aramco, surrounded by fences and tightly controlled entrances. Everywhere else, Westerners live together in more or less discreet and hermetically sealed compounds; in Dammam, where a whole city is closed to free circulation, the segregation is crudely blatant.

The expansion of the cities therefore mainly corresponds to the distinctive logic of real estate investment, which is both the main vehicle for distribution of the oil rent and a token of the property owner's autonomy from society and the regime. This resonance of landowning reflexes, and the development of a property bubble as their corollary, reflect the alienation of an uncreative urban economy and its detachment from the oil production sites of Hasa and the industrial towns of the Gulf and the Red Sea: al-Jubail and Yanbu.

For several years, however, this expansion of the city has been accompanied by an inverse attempt to reclaim the traditional town centres: old Riyadh and old Jeddah, in particular, are undergoing a late rebirth. The destruction of dilapidated blocks opened the way in old Riyadh for the erection of the Palace of Justice, a large new mosque and modern souks representing a pastiche of the buildings they replaced; while in Jeddah skyscrapers and other office blocks have mingled with the old town, whose fine Musharabieh-style houses are being restored in stages. The old towns are being colonized by functions derived from the modern town, and this return to the centre – especially in Najd – goes hand in hand with a neo-traditional architecture that reproduces, with varying degrees of success, the classical model of the peristyled house in cob (tin). To orthogonal proliferation of the city, this trend therefore opposes a wish to move back into the forgotten mainstream of

Saudi town planning; sometimes it induces a wish to falsify the urban architectural heritage.

Atomized families

Throughout the second half of the twentieth century this jerky, sometimes contrived and contradictory urbanization was the setting in which the modernization and individualization of Saudi society unfolded. Constantly breaking down traditional social structures, the swift and massive urbanization served to detribalize society, to make the family cell its basic unit, and finally to split the family itself into conjugal micro-elements.

By virtue of Abdelaziz's matrimonial strategy, the real estate strategy of the state administration and the sidelining or instrumentalization of the great nomadic tribes, the capture of power by the Sauds was in every respect not only a victory of town over desert but *a victory of the family over the tribe*.[15] The urbanization of Arabia therefore also corresponded to a sedentarization or detribalization of the nomads, and it was accompanied by a family-centred political discourse of legitimization: *'a'iliya*. In fact, the family model operated from top to bottom of the new state, from the royal family through the great families of merchants and entrepreneurs to nomadic families detached from their tribal history and sense of belonging; it allowed the regime to portray itself as a paternal force, using this as its main justification and a screen on which to project its image. 'The state represented power and grandeur. This marked a transformation in the nature of political authority. The state acquired legitimacy and loyalty through the distribution of wealth. The response was no longer political submission but gratitude.'[16]

In the 1950s the construction of a Saudi national identity therefore took the path of celebrating the family as the natural site for the learning of sociability and subordination to a gently coercive authority. The generation born between 1930 and 1950 took full advantage of this subsidized promotion of the family cell: polygamy became a common practice in the course of economic growth and social modernization, unlike in the period before the foundation of the kingdom. Facilitated by economic growth and encouraged by the

dominant discourse, polygamy seemed to be one of the practices
that had formerly been reserved for the princes but were now open
to all – just like car ownership or the traditional 'princely' costume
of white thob and bisht (the gold-embellished black or brown cloak).
But this 'aristocratization' of society was only one aspect: polygamy
equally testified to the mobilization of 'traditional' or 'fully Islamic'
social traits in dated and 'modern' social-economic circumstances,
thereby demonstrating how far the invention of tradition could go.

The urban explosion of the 1970s and 1980s put an end to the
golden age of the family. At the beginning of modernization, it
had mainly been a question of extended families grouped around a
'common house' that was reserved for festivities and great occasions;
these extended families were in turn grouped together by geographical or tribal origin, each new urban district being closely linked to
the original home area of its inhabitants. But as prices rose, and as
the property market took off, families were dispersed to wherever
marriages, partnerships and job opportunities took them, so that
the norm today is no longer a three-generation or four-generation
extended family living in close proximity but the narrower unit of
father, mother and children.

Within urban space, this general atomization and individualization
of society are expressed in the domination of the self-enclosed private
'villa', usually windowless and hidden behind high walls that may
even have a metal fence on top. Protected by numerous unwritten
customs, the closed space of the narrow family is strictly segregated
between a male and a female pole; the two-track circulation of
individuals observable in Saudi cities is found in most public places,
so that the urban space lives more on a juxtaposition of family cells
than on a public space shared by all.

In the old towns, which are systems of partitions as much as
of passages,[17] there is an imperceptible transition from the public
space of the street through the semi-public space of the cul-de-sac
or yard to the private place of the dwelling. The 'traditional' wall
was an open frontier keeping out the gaze of anonymous passers-by
and enclosing ever narrower and less engaging alleys, in order to
deflect the undesirable without actually turning it away. The modern
wall, by contrast, which is especially present in Najd, is hermetically

sealed and has only one opening in the shape of a solid metal door. It signals an inviolable space and defends it against any intrusion, so that public space can now directly adjoin the private dwelling. Just as a European homeowner uses his façade and windows as a social marker of affluence, so does the head of a Saudi family entrench himself behind a wall whose height and thickness are an indication of his own importance – a wall that is one of the sites of the ostentatious display of wealth.

The private space of the family remains the area of application of family-centred ideology, but it now faces competition from the open spaces of the school, the association (sporting or literary club) and the mosque. Since the fall in oil prices and the economic crisis of the 1980s and 1990s, the forces of dispersion have had the upper hand over the forces of cohesion in the family home. 'Families are no longer the dominant sphere of socio-economic life; their role appears to be becoming gradually marginalized. *Valorizing the family is a recognition of its diminished role in life.*'[18] Having passed over the last thirty years from an offensive to a defensive posture, the family-centred ideology of the government and society ill disguises the disarray of the economic boom generation, which since the early 1990s has faced the revolt of young people born in the crisis years who now make up more than half of the population.[19] Evidence of this may be seen in Saudi newspapers and magazines, which for some years have been directly broaching once-taboo issues such as drugs, urban violence, youth unemployment and homosexuality.[20]

After urbanization, the *atomization of the family* is therefore the second gateway into Saudi society. Combined with growing political and economic uncertainties, it constitutes the starting point for un-precedented *individualization* and a profound change in social relations. The decline of the extended family and the polygamous model has also been expressed in a demographic revolution: urbanization and sedentarization, taking place against a background of economic crisis, have led Arabia to accomplish its demographic transition.

In the twenty-year period from 1980 to 2000, the fertility rate of Saudi women (not including immigrants) was nearly halved from an average of 8.26 to 4.37 children, while the birth rate displayed a similar downward trend from 50 to 28.9 per thousand. The rate of natural growth has now settled at 2.5 per cent,[21] and Arabia now fits into a pattern visible throughout the Arab world, from the Atlantic to the Arabian–Persian Gulf – a pattern marked by smaller families, a higher age of marriage and a spectacular fall in birth and death rates. After thirty years of exponential demographic growth, the population continues to grow but at a stable rhythm: it should reach 25 million (including 6 million foreigners) in 2010, and 34 million (including 7 million foreigners) in 2025.[22]

This new demographic pattern is a consequence of falling oil prices and urbanization, but it also marks a shift in the relations of power within the family. The transition from extended to small families led Saudi women to assume a place in the family that they had previously held only in the narrow circle of the gynaeceum; economic uncertainty has also impelled them to look for work and to bring in *external* support for the material life of the family – a purely male function during the years of growth. Higher educational levels (there are today more female than male students) and the wider use of contraceptives (by one in five Saudi women[23]) have often allowed women to win their husband away from a staunch opposition to birth control and to convince him of the need to abandon the model of the extended family handed down by his parents. 'The inordinate ambitions of the Saudi "male" (who looked to have the largest possible number of children), together with the government's pursuit of a national population as high as Arabia can contain, have been undermined by the *silent revolution of women*.'[24]

We shall return in Chapter 7 to this 'revolution', which is not limited to the narrow circle of family relations. It is enough to note here that the atomization of families leads to a process of *individualization* and *equalization*, to emancipation of the two silent halves of society that are women and young people.

The society of the poor

As we have seen, everyone can claim an entitlement to such tokens of power as an American automobile, princely clothing and a 'Western' lifestyle more or less copied from the outposts of the West that Egypt and Lebanon represent in Saudi eyes; the 'aristocratization' of society corresponds to an apparent equalization of people's conditions. But it is an apparent or ideal equalization, because until recently the image that Saudi Arabia meant to convey to the world was that of a united and prosperous country, a family of happy families led by princes who were both devout and modern.

Yet this ideal equality masked inequalities that had already been growing before the fall in oil prices. In 1980 – on the eve of the oil crash – poverty affected two out of five households, mainly concentrated in the outlying provinces of Hail, Qasim and Asir.[25] The distribution of the rent was therefore both a distribution of disorder and a distribution of inequalities, and the end of opulence signalled by policy failures and the emergence of unemployment led to a worsening of social-economic differences. With industrialization and growth, and even more with recession, veritable social 'classes' came into being.

The third gateway into Saudi society, then, is the phenomenon of *pauperization*. This has a number of faces: the civil servant who, like his Egyptian counterpart, has to take a second job to supplement his meagre and often late-paid income; the modest family that is forced to move into a central district of Riyadh or Jeddah formerly reserved for immigrants; or the young unemployed graduate who wanders between informal jobs and periods of inactivity, sometimes falling into petty crime. Precarious and distressing situations are more and more frequent, and conflict with the official discourse of a government proud of its people's wealth and development.

In the recent period, however, official discourse itself has become noticeably more restrained. In November 2002, after an incipient riot in Riyadh, Crown Prince Abdullah decided to make a high-profile visit to some 'underprivileged districts' in the capital, and Prince al-Walid ibn Talal, one of the richest businessmen in the kingdom, followed this up with a promise to build at his own cost a thousand public housing units a year for ten years. The crown prince's visit marked official recognition of the existence of poor Saudis, as well as a public determination to solve the problem; the labour and social affairs minister, Ali al-Namla, was put in charge of a committee against poverty and the implementation of a national employment strategy. Yet, just a few days earlier, in a survey conducted by the American–Egyptian magazine *Al-Saqr*, a sample of several thousand citizens of the Gulf Cooperation Council had voted Riyadh the most beautiful city in the Gulf. Ironically, for once the blame lay not abroad but inside the country. While the GCC citizens were praising the sweetness of life in Riyadh, its high altitude, cool nights and palm groves, top Saudi leaders were finally gearing up to take a more social approach to the delicate issue of town planning.

Nevertheless, it is unlikely that the sudden voluntarism of the government can put paid to the problem of pauperization and the growing urban insecurity that is often its corollary. Since the unfocused initiatives (a war on poverty fund, occupational training schemes, etc.) go together with an unrealistic policy for the 'Saudiization' of employment, there is a risk that – whatever the champions of forced repatriation of immigrants may say – these interventions may actually reduce the government's room for manoeuvre instead of increasing it.

Against a background of mass youth unemployment, a veritable 'immigrant problem' has made its appearance and sometimes led to the taking of downright populist positions. In November 2002 the journalist Ali al-Musa, who is sometimes described as a modernist and an enlightened liberal,[26] published an article in *Al-Watan* with the outspoken title 'Saudi cities are no longer Saudi'. In the form of an open letter to the labour and social affairs minister, Ali al-Musa described the 'Little Delhi' appearance of certain Saudi city centres and went on to lambast the government's policy of encouraging foreign investment, which allegedly served 'the same big fish who control the private sector'. Pointing to 'the stack of 200,000 files of Saudi graduates at a time when as many foreign workers were entering the country each month', he effectively demanded that the government should Saudiize the economy and the jobs market as soon as possible.

Not all the support for 'national preference' Saudi-style is as crude or demagogic as Ali al-Musa's, and some voices have been raised in the press to expose the xenophobic premises or economic incoherence of the 'Saudiization' discourse. But the problem of immigration is a real problem, and the construction of ethnic areas in the big cities heightens the social segregation and makes of Riyadh or Jeddah a patchwork quilt in which Saudi, Filipino, Pakistani, Yemeni, Indian, European, Syrian and Egyptian districts form a landscape worthy of the big American cities.

From a position very distant from Ali al-Musa's, various leader writers and journalists regularly demand that foreign workers should be given the same social rights as Saudis, and that society should change its often condescending and sometimes violent attitude to immigrants. Thus, although the recognition that poverty has been growing in the Saudi population may give rise to xenophobic positions, it inevitably poses the problem of access to wealth by Saudis as well as immigrant workers, and may generate an economically more realistic and socially more just approach to the presence of 6 million foreigners in Arabia. In any event, it seems to us that 'Saudiization' is not here the appropriate response – and that Saudi Arabia's economic and social problems must be posed within the strictly regional framework of the GCC, or in the broader one of commercial and financial relations with nearby Arab and Asian countries.[27]

The invention of tradition

Contemporary Saudi society is the outcome of a complex evolution, in which the most important processes have been urbanization, pauperization and a gradual break-up of family structures. It has been quite an ordinary modernization, then, similar to that which has affected most Middle Eastern societies over the past thirty years – except that tremendous oil wealth has allowed Saudi society to escape the cataclysm that struck Egypt, whose capital city alone has as many inhabitants as the whole of Saudi Arabia. Moreover, government paternalism has spared society the humiliations of the Syrian or the Iraqi people, whose regimes have violently manipulated ethnic and religious identities and sometimes gone as far as massacring whole sections of the population.[28]

So, is Saudi society traditional? One might say so, but only if the word 'traditional' is explained and only if the preservation of customs and behaviour untouched by modernization is clearly distinguished from the artificial reinvention of tradition in response to modernization and as a final manifestation of modernity. As we have seen, when the code of honour or the laws of hospitality are largely relics of a bygone age, strict segregation of the sexes or a special definition of women's status becomes one of the throwbacks ultimately imposed by modernization itself. Both the government and society have engaged in this kind of rewriting of tradition: the government by trying to sew together national unity within a 'traditional culture' or an Islamic, family-centred and ideological 'common heritage' (*turath*); and society by devising various matrimonial or patriarchal strategies to preserve what modernity has been stripping away piece by piece.

The state's manipulation of the figure of the Bedouin illustrates this 'stitching together' of a Saudi heritage out of tattered traditions, Bedouin and sedentary legacies and disparate Islamic forms of conduct. It has been all the easier to present the Bedouin as a symbol of 'eternal' Arabia because a fierce struggle has been systematically waged against the Bedouin way of life.[29] A good example of this is the annual Janadriya festival, organized by the National Guard in the northern suburbs of Riyadh, a kind of endogenous Disneyland where 'natives' are invited to stroll around as tourists in their own country and to contemplate an inauthentic cultural tradition that has become no more than an object of the crafts and entertainment trade – the perfect image of a reinvented and hackneyed tradition.

In 1988, at the start of the period of greater openness (*infitah*) of the Saudi press, an article by the woman writer Fawziya Abu Khalid brilliantly dissected the artificial construction of a national culture around historical splendours and scraps of tradition:

> Heritage [*turath*] is not a hearth made of mud, its fire turned to ashes in a gas burner. Heritage is not *dalla* [coffee pot] or *mat'ouba* [ewer] or *es'hala* [milk pot] or *mehmass* [coffee roaster] or a *zinbeel* [basket] with broken handles. Heritage is not a Nabti poem [from the name of traditional Bedouin poetry] or a Nejdi dance or some other southern dance. Heritage is not houses made of hay and mud or *okt* [cheese snacks] made of the racing camels' milk. Heritage is the traces the trembling girls leave on the chunks of *okt*; it is

the travail of lads who mix hay and mud with sweat and sad *danas* [melodies]. It is the darkly painted eyes [with *kuhl*] that weave. It is the roughness of the hand that creates.... It is the relation of the spine to the ploughing of the land. *Turath* is the people in their joy and sorrow, defeat and victory, in their dreams that take refuge in the future. Simplifying heritage by converting it to its elementary substance, in which life manifests itself in the daily struggle for continuity and growth, is one of the means of communicating with our heritage. This is the means by which we create a movement of social change.[30]

Out of a constant historical flux, preserved in the tales of the ancients, in love scenes or battle scenes, in a treasury of popular wisdom or an apparatus of norms and attitudes, customs and examples, the 'tradition' to which the Saudi state lays claim picks out significant units and instruments of power and coercion, symbolic violence and cultural integration of the whole of society. Just as a torch beam in the dark produces only scraps of vision, not all-round visibility, so does this ideological 'tradition' have to do with the recollective filtering of scattered elements, of Islamic norms detached from their scriptural context, of patriarchal values separated from their historical cause. It does not grasp the continual historical movement of the national heritage, the eternal present heavy with the past and pregnant with the future; nor does it manage to conceptualize the elemental simplicity of culture, the relationship of one people to the world and to other peoples, the limpid expression of the evolution of a nation.

This is what Fawziya Abu Khalid finds wrong in the state's skilful manipulation of the Saudi cultures, or in the 'antiquities traffic' in which the regime engages with the blessing of Saudis (mostly in Najd) who have profited from this commerce in images. What Fawziya Abu Khalid describes is essentially the crisis of a culture torn between painful modernization and artificial reference to an idealized and fossilized past.[31]

The same analysis could apply to the reinvention by society of a vernacular Islamic tradition, as it could also to the instrumentalization of Islam by the regime and by the Islamist opposition, each of which takes from the Koranic legacy whatever serves its current political or social strategy. In much the same way that Arabic dialects select what suits them from the vast treasury of classical Arabic, each being essentially no more than an anthology sometimes livened up with borrowings from other languages (Berber or French in North Africa; Turkish, English or French in the Middle East; Persian, English or French in the Gulf), Saudi Islamic identity is a selection of rites, rituals and prescriptions that are experienced as simultaneously universal (because Islamic) and particular (because chosen here and now).[32]

Between this religious statement and the social practice there is the same gap as that between Catholic norms and the strategies of the Mediterranean *haute bourgeoisie*, or proclamations of Marxism–Leninism and the mores of the French left: it is the gap created by the specificity of a social *praxis*, which is no less autonomous in Saudi Arabia than anywhere else. In moving from Islam to society, or from tradition to modernity, we must therefore be attentive to strategies for the reconstruction of identity or the reinvention of tradition, attentive to the gradations separating what is said from what is done, proclamations of identity from everyday behaviour, venerated norms from social practices that are inevitably deviant just because they are *autonomous*.

When we consider the strategies for the rereading of history, the reinvention of tradition and the manipulation of heritages, when we look at the crisis of culture through which Saudi Arabia is passing today, we find that they are essentially about the fate of a society doomed to *individualization* of attitudes and values, in which each individual – following the example set by the state – is entitled to choose his own identity from the treasury bequeathed by tradition. People will invent themselves as reactionary or progressive, pro-American, liberal or Islamist, Bedouin or sedentary, supporter or opponent of the royal family, just as easily as they will travel by plane from Dammam to Riyadh or from Riyadh to Jeddah, in a quasi-topographical selection of their social *position* and the values serving or accompanying it. This autonomy, which is peculiar to the new generation, shapes the contours of a fragmented society, not only in the postmodern space of the Saudi metropolises but in the very values that constitute them as a single whole. We shall now try to plot the trajectory of this individualization process, directed against the society of men and of parents, which since the late 1980s has enabled the two silent half-parts of Saudi society, women and young people, gradually to win their independence.

7

The appearance of women

Al-mamnu' marghub — what is forbidden is desired.

Najd proverb

For the vast majority of Western observers, the position of women sums up what is most conservative in Saudi society and is a symbol of the obscurantism of the regime. Veiled, confined to the home, treated as minors, subject to the authority of their father, brother or husband, in short, 'prevented from existing',[1] women seem to bear mute testimony to the violence and oppression that a reactionary state and medieval society inflict on their weakest members.

It is true that, in Saudi Arabia today, women do not enjoy all the rights that the law recognizes in the case of men; that women cannot travel or study abroad without the written permission of a male guardian (mahram); that their share of an inheritance under Islamic law is only half that of a man; that their main sphere of freedom is sometimes the confined space of the marital home and the family; and that many wills conspire to keep these frail and tender beings in the exclusive realm of children's education. These peculiarities would seem shameful to anyone who wanted to fix a mental picture of the female condition in Arabia at the present point in time. But, for those who make the more cautious and painstaking effort to place each social phenomenon in its historical and political context, the characteristics of the female condition in Arabia call more for analysis than for indignation or invective. Having dismissed any desire to condemn, let us therefore seek to understand.

The nagging question of women's status

The very terms in which the problem of the status of Saudi women is posed seem to be very ill chosen in three respects.

First, condemnations of women's status in Saudi Arabia often involve the previously discussed confusion between Islam and tradition. Outside observers sometimes forget the gradations and nuances, the tensions and possible contradictions, that lie between Islam and tradition, between the religion and the set of rules with which society ensures its survival. They may think, for example, that the full veil ('abbaiya on the body, khimar on the face) is a straightforward example of both 'male domination' and 'subservience to religion', without realizing that the inference is not so clear from male domination to divine domination, or vice versa. According to Tocqueville:

> The clergy opened their ranks to all classes, to the poor and the rich, the commoner and the noble; through the church, equality penetrated into the government, and he who as a serf must have vegetated in perpetual bondage took his place as a priest in the midst of nobles, and not infrequently above the heads of kings.[2]

In the same way, religion can be a means for women to counterpose God's rule to the rule of men, gaining a freedom that would otherwise be denied them. A fine distinction therefore needs to be drawn between religion and tradition, if only to be able, should the need arise, to identify the two in full awareness of what one is doing.

Second, no caution at all is shown before judging state action as an oppressive enterprise. Yet in 1960 it was the state that, at the instigation of King Faisal's wife, imposed the idea of female education on the ulema and the whole of society. The fact that after 1980 the same state made women a moral problem, as it were, was therefore not something ordinary and to be expected: twenty years after contributing to women's liberation through education, the state again made them minors by bringing into force a number of extremely restrictive laws. Thus, in a couple of decades, the state passed from a lexicon of Western-style modernization to one of a deliberately 'Islamic' moral order. Far from demonstrating that the state is *essentially* modern or Islamic, favourable or hostile to women, socially emancipatory or oppressive, this shift signalled the cynicism and impotence of a political class that agrees to speak any language and to parade any sign, so long as it appears to serve its ends.

Yet such behaviour also shows that in 1960 the state felt strong enough to shake up a still traditional society, by forcing through the education of girls, whereas in 1980 the primacy of politics had been called into question by the oil boom, the intense politicization of society and the internal and external challenge represented by the Iranian Revolution, the Shiite intifada and the seizure of the Great Mosque in Mecca. In 1960 the state could impose exogenous modern norms on society, but twenty years later it was forced to take up and try to utilize the norms of society itself – that is, tribalism and Islam.[3] Care should therefore be taken to situate the state's attitude to women within a longer history of relations between the political sphere and a civil society liberated by oil wealth but also rendered dependent on the state.

Third, to make the status of women the yardstick of Arabia's modernity or backwardness often comes down to adopting the framework that Saudi society and the state themselves use to judge the moral or religious health of the country. For it is above all *inside Saudi Arabia* that the media constantly refer to the 'status of Saudi women', by turns suspecting them of being the 'Trojan horse of Westernization' or congratulating them for being the 'last bastion of religion'. What the West has to say about the issue is nothing in comparison with what Saudi society itself articulates. Whether it is a question of academics, men of religion, senior civil servants, princes, journalists or businessmen, not a week goes by without several men taking up their pen and writing in the press or on the Internet about the 'problems' of women, their 'natural inclinations', the 'place' they should have in society or the freedoms they can legitimately acquire. Rather than women themselves, who are scarcely visible and usually absent from the male public space, it is the extraordinary male solicitude for the female half of the population which leaps to the eyes of someone reading the Saudi press.[4]

It is not surprising that when Saudi women took up the pen, in the late 1970s, they were mainly concerned to challenge the categories in which both the East and the West had confined them; they therefore refused to embody inside the country either social progress or regression, or to represent, in the eyes of the world, some Islamic purity or medieval backwardness of Saudi society. They were not prepared to be the prism through which the whole society was read, in its steps forward and steps back, its injustices and its achievements – in short, to be a propaganda item, for use either for or against the regime in Riyadh.

As Juhayer al-Musa'ed, an editorial writer for the daily *Al-Jazira* and a journalist at *Al-Riyadh*, wrote at the end of the 1980s:

> Many topics are discussed as 'women's issues' whereas in fact they are not. They are simply issues of a society that is experiencing development and change.... Journalism concentrates on the woman as she goes to school and gets an education, as she works, as she eats, as she gets married, as she brings up her children, as she gives birth, and so on. *The woman becomes the 'creator' of journalism and also its victim.*[5]

In other words, women may be the victims mainly of a discourse that systematically takes them as an example and a target. In a society where – from pre-Islamic poetry to Koranic revelation and from incendiary preaching to political harangues – discourse is at the same time an act, and a political act at that, it is natural that the revolt of women should at first have taken the reassuring shape of a paper revolution. But we should not be deceived by this. In speaking out publicly, women changed their status 'from that of a "symbol" to that of a "real" human being. The idea is not only a revelation but revolutionary.'[6]

Perhaps the confusion is due mainly to the use of terms such as women's 'status' or 'place'. For in a way these underwrite what is being made the object of attack: that women should be assigned a mere 'place' in society that is governed by a set of universally accepted rules (a 'status' or 'statute'). Such terms take the female condition out of history – a history in which, in Arabia as anywhere else, it is hard to think that women have not also been actors. If Fatna Shaker, the first female editor-in-chief and speaker on the national radio, is right in saying that 'often we hear about the woman's issue, the child's issue, the minorities' issue, but rarely do we hear of the man's issue',[7] this is because everyone – Westerner or Saudi – tacitly accepts that women can be *placed* in a category with rigidly defined boundaries, *frozen* in a juridical present from which they cannot escape into a *history*. Perhaps this is one of the paradoxes of a certain comfortable feminism, whose language of place and status silently confirms what it so vociferously denounces.

Our main concern here will be to treat woman as the equal of man – that is, as a historical actor – so that the female 'status' is systematically located within the process of which it is both origin and result. We shall then see that, far from being victims of Islam or the state, women since the early 1980s have, like men, set about using the state and Islam to hasten their liberation.

Modern signs, traditional signs?

Saudi women are invisible. However, even draped in a black *'abbaiya*, even covered with a black *tarha* or *hijab* (head veil) and a *khimar* (face mask), they occupy a noteworthy part of public space; their silhouette – alongside the white silhouette of men, also with a head veil but with face uncovered – gives Saudi streets and malls their distinctive aspect of stylized abstraction, without the varied colours typical of Western streets. Women do not drive cars, rarely move around alone and are usually accompanied by a brother, husband, father, female friend or relative, driver or maid. In shops, banks, restaurants, universities, libraries and government offices, they are received in a special area forbidden to men that is marked *Qism al-'a'ilat* (family section).

None of these characteristics has acquired the force of an un-varying rule, even if a number of them have *recently* been legally formalized (the driving ban dates from the beginning of the 1990s). All those regularities admit of exceptions. In Jeddah, and in some parts of Riyadh, female members of the prosperous classes do not hesitate to uncover their face, much to the displeasure not only of older men and some clerics but also of most other women. The ban on driving? It applies only in the city, not in the countryside, where it is not unusual to come across a woman behind a steering wheel, taking a child or elderly relative to school or the doctor's surgery. Segregation of public space? This tends not to be enforced in the big cities: all supermarkets are open to women as well as men, and some malls have completely mixed restaurants for their customers' use.

Only the veil remains a constant of women's appearance in public. Who issues the order to wear it? The answer to this question is not so easy: both nobody and everyone. A young girl whose elder sister already wears the veil will not rest until she wears it herself, for the simple reason that, along with high heels, make-up or short skirts, the veil is here a sign of womanhood. In a context of gender segregation, the meaning that girls attach to the veil refers not directly to male oppression – the need to wear it is nearly always conveyed by the mother or sister – but to the freedom to go out of the house, to be free in one's movements. The veil is the means for women to be untouchable representatives of private space within public space; it provides the social comfort of being able to see without being seen.

In fact, there are several different attitudes that Saudi women may take towards the veil, spanning the whole range from the strictest conservatism to a claim of modernity, although none of these questions the actual wearing of the veil. The conservative attitude, common in some rural areas and less prosperous urban milieux, raises no questions at all about the fabric that conceals women: 'you don't just wear it, you are born and brought up in it'.[8] Here the veil is what it is in the truly traditional areas of the Arabian Peninsula (certain parts of Yemen or the Sultanate of Oman): that is, a tool for the *privatization* of women, accepted without qualms by the male and female population as part of their environment. Indoors, the veil is not worn among women, though it is in the presence of some men in the family; outdoors, women disappear behind a layer of black cloth. Wearing of the veil is the *natural* thing to do: it is not affected by the change in dress codes which, like the individualization of life strategies and choices, signals the emergence of modernity.

At the opposite extreme, a claim to modernity can express itself in an *eroticization* of the veil. Although woman is invisible, she sometimes offers herself to be seen in her very invisibility. Here the veil is not patiently tolerated but assumed, brandished or subtly corrupted: the area around the eyes, the tip of a pair of trainers, the tight or not so tight-fitting cut of the *'abbaiya*, the thinness and transparency of the gauze covering the face become so many signs that veil as much as they unveil, in a fine dialectic of the diaphanous and the opaque, the close-fitting and the loosely flowing. From a 'French *'abbaiya*', neatly trimmed to the last millimetre, through to a classical *'abbaiya* carrying the inscription 'Touch Me If You Dare', the sartorial abuses are frequent among well-off young women in the cities and go together with a wide range of head veils (from the simple *tarha* occasionally turned down in front of the face to a fine see-through fabric placed on the head like a bridal veil).

The seductive effrontery with which some are able to deflect the veil from its primary function represents one possible extreme, whose distilled erotic charge spreads among close relatives and friends to infect the attitudes of all women in Arabia. Only one has to veil herself for the purposes of enticement and everyone else will react accordingly, either by following the new and freer fashion or by keeping a close watch on their daughter, sister or girl friend. Unlike the veil worn by women in traditionalist regions, the city veil inevitably becomes a second-degree adornment, no longer a thing but a *sign*. As such, it calls for neither out-of-hand condemnation nor blind praise but for careful exegesis. Women in today's Saudi cities no longer wear the veil 'just because it's there', and even if they do they invest it with a meaning of their own. It is in this female approach that we should seek the significance of the *'abbaiya*, the *tarha* and the *khimar*.

The second modernist attitude consists in the attribution of not an erotic but, on the contrary, a religious meaning to the veil. That the traditionally unquestioned veil should become a token of submission to God is a quite novel development – and testifies to the modernity of some women's attitude to religion. We shall return below to the appearance of the 'Islamic' veil in Arabia, but this review is enough to show that, with the noteworthy exception of an older and Westernized minority, Saudi women not only accept the veil but experience it as an instrument of freedom. So great is this sense of freedom that, after the terrorist attacks of 12 May 2003 in Riyadh, some women went so far as to demand that police at checkpoints should check their identity and search them and other women, precisely because one of the terrorists had disguised himself as a woman to pass through undetected.

The veil and Islam

What is the origin of the veil and of the segregation that it signals? We should begin by making it clear that there are two types of veil, each with its distinct appearance and status. First, the social veil (the khimar) covers the face with a black mask, showing the eyes or hiding them behind a piece of thin translucent gauze. This veil is inherently foreign to Islam, in the sense that it is not mentioned in any of the passages in the Koran or the Sunna that deal with modesty in both sexes. In one passage we read:

> Tell male believers to lower their eyes and to contain their private parts: that will be cleaner. God is well apprised of their conduct. Tell female believers to lower their eyes and to contain their private parts; to refrain from displaying their charms, save that which stands out; to pull their headgear down over the neckline of their clothing.[9]

And the Book continues: 'A sure means of being recognized as ladies and escaping any insult.'[10]

These two verses contain the origin of the second veil, the religious veil or tarha, which is a sign of submission to God and of modest conduct. While the social veil protects women who wear it from 'ayb (social shame), the religious veil preserves them from the haram (sin) of lack of modesty. No confusion is possible between 'ayb and haram, traditions ('adat) and religious prescriptions ('ibadat), any more than it is between the khimar and the tarha; these are two historically and theologically distinct orders. With a few exceptions, as we have seen, the social veil is worn all over Arabia. But within the precincts of the two mosques of Mecca and Medina and along the routes of the greater and lesser pilgrimages women actually have a duty to uncover their faces; the khimar disappears and gives way to the tarha.

The social veil and segregation are not only part of a distinct order of religion; they are also, as Germaine Tillion has shown in a now canonical work, anti-Islamic instruments.[11] A veritable Napoleonic Code of the southern Mediterranean, the Koran read literally led to the dispersion of landholdings and tribal legacies by allocating a share of the inheritance to the father's daughter. It was therefore to retain their heritage, not to avoid scandal, that tribes in the process of destruction and sedentarization were tempted to control their women by keeping them from the attentions of strangers: '1. religious fervour imposes female inheritance; 2. female inheritance destroys the tribe; 3. the destroyed tribe accepts outsiders; 4. fathers then veil their daughters, *to preserve them for the boys of the family notwithstanding.*'[12]

In Arabia, as in the rest of the Arab world, the pre-Islamic institution of the veil was reintroduced when the Arabs settled down and urban promiscuity began to endanger family inheritances. The defence of landed property and patriarchy against the egalitarianism imposed by Islam therefore acquired the purpose of protecting women's purity and honour ('irdh). A secular not an Islamic value, traditionally urban rather than rural and Bedouin, 'irdh is embodied in the women of the family and today constitutes one of the horizons of social existence. Woman is that part of society in whom blame and honour, virtue and vice are concentrated, and so a family's reputation hinges first of all on the chastity and irreproachable behaviour of its female members.

In the early 1980s, the return in force of the *social* veil was the opportunity for the state to deploy a *religious* line of argument. The official ulema especially invoked the Hanbalite concept of *sadd al-zhara'i*: that is, literally, 'means block' or prohibition of the paths leading to sin. The fact that this veritable preventive war against fitna (sedition) was waged with a mixture of tradition and Islam, in which the *social* lexicon of segregation merged with the *religious* vocabulary of modesty, tells us a lot about the state's attitude to tradition and religion, as well as the regressive stamp it imprinted on religious discourse itself.

As we have seen, this recent period was also the one that produced the laws banning women from driving, travelling abroad without a *mahram* and running a business of their own without male intercession – laws which put an end to 'over a fifteen-centuries-old traditional right for the Arab woman to be an independent entrepreneur'.[13] Significantly, it was just when the generation of state-educated women was beginning to rise up the ladder and to take an active part in the economy that the state and society, with the help of the recession and political threats, hardened their line on values artificially wheeled out for the occasion. As Fatna Shaker wrote in connection with the social norms promulgated in the early 1980s:

> The humanity of women was established by Islam when it freed her from 'female infanticide' and acknowledged for her a human existence independent of men. Islam made her a partner and not a subordinate.... 'Female infanticide' may have stopped physically but still be practised, however differently in kind and degree.[14]

The veil is certainly traditional, then, but we need to be cautious about the circumstances in which the tradition is mobilized and to avoid confusing with straightforward backwardness what is really part of a *reaction* against social modernization and, above all, its setbacks and failures. In other words, the veil and segregation testify to a *traditionalism* which, in this sense quite distinct from *tradition*, is itself an expression of ambiguous and chaotic modernity. We should also note that the *religious* police were given the task of keeping a watch on women, and that an *Islamic* line of argument was here used to maintain *patriarchal* social values, whereas in fact social and religious practices were here not only distinct but contradictory. In order to preserve the basis of its power and to show that it spoke the same language as society, the regime therefore undertook – in defiance of all Islamic logic – to weld together Islam and tradition in a compact block. Women will never cease trying to break up this amalgam of Islam and tradition.

Emancipatory strategies

As we have seen, female emancipation may be dated from the time when women spoke out in public. In 1956 the first article by a woman was published in the Jeddah daily *Al-Manhil*. Since the early 1960s – the very time when female education was introduced in the kingdom – women journalists have been regularly writing in the daily or monthly press. And it was in 1981 that *Al-Riyadh*, a daily published in the capital, hired women for the first time as regular correspondents.[15]

Women were not destined only to run the home or to bring up children, nor confined within an exclusively feminine public sphere; they used the columns of daily papers or periodicals to participate in public life as such, female and male, social and political. In this capacity women were at the heart of the 'modernism controversy' initiated in 1987 by the young sheikhs Said al-Ghamdi and Awad al-Qarni[16] – a controversy in which the 'women's question' was one of the main issues. As well as being brought to the fore of the literary and intellectual scene, women asserted their economic independence.

By the 1960s some women of independent means were running their own business, especially in Hijaz, where pilgrimage merchants had already diversified their activity and involved their children, daughters included. It is estimated today that women hold roughly 40 per cent of Saudi private wealth, and that, though no longer entitled to run their own business directly, they are able to do so through a male representative. Women own and run in this way some 15,000 firms, and they can be elected to sit in the female sections of the Riyadh, Jeddah and Dhahram chambers of commerce.[17]

Saudi Arabia's ever more educated women have been gradually overtaking men at university and in 1995 accounted for 55 per cent of all graduates.[18] Today, they represent a little under 10 per cent of the national labour force (not including immigrants), and although long confined to 'female' jobs (medicine, teaching and research, interior decoration, etc.) they are gradually spreading into all the 'male' occupations and can now have a career as a journalist, engineer or even aircraft pilot. Segregation has played an indirect role in boosting female labour, since the splitting of most shopping areas into two means that 'women's sections' are run and managed by women. This backdoor parity has also enabled women to pursue a career in banking, commerce, public services and the senior civil service. By expanding a female public space, as distinct from male or mixed public space, segregation has thus created areas of quite major women's autonomy.

As we have seen, the spearhead of this public self-affirmation was journalism and literature. As large numbers of girls have passed through the school and university system, their often greater interest in intellectual rather than technical subjects has given them a real social and political visibility in teaching, research and writing. The generalization of education, the falling rates of illiteracy (16 per cent for men, 32 per cent for women) and the emergence of a huge female readership have given a spectacular boost to publishing: in 1989 Saudi Arabia had 350 houses, and in 1996 a total of 3,700 titles were published – almost as much as in the whole of the rest of the Arab world, excluding Egypt and Lebanon. In the same year, the street kiosks had on sale 90 different periodicals, including 10 daily newspapers. Distribution outlets have grown *pari passu*, now numbering more than 2,000 bookshops and approximately 5,000 kiosks and other sales points. More than 200 public libraries cater for a now mixed public, with certain days reserved for women, and women's literary clubs have undergone considerable growth and are officially registered with the youth and sports ministry.[19]

Female emancipation has therefore been pursued on the very terrain of male domination: the intellectual and administrative professions, work and education. The writer Sharifa al-Shamlan had one of her characters sum this up in a few calmly iconoclastic lines: 'If women really have less intelligence and religion than men,' she thinks, 'then most of the men must lose theirs by choice. Most women's intelligence is greater than their experience and that strengthens and deepens their religion.'[20] It was therefore mainly through the exercise of their intelligence that Saudi women carried out their paper revolution, whereas the state had tried to confine them to the home and to make them symbols of social purity, and society had tried to make them emblems of the modernist threat.

Evidence of these social advances should not, however, blind us to the fact that it is difficult to speak there of 'women's liberation':

> What we do not agree on is what the woman wants from liberation. Who is 'occupying' her and from whom is she seeking liberation? Why does the woman complain of oppression? And who is she complaining about? I expect that the thought is widespread that the woman is suffering from man's oppression of her.... These expressions are not only widespread among Arab women but have also become *a part of our parlance that we imported, among other things, from foreigners....* But at the same time we find that the woman marries the man, loves the man, and bears him children![21]

Thus in 1984, Juhayer al-Musa'ed objected to the very vocabulary in which women's liberation could be expressed, seeing it as an exogenous import from the West and arguing that it was contradictory for women to wish to free themselves of men to whom they were tied by their female condition. Fundamentally, her point was that women cannot free themselves from men but must free themselves *with* men. The second phase of women's liberation therefore expressed itself in a vocabulary that was no longer imported but perfectly exogenous; it objected to the very word 'liberation' that others attributed to it, as well as to the idea that the emancipation of women was exclusively female in its impact.

The rise of an Islamic feminism

The first phase of the feminist movement therefore took place inside the intellectual and economic establishment of the kingdom and expressed itself in a vocabulary largely borrowed from Western feminist struggles. This modernization 'from above' found a counterpart, from the mid-1980s, in a mobilization 'from below' – a second phase that saw itself as both more authentic (because it spoke the language of Islam, not of imported modernity) and more universal (because it thereby affected the whole of the female population, not just an educated, Westernized elite).

So, whereas the modernists of the 1970s and 1980s combated tradition in the name of modernity yet took care not to contradict

religious norms, the feminists of the 1980s and 1990s opposed tradition in the name of religion itself. Women were no longer content
to quote Khadijah (the Prophet's wife) as their example; they also
set about reinterpreting the teachings of Islam, in a guerrilla war
against the ulema similar to that which the young sheikhs were
waging at the same time:

> Women writers ... feel the need to first liberate Islam from shackles
> of cultural politics by speaking directly from and to the texts. This
> has posed a considerable challenge to the religious leaders not only
> because it breaks their monopoly of religious interpretation but,
> more important, because it exposes their attempt to reduce religion
> to its ideological use.[22]

> It is this position, combining religion and a spirit of reform,
> which makes it possible to speak of 'Islamic feminism'.[23]

The first difference between this Islamic feminism and Western
feminism was that its arguments were based on the Koran and the
Sunna. In downplaying human law and opposing to it the radical
transcendence of divine law, in reclaiming an Islamic identity and
asserting it against Western ideological influences increasingly seen
in terms of real and symbolic violence, the new feminism adopted
a considerably more trenchant and assertive tone. As one 'liberated'
woman, a medical specialist in Riyadh, put it:

> Who are you to come giving us lessons? I really believed in
> the values that the West upheld, but you have been betraying
> them – especially in Palestine. Have you seen the pictures of the
> prisoners at Guantánamo? They're treated like animals. You've never
> accepted us for what we are, *you just want us to become like yourselves.*
> Islam is the basis of our life. I don't want that to change. *We have
> nothing left except Islam.*[24]

At once a reaction and an affirmation, Islamic feminism has taken the
same paths as Islamism: its religious vocabulary too involves a rejection and a recovery, a preservation both critical and progressive.

The 'new veil' or 'religious veil' is the most eloquent sign of this
Islamic feminism. Just as some women make the veil a factor in
seduction, others turn it into a religious sign and wear the *tarha* under
all circumstances, even in private or abroad, thereby emancipating

themselves from the 'feminine model' imposed by men. This does not cancel the meaning of the social veil (khimar), but it does put it in a very different perspective. By taking up the religious veil, Islamist feminists transcend the social veil and criticize the profane significance it has for men of hiding their wife, daughter or sister from the desire of strangers. Far from signifying subservience to the family, the religious veil usually goes together with a wish (in accordance with Islam) to choose a husband outside the circle of first and second cousins.

Marital practices are central to the concerns of Islamic feminists – especially in view of the crisis of marriage that the kingdom has experienced since the early 1980s. Because of the ever larger size of the mahr (bride price payable by a husband), as well as the socially timorous practices of many families, the number of unmarried women has been on the rise: as many as a million and a half in 2002. At the same time, the divorce rate has shot up to one in three marriages, also in 2002. Hence the recurrent appeals for a reduction in the mahr, and sometimes for a free choice of spouses over and against the social and matrimonial strategies of each family.

Here, too, Islam provides a means to deflect family strategies by making them secondary to something higher. In order to counter the disastrous effect of the restrictions imposed on women in the early 1980s, the new generation of 'Islamist' women have brought an older religious practice back into force: that is, they increasingly get the sheikh to insert into their marriage contract a number of binding clauses such as freedom of movement, freedom to study abroad, power to repudiate the husband if he takes other wives, freedom to continue their studies, to take a job, and so on.[25] In their assertions of autonomy with regard to men and social conventions, it is Islam that women invoke rather than a hypothetical world struggle for women's liberation.

Less spectacular than Western-style liberation but certainly more effective, this Islamic movement is similar to that which has mobilized women in Turkey or Iran.[26] From a base in the women's universities and literary clubs, it is reaching large sections of the female population and finding expression in public meetings and numerous publications, Islamic or secular, which divide their space between exegesis of the revealed texts and women's verse or prose literature. They reject Western feminism as irresponsible and dismiss what they see as the West's inconsistent and insulting verdict on Saudi women. What they are saying, in essence, is that the 'women's problem' is not actually a problem.

When faced with the artificial sense of pity that the West feels for them, they reply that Saudi women – who belong to a rich and well-educated society – are certainly among the happiest in the Arab and the third world, and that the pauperization of Arabia is a much greater danger for them and the whole of the new generation than is an imposition of strict Islamic standards by the Saudi state. One young woman interviewed by Alain Gresh said with a mixture of humour and bitterness: 'Driving a car is not a top priority. In fifteen years' time we will have gained that right, but we won't be able to buy a car any longer.'[27] The Islamic mobilization of Saudi women is a way of cocking a snook at Western expectations: it shows that the real problem is not the position of women but the future of Saudi youth as a whole. In other words, it may well be the case that the gender issue is mobilized only to conceal what is really at stake – the problem of the younger generation.

8

The Gulf War generation

Une génération est un drame.

Honoré de Balzac

More than the condition of women, it is the condition of Saudi youth that worries not only society but the regime – and also, since 11 September 2001, all the Western countries. Excluded from most positions of responsibility, struggling to find a place in the jobs market, the new generation nevertheless represents a majority of the population: one Saudi in two is less than 15 years old, and 60 per cent of the population are under 20.

It is a commonplace to say that the younger generation throughout the Middle East, from Palestinian *shabab* to Iranian students, has become a major focus for politicians and the media. The paradox is that the biological definition given of the younger generation clashes with the political role that people would like to see it play or, on the contrary, are afraid that it might play. A few years ago, the Western media hoped that a new generation of Arab leaders[1] would help to change political practices – but in most cases, especially in Morocco and Syria, a brief and inconsequential 'Arab Spring' was followed by a reaffirmation of the inherited political line, disappointing the expectations built on a confusion between the biological and the social, the natural and the political order.

In other words, biological age cannot very well have an intrinsic political significance, and 'Arab youth' would appear to be a practical myth of the media, with as little scientific basis as the journalist's convenient 'Arab street' that is supposed to tell us what Arab peoples think without the need for them to be given an actual voice. Youth does not necessarily go together with progressive thinking, nor old age with conservative thinking; simple analysis of the polices of the 'young' Bashar al-Assad and the 'old' Abdallah Al Saud strikingly shows that youth can imitate and old age innovate. Biological definition is therefore not enough: it is absolutely essential to complement analysis of the age pyramid with an examination of what makes each age group conscious of itself as a *generation* with its own specificities. How does 'youth' become a player in politics and society?

This prelude now allows us to consider the Saudi youth issue, which inspires fear in the West for four reasons. First, young people form a majority of the population and, like women or the minorities, have little political representation. Second, arriving too late and unprepared in a prematurely exhausted economy, they face unemployment and a general lack of things to do. Third, as the Saudi sociologist Mai Yamani has shown through extensive fieldwork, the new generation tends to formulate its identity in religious terms:

> Islam, for all these young people, is key to their self-perception. It remains the main ideational force that gives coherence to their world. All those interviewed are aware of the wide-ranging changes that have swept through Saudi Arabia during their lifetime. It is Islam and 'tradition' that help them to put these changes into perspective. Islamic discourse is central to their self-understanding.[2]

Fourth and last, unemployment, Islam and a lack of political representation make it susceptible, in Western eyes, to recruitment by violent movements that endanger the sacred stability of the Middle East.[3]

The young old and the old young

The adjective 'young', or the noun form 'the young', does not mean anything in itself or biologically, for, as it has often been pointed out, we do not know at what age youth ends and maturity or old age begins. It is in *relation to* other generations ('mature people' or 'old people') that an age category takes shape which might be described as a 'younger generation'. In Arabia as elsewhere, then, generations are born in mutual encounter or even conflict, and it would be unrealistic to claim to draw a picture of youth without taking into account the primary relationship which, in the family, the educational system or the labour market, constitutes it as such: that is to say, its intercourse with 'old people'. If a generation is a drama or tragedy, it is precisely because the constitution of an age category is neither natural nor irenic but necessarily involves self-affirmation against another generation.

In a traditionally patriarchal society, youth is defined by the *defect* of a lack of experience and knowledge. According to Saudi tradition, to be young is 'not yet to be', and no positive value is attached to this provisional non-being; youth is defined not by any present state but by the future maturity it carries within it. It is the older person who is wise, skilful and experienced, and the adjective 'old' (*shaikh*) designates tribal chiefs as well as men of religion, men of power as well as men of knowledge. The traditional attitude of young people to the old is made up of respect and polite subservience. Historically, then, the Saudi younger generation has been the generation that listens and obeys.

This means that power in the tribe or family is not autocratic but 'gerontocratic'; each decision, jointly taken, does not oppose a leader to his subordinates but, rather, the assembly of elders to the still confused mass of young people. In fact, it is imprecise to speak here of an opposition between young and old, since their interrelations are much more ones of harmonious complementarity than of conflict. Thus, within the Bedouin tribes, young people are destined for action (the martial action of the raid or the romantic action of the *ghazal*) and are deflected from anything to do with the exercise of power and formal speech (words of command, words of storytelling), which is traditionally the preserve of old people. Bedouin poetry already served as a means of subverting this division of roles, since it was often the *young* poet who spoke and acted through it, no longer taken in by his elders and bent on making himself master of the tribal destiny through the word and the sword.[4]

This traditional subservience of 'the young' to 'the old' allows us to gauge the excitement and interest that surrounded the 'young sheikhs' movement of the mid-1980s. As we have seen, these 'young old people' appeared on the Saudi public stage to launch the 'modernism controversy', sharply criticizing the hold of imported Western ideas over the government, the state administration and the media. The object of their attack, then, was modernity itself, not only as a set of values alien to Saudi Islamic culture but also as the values of the Saudi government, of the shiyukh or old people. To some extent, the emergence of Saudi Islamism at the end of the 1980s may be read as the rise of a new generation of sheikhs, trained in the school of the Muslim Brotherhood, who were determined to fight it out (theoretically) with the religious establishment of the kingdom.[5]

Let us briefly glance back at the movement through which a section of young people opposed the powers-that-be, attacking modernity itself as a monopoly of the old. Reality seemed to be walking on its head, so clearly did criticism of the new emanate from the very ones who might have been expected to favour it. This clearly stated opposition to 'old people', testifying to the decline of the patriarchal model, is one of the most striking aspects in the constitution of Saudi youth as a meaningful category, and it makes itself felt in a number of ways. For example, young people who define themselves as 'religious' say that they will respect only those who follow the precepts of Islam and not hesitate to call even an old person to order.[6] Such sabre-rattling must be understood as a challenge to the traditional order – a challenge that opposes human law with the law of God. Before reading the youth revolt in religious terms, we should therefore see it as a *social* movement through which young people position themselves in relation to a field of power and attempt to subvert its defining polarities (young and old, authority and obedience, speech and silence).

So, should youth be understood as the age of confidence in life, unconcern about the future and rather scant attention to moral values? In today's Saudi Arabia these three characteristics appear to be inverted: that is, young people have very limited confidence in life, show little sign of unconcern and set great store by moral and religious values; whereas older people offer the image of a generation that grew up during the age of prosperity and is marked by confident attachment to the economic growth and social modernization in which it participated. Curiously enough, therefore, old people in the biological sense here appear 'youthful' in their attitudes, claiming the right to a certain adolescence and displaying the unconcern of people who have grown up in a world without problems or 'big issues'.

If the old behave like young people, conversely the young behave like old people. This is the painful paradox of the new generation, which gives it shape as a generation in the full sense of the term: if youth defines itself in opposition to old age, Saudi youth is an early old age, and old age is an artificially prolonged youth. What has made youth grow old too soon is its bitter experience of the labour market, the inadequacy of its training at school and university, and often the spectre of unemployment. Hence the atypical condition of Saudi young people, young in body and old in spirit. Hence too their defining struggle against old people, which, even if hushed up for reasons of propriety, involves them in a head-on clash.

The founding event of the malaise

The present conflict between the generations is bound up with the fact that neither knowledge nor action is open to young Saudis, who often see themselves as playthings of a history decided elsewhere, in the mysteries of the royal government or influential circles in Washington. The trauma of the second Gulf War, in 1990–91, has come to symbolize the emergence of this painful new perception.

As we have seen, the deafening silence of the royal palace and the official media after the Iraqi invasion of Kuwait shook the confidence that society had previously had in the regime. One of the young people interviewed by Mai Yamani put it like this:

> Television stations such as Jordan TV were transmitting pictures of demonstrations across the Arab and Islamic worlds in support of Iraq's annexation of Kuwait and protesting about the war effort against Iraq. Since there was hardly any news of this on Saudi state television, not even announcements about the invasion, we realized

that there was a heavy censorship of news, and we lost trust in the official media. As a result, we stopped watching state television and opted instead to watch only foreign news broadcasts.[7]

The arrival of American troops on Saudi soil, despite the government's massive spending on weapons of its own, came as a second shock:

We felt betrayed; the Saudi government invested our oil money in large amounts of military equipment that we saw paraded frequently on the television screens, and now we discovered that it was ineffective. We have no real power to stand against Saddam Hussein. We had believed the authorities' claim that our military was so powerful it could stand against Israel but, *subhan-Allah* – the wonders of the Almighty who will help us – we still need to understand how the Americans have come to be in charge.[8]

The media trauma (our television does not tell the truth) and the political shock (our government has lied or been duped) were compounded by fear of Iraqi bombing in Riyadh and a few towns in the Eastern Province. These missile attacks were nothing in comparison with what the Iraqi population endured, or what the Lebanese population had been through in the civil war, or what the Palestinian and Israeli populations are still experiencing today. But, for a barricaded society that believed in the promise of stability and perpetual peace, the noisy intrusion of the outside world suddenly revealed the fragility of the edifice that the kingdom had patiently built up.

The writer Badriya al-Bishr has dealt with this new awareness in one of her short stories. While 'mouths never stopped dilating to proffer new lies and to cloud the target of truth', during a 'war that half of us would have bet we'd never see', after Riyadh itself was bombed one Thursday, the novelist described as follows the irruption of violence into a developed society convinced of its own stability:

Thursday's terror has not gone away.... The war turned into invocation and insults – and rumours that acquired their full scope only when it was over. It went on like that until the danger had passed, until the guns fell silent, until *Patriot* was no more than an inscription on young people's T-shirts and women's dresses, or something for boys to joke about. War became the memory of inextinguishable suffering, a worm that continued to eat away at us and never had its fill. How many stories were built around it![9]

Although the second Gulf War had little material impact on the country, it deeply shook Saudi society at a symbolic level by demonstrating to everyone that the age of opulence was well and truly over. The irruption of war and political violence (in the shape of Iraqi missiles and media lies) put an end to a kind of innocence: the political and social struggles held back by growth and oil prosperity could emerge into broad daylight. The Gulf War generation had come into being – a generation which understood that, unlike its elders, it would have to live in an uncertain world. If, as Paul Nizan wrote, 'everything threatens a young man with ruin',[10] young Saudis had never felt as threatened as they did on the morrow of the second Gulf War.

A shipwrecked youth

Born in the years of plenty between 1970 and 1986, the new generation was ill prepared to enter an adulthood that was now demanded of it too soon. Indeed, under the impact of recession, the carefree existence for which long years had previously prepared it suddenly turned into a premature old age. It is the present younger generation that has suffered most from the social upheavals we have described above: massive and rapid urbanization, crisis of the family and impoverishment of society. With its roots in a crisis born of opulence, it has had to live through a huge shake-up in social and religious values and a sometimes violent competition among real traditions, ideological traditions reinvented by the state, traditional Islam, imported modernity and exogenous modernization.

The younger generation can be constituted only in the conflict that opposes it to a previous generation that knew only abundance. The identity of youth therefore passes first through what Pierre Bourdieu (in reference to France) called the 'conflict between systems of aspirations'[11] – that is, not only between levels of material existence but above all between levels of expectation. The living standards of young Saudis are significantly lower than those of their parents, and their aspirations now conflict with the economic decline of the country. Deprived of a future, young people really are a *generation in decline*, and the thought of what lies ahead (unemployment, crisis of marriage and the family model, etc.) cruelly contradicts the prosperity that seemed to be in store for them.

The youth identity that accompanies this sense of decline, stretching it into at least verbal militancy, is also bound up with an intense political awareness. This recent politicization of society grew stronger in the 1990s as a result of the presence of foreign media, the creation in 1996 of the pan-Arab satellite television station Al-Jazeera, with a mostly Saudi audience, the introduction of the Internet in 1998 and the gradual liberalization of the press since the mid-1990s (symbolized by the creation of the daily *Al-Watan* in 1998, which does not hesitate to take up such burning issues as suicide among young people, marital problems, drugs or homosexuality, and even, since 9/11, internal government policy).

The politicization expresses itself first of all in the emergence of a genuinely national consciousness. This is now spread by what one might call a 'national language', since internal migration means that the Riyadh dialect has absorbed regional elements and become a *lingua franca* among young people;[12] they use it to express their common condition in a common language, as opposed to regional remnants and sometimes Bedouin dialects. Second, the politicization is apparent in distrust of the political regime, which can be traced back to the upheaval of the second Gulf War. 'The government has become that "other" which is no longer trusted', writes Mai Yamani.[13] The previous generation, which owed nearly everything to state intervention in society, could not have shared this attitude of distrust and contempt.

Third, young people have become politicized through their lively interest in the conflicts shaking the Arab and Muslim world. The Israeli–Palestinian conflict, in particular, is the backdrop against which many have developed characteristic forms of discourse, taken up political positions and identified with other causes; its injustice here becomes the key to a general reading of political events, from the Bush administration's 'war on terror' to the fighting in the former Yugoslavia or Chechnya, from the Western occupation of Iraq in 2003 to the debates concerning Islam in Europe. Much better informed than their parents, much more open to the world and current politics, the younger generation sometimes uses its pro-Palestinian or pro-Iraqi commitment to criticize Arabia's foreign policy for being too subservient to American wishes or even (when a hand is publicly held out to Israel, as in 2002) for betraying the Arab nation and Islam.[14]

The fact that young people are not politically represented – except perhaps by young princes too numerous to gain a real hearing – fuels endemic opposition in certain parts of Saudi Arabia. In Hijaz, for example, in the run-up to the seizure of the main mosque in Mecca in 1979, Sunni-Shafeite and Sufi religious minorities allied with young army officers to express their revolt. In Hasa, the intifada of 1979 was followed by high levels of secret organization throughout the 1980s and 1990s. And in Najd itself, rebellious Sunni groups appeared on the scene in the early 1980s, and the following decade witnessed an open challenge to the government (in 1992) as well as the intifada of 1994, which in Qasim seemed to hark back to the great student demonstrations of 1956.

In each of these cases the revolt expressed itself in religious terms, and, although the re-Islamization of Saudi young people today only rarely takes radical forms, it underpins their identity and an ever more pressing desire to become a fully fledged political and social actor. Before we examine this re-Islamization, however, we must account for the last element in the malaise of young people: the crisis of the educational system.

Does the educational system turn out terrorists?

Since 11 September 2001, both the content and the form of the Saudi educational system have been subjected to sharp criticism outside the kingdom, especially in the United States.

As regards content, it is argued that curricula attach great importance to religion and thus help to produce young fanatics ready to take up arms against the 'infidel' West. It is true that nearly 30 per cent of teaching time in primary schools is devoted to religion and the Arabic language – a figure that falls to 24 per cent in lower-secondary education and 14 per cent in upper-secondary education for general courses of study (34 per cent for pupils specializing in Islamic law and Arabic). Three of Saudi Arabia's seven universities are Islamic, and the weight of religion and Arabic in higher education varies from 10 per cent for students taking technical courses to 45 per cent for those studying literature or law.[15]

As to the form of education, suspicions have been raised about the centrality of lectures, the total authority of the lecturer and the traditional methods of learning by rote. These are said to dry up students' brains, as it were, and to help produce machines for the recitation of sacred texts, so that young people become more willing to engage in some jihad or other when the skills they have learned do not suit them for a narrow labour market.

Such criticisms have gone down badly inside the kingdom, and the great majority of intellectuals – from the most Islamic to the most liberal – reject any Western attempt to interfere in the educational system by defining its goals or drawing up curricula. In spring 2002, for example, the pro-Western liberal Ali al-Musa stated that 'we are defending our school curricula against Western attack as if we were prisoners before an interrogation', while Sheikh Saud al-Shreim, imam of the main mosque in Mecca, described as 'high treason' the secularization of school syllabuses.[16] The place of Islam in educational programmes is unanimously defended as a matter of national sovereignty – a reaction which indicates both the importance that Saudi society attaches to its educational system and the weight of Saudi nationalism even among Islamists or liberals, who might have been thought to define their political identity in supranational terms.

This general attachment to the Islamic character of education is therefore part of the conception that Saudis have of national consciousness. Just as in France, since the Ferry laws of 1880–81, one of the priorities of National Education has been to train citizens who are both conscious of republican values and fit to take on political and social responsibilities, so in Saudi Arabia it is an explicit goal of education to train Muslim citizens who are both conscious of Islamic values and fit to be integrated into a society that accepts change only when it is grounded in Islam.

One feature of the 1990s was a new diversity in the 'masters of truth' – that is, in the normative discourses of civil society. Since the creation of public schools in the 1930s, social references had tended to become increasingly fragmented because of competition between traditional religious education and modern education that was only partly religious. In the 1960s the introduction of education for girls, then the school reforms inspired by practices of the Muslim Brotherhood, had further intensified this competition, even within the same school, between very different discourses. But the school remained one and indivisible as it absorbed, not without difficulty, the massive influx of the 1970s and 1980s that followed the oil boom and the government's decision to strengthen national identity by educating the whole of society.

In the 1990s the range of the 'masters of truth', already diversified through the sending of students on a large scale to Europe and the United States, was further increased by satellite television (which has become a 'moral authority' in Arabia as has television in Western Europe) and by the host of discourses to which the Internet gave access but not always the interpretative key. At a religious level, for instance, the popular 'Sharia and Life' television programme, which Al-Jazeera broadcast with sponsorship from Egyptian–Qatari Sheikh Yusuf al-Qaradhawi, contributed in its way to the multiplication of references and the growing competition among Islamic discourses. Here as in Europe, therefore, it would be a mistake to think that the development of means of communication has led to the emergence of a uniform and homogeneous culture; the spread of the mass media has, on the contrary, resulted in an unprecedented diversity of references and authorities.

Within this framework of competition among discourses of truth, intellectuals defend the national character of religious education and treat its disappearance as 'high treason'. *Mutatis mutandis*, the Saudi educational system faces the same issues as its French counterpart: the maintenance of standards in a context of massive expansion, the intervention of society in education, and the emergence of television as an alternative 'master of truth'. In particular, the sometimes disloyal competition of media discourse is no weaker in Arabia than in France, and it poses similar dangers for the development of a national consciousness (moral and Islamic in the one case, republican and secular in the other).

The attachment to religious education is also connected with the fact that it includes the teaching of literature and law. Courses in religion are combined with Arabic language courses precisely because the Koran, as the first formalization of 'classical Arabic', provides the foundation for Arabic literature and the common reservoir for all intellectual expressions, even those most secular in appearance.[17] What is really decisive for Saudis, however, is the civic and legal dimension of religious education. In a country where – with the exception of administrative and commercial law – all public and private law is derived from the Koran and the Sunna, religious education has the function of opening to ordinary people the secret dispensaries in which sharia law is formulated. No one is supposed to be ignorant of the law, and its principles are to be found in the sacred text. But knowledge of it is essential mainly for individual mastery of the Islamic canons, and it is in this sense that even (or especially) religious education has permitted the constitution of an autonomous civil society. For how is it possible to free the individual from the arbitrary power of the 'alim (theologian) or overzealous members of the religious police, if not by imparting the knowledge that will put him or her on an equal footing with them?

If women use certain religious norms (the marriage contract, the idea of partnership rather than subordination to the husband, the freedom to travel or study) to free themselves from restrictive traditional practices, they owe this to the school and to religious education. The mobilization of endogenous categories has proved much the more effective method of fighting against vernacular traditions. Besides, mythical reference to the first century of Islam, which is a compulsory part of any religious education course, functions as an instrument of both preservation and reform: it was the blessed age when women were freer and Islam was not yet split into different schools of thought.

Nostalgic references to that early time can induce a proud, intransigent claim to represent the one true Islam, reformed Saudi Islam, but it can also assist the emergence of real, if unexpected, ecumenical sentiments. Only this invocation of a golden age can justify, for example, a rapprochement between Sunnis and Shiites that rises above the turbulent history of their relations, or a move towards a more inclusive and 'original' Islam that removes all distinctions between the Hanbalite and other Sunni schools of Islam. In fact, it was such considerations which led the Saudi religious and political authorities in 1993 to begin a rapprochement with the Shiite community in al-Hasa, or which persuaded the Najdis to tolerate the Shafeite, Hanafite and Malikite ulema and Sufi fraternities of Hijaz.[18]

The most that intellectuals and political leaders accept, then, is a touching up of the content of religious education, like that which accompanied the official rapprochement between Sunnis and Shiites in 1993, when all negative references to the latter disappeared from school manuals. There can be no question of a challenge to the principle of religious education as such, and Western criticisms on this score are systematically and unanimously brushed aside.

What reform of education?

This is not to say that all debate on the matter is impossible. As Education Minister Muhammad Al Rashid declared in spring 2002:

> It is of great importance to utilize those impacts [of 11 September] to serve our community. We do not claim that we are living on an isolated island, as the whole world has become a small global village. However, our national educational curricula never urged extreme thinking.[19]

According to a study commissioned after 9/11 by the Faisaliya Foundation (which is owned by the sons of King Faisal), only 5 to 10 per cent of religious content is debatable and considered false.[20] The educational institutions do not provide for questioning of religion, only for the adjustment of curricula to the needs of the labour market.

In the view of most intellectuals and political leaders, those who dwell only on the place of religion in education not only offend Saudi national dignity but deliberately confuse the issue. The debate inside Arabia assumes that the main defect of the education system is not that it turns out Islamists but that school-leavers are unable to find a job. For the reasons we have just given, Saudis have no time for a 'secular' education system: they may want a greater degree of consensus at school, but what counts most for them is that it should produce better results. In other words, it is primarily economic motives – more than American pressure, to which neither Prince Abdullah nor his entourage is willing to give in – which have led to the contemplation of reforms in education. On this issue, as on the Islamic character of the education system, the political class is backed up by Saudi intellectuals in general, who since 9/11 have begun freely to debate in the press the content of such reforms.[21]

The main issues facing the education system today are the provision of schooling for all young Saudis, the promotion of vocational training and the integration of graduates into economic life.

Despite the spectacular progress of the past fifty years, the provision of schooling for everyone is still an issue, as only 76 per cent of children attend primary school, 61 per cent secondary school and 16 per cent an institution of higher learning. These figures suggest that the problem needs to be formulated in a new and different way: namely, the weak link in the system is not higher education but primary education;[22] its crucial failing is not the overproduction of graduates from Islamic universities but, more simply, the fact that not all children in an age group even attend school. If a quarter of children still do not go to school, an equally serious fact is that 40 per cent of children who do receive a full-time education leave the system without completing the first cycle of secondary education.[23] This means that a majority of young Saudis (55 per cent, including those who are never in full-time education or drop out of primary school, but not including those who drop out of upper-secondary or higher education) enter the labour market without any qualification. It is therefore mainly in relation to the primary level that the problems of the education system and youth unemployment need to be posed.

The second issue is the promotion of vocational training, to counter the attraction that students feel for the general courses that operate as 'factories of civil servants'. As we have seen, since staffing levels in the public sector and state administration were frozen in the budgetary crisis of 1986, the state has no longer been able to provide artificially for full employment. Today, 8.5 per cent of university graduates have followed technical courses and represent only 2 per cent of labour market entrants[24] – which certainly means that the content of education is ill suited to market requirements. The reforms and the boost to vocational training that have been on the agenda since 1998[25] aim both to bring new layers of children into full-time education and to involve companies in the design of courses.

The real issue facing the education system is therefore the insertion of young people into the labour market. As the share of immigrants in the active population continues to rise, against a background of weak economic growth and state disengagement, the problem of education today is primarily economic, not ideological or religious.

Public education has had the huge merit of fusing together the middle classes around common values and references, thereby enabling a genuine civil society to emerge on the scene. The role of religious education in this has gone together with a re-Islamization of the new generation and enriched it with precise knowledge of the Islamic corpus, which has served women well, for example, when they have opposed various traditions in the name of religion. It would be pointless to look here for the roots of the violence to which a tiny minority of young people have turned. As we have seen, the reason why some of the younger generation are left on the sidelines – whether or not they have a university degree – is that studying no longer necessarily leads to a job and that the 'social elevator' is no longer working properly. It is true that violent action is one possible response to this blockage, but that has little to do in principle with the fact that religious education is everywhere on the curriculum.

The re-Islamization of young people

It is therefore impossible to read the re-Islamization of young people as a 'mistake' on the part of the government, or to suggest that in the Islamic universities it inadvertently fed the hand that later bit it on several occasions. Like most social movements, re-Islamization must be attributed to a multiplicity of causes, not to some official aim of strengthening the hold of Islam over society.

In the context of the social and economic upheavals that were shaking Arabia in the late twentieth century, Islam represented for young people not only a means of understanding the world and clearing the turbid waters of Saudi modernization but also a cement that held together civil society in the face of predatory activity by the state. Mai Yamani reminds us that 'where the government seeks to coopt and control all areas of society, to minimize opposition to its rule, it is often only religious organizations that retain enough autonomy or cohesion to shelter the vestiges of civil society.'[26] Charitable associations, informal clubs and periodic meetings are all ways in which society engages in free discourse about itself and politics. The mosque is still often the only place where it is possible to offer and hear free speech that is *accessible to everyone*, as we can see from the government's repeatedly stated wish to control what is said there. Thus, if Islam is pivotal to the identity of young people, it is because they see it as both an unquestionable space and a space for free discussion, because they can express within it either submission or opposition to the dominant norms.

In any event, four kinds of attitude seem to be identifiable. Two minorities occupy the extremes: the 'Westernizers', who are both liberal and modernist, and the 'Islamists', who are both reformist and militant. The great majority of young people divide between a respectable conservatism with no special ideological orientation and an attachment to religion which, though ideologically firmer, cannot be compared to the seditiousness of the young Islamists.[27]

The Westernized attitude is shared by a tiny percentage of young people who have studied in the West and who, out of a craving for reforms or pique at their own unemployment, adopt a liberal reformist discourse. They are great favourites of Western journalists, especially because they speak English, and most of them come from the affluent business class or the ranks of the royal family. The modernization in which they invest their hopes must be derived from Islam, however, or at least *expressed* in the vocabulary of religion.

The second attitude – certainly the most widespread, among those who play or would like to play the game or who honestly support the policies of the Riyadh government – prefers the status quo to any challenge and involves a respectful wait-and-see approach to the 'traditions' reinvented by the regime. The third attitude is that of people from a more conservative rural background who, in a reaction against what they sometimes see as their parents' 'levity', think of their own life in religious terms and, without setting their sights on political change, trail around a kind of gentle reproach.

For these last two groups, which are closely related to each other ideologically, the role of the family is all the more important because its real authority has evaporated. Islam thus becomes easily reducible to the bowdlerized version spread by the religious establishment, and modernity is seen as ultimately nothing other than Western influence. Neither of these groups really advances an endogenous conception of modernity – unlike the two extreme groups, for which modernity can be either Islamized (the liberal position) or derived from Islam without Western mediation (the Islamist position).

The fourth attitude is that of a minority of young people who think in a religious way about not only their social existence but also their political life. These 'Islamists' describe themselves as an 'active minority' numbering some 15 per cent of the country's youth[28] – a self-perception that strongly contrasts with the image of power that the Western media automatically associate with Islamists. Political re-Islamization therefore seems to be a marginal phenomenon and – to use a Marxist vocabulary – appears as the 'self-consciousness' of a process of social and identity-centred re-Islamization: 'Although the radical Islamists are in a small minority, their language, identifying corruption and demonizing the West, finds an echo among many of the new generation.'[29] What young people *do*, Islamists *say*. And, through the very act of verbalization, individual and social practice becomes a public political act.

The core of the young Islamists' argument is that religion is both a *heritage* and a *critical instrument*. In this way, in words as well as deeds, they clearly distinguish between tradition (which changes) and religion (which is immutable), and for them religion is a higher standard to which practices, habits and customs can be referred. As we have seen, this distinction also enables young women to claim emancipation and the younger generation to establish the framework for a *rational*, no longer traditional, political discourse. Whereas traditionalist conformism makes sense only by implicitly referring to 'what should and should not be done', the discourse of the young Islamists refers on the contrary to Islamic norms that are explicitly declared to be Islamic.

The Islam of young people tends to separate itself from tradition, and the political freedom that some of them demand is expressed in a religious vocabulary, from spaces that are themselves sacred. For radicals, this attitude involves a head-on confrontation between religion and tradition; for everyone else, the more sober point is to use Islam as a means of inserting themselves into an unwelcoming society, one that still thinks of women as dependent beings symbolically apart from men. Westernized young people, for their part, tend to make Islam a merely formal framework of their identity and often succumb to a form of re-Islamization more akin to a fashion than a real social or political movement.

In a sense, we could say that almost the whole of Saudi youth is 'Islamist' – although then the term 'Islamism' loses in meaning what it gains in extension. It is therefore better to speak of several different ways of referring to Islam, several modes of *identification* ranging from extreme Westernization to political and religious radicalism; most positions would then fall in-between, encompassing those for whom Islam – like social Christianity in France in the 1930s or ecologism in Germany in the 1980s – is the language in which social progress can be profitably articulated.

To sum up: the re-Islamization of Saudi youth, favoured by the major changes in the country since the 1970s, may be assigned three different meanings: a re-Islamization of identity (the 'degree zero'), a social re-Islamization ('for the greatest number') and a political re-Islamization (its 'self-consciousness'). Beyond these differences,

however, re-Islamization symbolically constitutes the younger generation as a significant whole, distinct from the 'older' generation.

It is therefore through an individual appropriation of religion, neither
conformist nor imposed, that the Gulf War generation distinguishes
between received tradition and reinterpreted Islam, between inherited
social forms and a purified religion that has been absorbed and
placed within reach of the individual. Far from being an ideological
emanation of the central government, religion is thus more akin
to what Pierre Bourdieu calls a counter-culture, a 'culture capable of
placing the culture at a distance, of analysing it and not imposing
an inverted form of it'[30] – a counter-culture that is fundamentally
a modern and endogenous culture.

Conclusion

Arabs cannot be bought.

Jacques Berque

Since 11 September 2001 journalists, experts and researchers have been travelling the length and breadth of the Arabian Peninsula, in search of a key to Saudi society that will allow them to explain the attacks in New York and Washington. Some are filled with wonder at the conservatism of young people, the silence of women or the perilous advances of religion, while others, sometimes using the same hypotheses or reaching curiously similar results, attempt to find among 'Islamist terrorists' the ray of light that will dispel the mystery. Along the way, Saudi studies have undoubtedly made some progress, moving from aerial views and distant fantasies to an encounter with real facts and real people, but it is not clear that this has increased our understanding of the roots of 9/11 or made our knowledge of Saudi society sharper and more precise. Indeed, it is more than likely that the ravages of media superficiality and 'jihadology' have obscured both the nature of the event (political violence hitting the territory of the United States) and its supposed cause (Saudi society).

The enduring subservience of the 'ally of fifty years'

The fact is that the attacks of 9/11 were directed less against the liberal democratic values of the West than against the way in which the United States and Europe have used them in their confrontation with the Arab-Muslim world in general and Saudi Arabia in particular – that is, to intervene systematically in Middle Eastern political and economic affairs, offering unfailing support to the most authoritarian dictatorships in the region, which are supposed to be guarding democracy or stability from the dangers of 'fundamentalism'.[1] Whether we consider the fraudulent sales of frontier defence systems or the trade in army surplus or the cooperation in the gathering of intelligence, the West's dealings with its 'ally of fifty years' have consistently shown contempt for the very values which it now rebukes that ally for failing to observe: democracy, financial transparency and political accountability.

Yet there is much worse. Whereas, for half a century, the Atlantic economic area has owed part of its formidable growth to the godsend of Saudi oil and Riyadh's willingness to pump extra supplies onto the world market at the slightest jolt (as after 9/11 or during the strikes in Venezuela); whereas Saudis have lent their support to all the high-risk American strategies, from the manipulation of Iraq against the Iranian Revolution in the 1980s through the joint anti-Soviet jihad in Central Asia and the Gulf War of 1990 to the invasion of Afghanistan in 2001; whereas, to cut a long story short, the government in Riyadh has invariably followed Washington to the peril of its own internal legitimacy and regional credibility, all the pressure is now on it to give further cast-iron proof of its allegiance. It would be singularly naive, however, to imagine that it is because of any irreducible opposition to the West and its values that Saudi Arabia finds itself at the centre of the post-9/11 turmoil. Rather, its use by the West as a playing field for the crudest manipulation and the most sordid trafficking is the reason why fifteen of the nineteen New York and Washington kamikazes turned out to have had their origins in Arabia.

The testimony of a former CIA operative, a man little inclined to sympathy with Riyadh or indulgence towards Saudi society, is quite unambiguous on this point.

> We pay market prices. But the point is that it's all based on supply and demand, and by increasing the supply, they keep down the price. It's something the Saudis have paid out of their pockets. We've never reimbursed them for this surplus capacity. We built it in the sixties and seventies [when Aramco was still an American conglomerate – PM]; but when they nationalized Aramco they paid for it, they bought it back. We can't simply just sit down and say, 'These guys have always been against us and the Wahhabi fundamentalists have been sent by the royal family to destroy the West.'[2]

> Well, Kissinger set this up in the first oil embargo. He said, listen, fine, you can raise the price of oil. You're going to get more money for your oil. But let's be reasonable about this. Take this money and all this profit you're making, and invest it in the United States, which is a perfectly good policy, by the way. Buy our arms. Keep your money here. It'll keep our economy floating. We won't go into a recession or a depression because of high oil prices. And we're all going to win by this. And that worked fine.... I think it's more political [that is, the motives of the terrorists – PM]. I think that the sooner we stop interfering in the Middle East, the more likely we'll be able to exact a truce with terrorism.[3]

In the light of this plain-speaking diagnosis, how derisory – or neurotic – appear the efforts of those who think that an identikit 'Wahhabism' or some dreamed-up genealogy of 'jihadist Islamists' can account for 9/11 or even the whole of Saudi society! The violence stemming from, and occurring within, Saudi Arabia is more political than religious or ideological. It has more to do with the closer contacts between Saudis and the rest of the world than with the supposed 'closure' of a country which, for fifty years, has been largely open to the worst features of the West: a crude will to power, corrupt arrangements, police violence and media lies. It is therefore wrong to focus on the social-political 'conservatism' or religious 'fundamentalism' of the active opposition, or to blackball Saudi Arabia as an incurably anti-democratic and inherently authoritarian nation. Far from being a solid block of tradition covered with a technological veneer, Saudi Arabia is literally transfixed by modernity:

the difference between its modernity and ours is only a difference of degree or pace, not one of essence or nature. The aim of this book has been precisely to show that hate and righteous indignation are bad gateways to an understanding of Saudi society and politics; that contextualization, secular analysis and patient social-political explanation should be systematically preferred to the categories of essentialism, culturalism or intellectual absolutism ('Islamic country', 'conservative society', 'reactionary customs'); that Saudi society has been not so much the subject of anti-Western violence as the object of a more diffuse and less spectacular but equally explosive violence – namely, the symbolic, political and economic domination exercised by an autistic and contemptuous West over the country's strategic and oil-related horizons. In short, we set out to avoid any a priori exclusion of the Saudis from modernity, at a time when they are trying to experience modernity for themselves, formulating it in their own concepts and against the background of a desperate regional situation.

Social history against political myths

Our main aim has been to enable social history to assert all its power against the political myths devised by the Saudi regime, its Western allies and the oil corporations. By restoring the complex and continuous temporality of Saudi history, in the face of the truncated fables that the dominant players mobilize for evident political ends,[4] we have put in their rightful place the supposedly 'Islamic' or 'Bedouin' character of the state and the 'conservatism' of the society – a place somewhere between imaginary social-political constructs and inventions of tradition. The official ideologies of 'Islamic progress' and 'Bedouin consensus' are thin layers of meaning tacked on to complex cultural repertoires; both are products of a political manipulation of history, in which the economic and political-legal content of Islam is at best adapted and at worst instrumentalized, while a Bedouin myth is promoted at the same time that the nomadic way of life is being wiped out and tribal identities re-formed for the benefit of the central state.[5]

Yet it is not enough simply to condemn these myths as truncated or erroneous; any invention of tradition is at the same time the expression of a crisis of culture, whereby traditional referents are placed at a distance and reassembled. Any invention of tradition, then, is also an invention of modernity.[6] Just as (to quote one of Marx's ideas) the French Revolution was acted out in Roman costumes, the construction of the Saudi state has been acted out in Islamic, Bedouin or Western-technocratic costumes – in fantasy images that have given the state an increment of respectability, nobility or legitimacy. The endogenous or vernacular culture is no longer that natural environment in which social and political players used to bathe: it has become a *sign market* where each tries to exercise a monopoly. And the Saudi regime is a past master at symbolic manipulation. During the period from the 1920s to the 1970s, a technocratic supratribal state established its hegemony over a less and less tribal, more and more governable society, by means of a monopoly at once political (conquest of Arabia and subjugation of its tribes), social (suppression of 'Bedouinism', annexation through marriage of the Najdi tribes, triumph of the urban model), religious (international recognition of Saudi guardianship of the holy sites) and economic (gradual extension of control over oil resources and the national economy).

Since the 1950s, however, this monopoly has been challenged by groups of people bent on exposing the artificial character of official ideology and replacing it with their own reading of history – groups which have more and more vociferously demanded that the majority of the population should have access to political representation, and no longer be denied any presence in the media or excluded from the circuits of political decision-making. In the 1950s and 1960s, in the context of the Cold War, the challenge from labour unions, socialism and Arab nationalism ran up against barriers erected (often very abruptly) by the Saudi regime and its Western backers. Since the 1970s a powerful wave of Islamist opposition has taken up the torch from the nationalist movements and successfully mobilized sections of society eager to enter the public arena. In this sense Saudi Islamism is not – as some believe – a product of the Saudi state designed to harass or threaten the countries of the West;

rather, it involves a mobilization of effective symbolic resources against the state's monopoly on the political, social, religious and economic markets – and hence against American support for the Riyadh government.

At a strictly religious level, the revolt by part of the official establishment against the subordination of religion to politics and of politics to Arabia's international alliance strategy is tantamount to a call for the *liberalization of religion* and, paradoxically, for an actual separation of religion and politics – for example, in relation to the independence of the legal system, or the autonomy of Islamic discourse from the official 'politically correct' language. In this connection Jacques Berque once wrote that

> by virtue of its very polyvalency, Islam has entrenched itself in broad social sectors not as an interpretative reality (as its basic definitions would require), but as a *de facto* compromise between the ulema and central authority. So it is the elimination, or at least demystification, of these compromises which, in the realm of Islam, would amount to secularism. That, in a sense, would be *to return to origins.*[7]

This return to origins – *pace* those for whom 'fundamentalism' equals 'theocracy' – essentially involves a recovery of the heuristic power of Islamic concepts beneath the coating of accumulated tradition and political intervention. It may even be said to border on secularism, inasmuch as it distinguishes religious authority from political authority and makes it possible for everyone to enjoy a new independence. Our own reforms and revolutions in Europe drew upon this two-way traffic between return to the past and projection into the future, between fundamentalism and progressivism. There is no reason why the same should not be true in Arab and Muslim countries.

The rise of new political movements, mobilizing discursive resources that are perceived as endogenous (the conceptual toolbox of Islam), has therefore involved a revolt of society against the symbolic monopoly of ruling groups, much more than a divine revenge against the 'infidel' state or Western 'crusaders'. Especially since the 1990s, the state's loss of religious and political hegemony has gone hand in hand with the decline both of its economic influence (due to the privatization drive launched by Crown Prince Abdullah's government in 1998) and of its capacity to set exemplary guidelines for society (because of the opening up of the social imagination, the new plural lifestyles and forms of representation, and the weight of globalization among the middle classes).

This crisis of the state monopoly is not necessarily an encouraging sign, especially with regard to the economy. Whereas the Fahd era was synonymous with a certain rationalization–bureaucratization of the energy sector and public services, which restricted the influence of the royal family to the (profitable) domain of arms and construction contracts, there is a risk that the opening up of the capital of large public corporations (telecommunications, electricity, water), as well as gas (and perhaps oil) operations, will allow oligarchic interests to flow into areas previously controlled by the state. Far from being a form of rationalization or progress, this wave of liberalization might well be restoring to commercial or princely circles some of the powers that the royal administration captured for itself, and eventually express itself in a retreat from further political reform and democratization.[8]

In any event, the crisis of the state's symbolic monopoly shows that the construction of the state as an apparatus of control and domination has not yet been completed – witness its loose control over certain regions (especially in central Arabia, Asir or the Jawf Wadi) and the permeability or indeterminateness of some of its international frontiers (especially with Yemen, but also on the Gulf and the border with Iraq). Equally, the formation of the state – a 'contradictory and largely unconscious process of conflicts, negotiations and compromises among various social groups'[9] – will remain unfinished unless and until society gains access to political representation and responsibility. Independently of its construction of an internal revenue department and strong public services for distribution of the oil rent, the dominant social group has systematically negotiated its identity with other groups whose very existence challenged its right to rule most of the Arabian Peninsula. Thus the newly emerging state successively assumed a supratribal identity vis-à-vis the Bedouin tribes, a modernizing and rationalizing identity vis-à-vis the educated bourgeoisie of Hijaz, an Islamic identity vis-à-vis the Western and Muslim international environment, and a Bedouin identity in its dealings with urban society. As Arabia was a plural reality, the state was itself forced to take up plural imaginative positions and a range of identities which, though not necessarily contradictory, were certainly inconsistent. It was undoubtedly within this flexible schema of identity that modernity emerged into the light of day – but also, more brutally, the will to power of a particular group and its self-assertion at the expense of others.

Faced with the ideological shadow play of the Saudi state, and with the appetite for domination of a group that did not hesitate to use force to assert its interests, opposition groups tirelessly sought to carve a place for society within the power game, and to complete the formation of the state by including in it the silent majorities made up of the urban middle classes, women, young people – and immigrants.

The Islamist movements:
from the 'Riyadh Spring' to reform from above

In a political space hemmed in on all sides by the power of the government, the liberals (libiraliyun) constitute a social minority that is overrepresented in the media. Their Western interlocutors, in foreign embassies and elsewhere, are charmed by the often secular character of their positions and turn a blind eye to their close links with the regime. However, the social representativeness of the liberals is inversely proportional to their media visibility: celebrated by the national and regional press, from Al-Riyadh through the Hijaz daily 'Ukazh to the Abha paper Al-Watan, they are cold-shouldered by a public that well knows who pushed them to prominence and often regards their displays of liberalism as an open provocation. The closeness of the liberals to the government apparatus therefore leaves huge scope for Islamist intellectuals and movements, who may be roughly divided into two groups: a large majority of 'reformists' (islahiyun or sahwiyun) and a minority prone to violent action, variously described as 'jihadists' (jihadiyun), 'extremists' (mutatarrifun) or 'lost sections' (al-fay'at al-dhala, in the official parlance). Like the liberals, this minority occupies a position in the media coverage (and has a related capacity to arouse fears) that is quite disproportionate to its actual presence in society.

Early in 2003 a tumultuous 'Riyadh Spring' saw the flowering of all manner of manifestoes, from a 'Vision for the present and future of the country'[10] (put forward by 104 Islamist and liberal intellectuals) to the Shiite document 'Partners of the Nation',[11] which followed in the tradition of a text that 153 Saudi intellectuals, Islamist and liberal, male and female, had composed a year earlier in response to a bellicose attack by sixty American intellectuals around Samuel Huntington and Francis Fukuyama.[12] The new crop of texts also reflected the relative openness of Saudi public debate, as well as the united front of Saudi intellectuals against American media attacks, a front that Crown Prince Adbullah had encouraged in autumn 2001 in his opening address to the constituent bodies of the nation, and again in December 2001 on the fringes of the GCC summit in Muscat.

The 'Vision for the present and future of the country' situated itself within a literal yet flexible interpretation of the sharia, combining the concept of general interest (maslaha 'amma) with the Islamic concept of shura (popular consultation). Instead of sticking to conventional formulations, the 104 intellectuals gave a precise democratic definition of shura – even if they preferred the endogenous concepts of shura and majlis and refrained from using the imported terms 'democracy' (dimuqratiyya) and 'parliament' (barlaman). Whether arguing for national and local elections under universal suffrage or for the accountability of national and regional executives to elected assemblies, they rigorously (and in the spirit of Islam) set out the principles of parliamentarianism and combined them with a set of important legal, economic and social provisions, such as an independent legal system, freedom of expression and association, control over the budget and employment policy.

The second of the two texts was signed by 450 Shiite intellectuals. Having originally emerged in the 1970s, Shiite Islamist groups shifted in the late 1980s from armed militancy to a challenge centred on issues of identity and legality (especially, but not only, under the influence of the Iranian 'Thermidor'[13] and the normalization of relations between the Islamic Republic and the Saudi kingdom). In 1993 these groups, together with their leading figure, Hassan al-Saffar, garnered the first fruits of this reorientation, when they received partial recognition from the Riyadh government. As the decade progressed, they continued to move along constitutional paths and took up the defence of minority rights, in a national Saudi and no longer an international 'pan-Shia' framework.[14] The text published in 2003 thus called for implementation of the 1993 agreements and argued that the defence of national unity (al-wahda al-wataniyya) required the recognition and satisfaction of religious minorities, not their repression. At the same time, as a corollary of rights for religious groups, the Shiite manifesto spelled out the concepts of citizenship and freedom of expression with greater precision than the Manifesto of the 104 had achieved.[15]

On 9 June 2003 King Fahd translated the two Islamist-liberal projects into a programme of government. On 20 June 2003 Crown Prince Abdullah accepted the conclusions of the first 'National Meeting for Intellectual Dialogue', a gathering of intellectuals from all sides, and formally recognized confessional diversity for the first time in the history of Arabia. In August 2003, in response to the petitioners' demands, a National Centre for Dialogue (Markaz al-hiwar al-watani) was created in Riyadh to replace the Commission for National Reconciliation and to promote the structural reforms that the Consultative Assembly had been postponing for so long. Finally, in October 2003, partial municipal elections under universal male suffrage were scheduled for the following year. According to an Al-Watan journalist, Abdallah al-Fawzan, the Riyadh Spring was beginning to look exactly like 'the dawning of reform'.

Yet the wave of violence that shook the country between May 2003 and June 2004, coinciding with the invasion of Iraq by Western coalition forces, led the royal government to admit that it was engaged in a battle with 'terrorism' inside Arabia itself. Several times, in Riyadh, the oil province and Hijaz, armed groups struck at symbols and agents of the Western presence (expatriate compounds, anti-terrorist centres, Western corporations), expressing in action an essentially anti-imperialist discourse and claiming to follow the revolutionary example of Osama bin Laden. The Saudi state cracked down on jihadist circles with the help of the American FBI, while a rise in oil prices gave it new room for maneouvre in the field of economic and social action.

The outbreak of armed violence within the Saudi internal debate naturally led to a hardening of positions and, in accordance with a formula tried elsewhere, compelled the majority of reformist Islamists to line up with the government's reform programme. Clearly there was a danger that this would deprive the Islamist reform movement of its political leaders and make Saudi society feel more remote from a gradual loosening that it already saw as developing without any input from itself.

The three sources of political society

The 'Arab political formula',[16] combining co-optation, repression and participation in US and European anti-terrorist strategies, persists all the way from Rabat through Cairo, Algiers and Sanaa to Riyadh. Nevertheless, Saudi Arabia has registered a number of really major changes.

First, in the space of twenty years, Saudi society has passed from rural existence and unmediated tradition to individualism and urbanization. Demographic trends have been accompanied by an upheaval in family structures, as a patriarchal model centred on the extended family has given way to a fragmented society in which the dominant form is the nuclear family of parents and children. This evolution, sustained by economic growth, rapid urbanization and a revolution in transport and communications, has led Saudi society to reformulate its guiding values. Especially clear evidence of this new voice are the (still timid) appearance of women in the media and intellectual life since the late 1980s and the greater boldness of the press despite self-censorship and cases of direct intervention by the regime.

Second, Islam has been adapted to Saudi society itself, through a movement to modernize and individualize religious practices. Today, most of the discourse of religion is produced and issued on the margins of the official establishment – whether in Islamist circles or in feminist and other readings that borrow the language and conceptual apparatus of Islam to gain a hearing for themselves. This autonomy is apparent, for example, in the abundance of new books about 'Islamic technology', dealing with questions of marriage, children's education, the 'place' of women in society, or even self-management and personal fulfilment. There is also a greater autonomy and diversity of religious vocabulary, as broadcasts on Arabic satellite television – both Saudi (Al-'Arabiya, Iqra') and non-Saudi (Al-Jazeera, Abu Dhabi TV) – have a much wider audience in the kingdom than the two more conventional national channels, and sharply contrast with the official religious establishment by virtue of their eclecticism and modernism.

Third, as interpreted by a modernized and individualized society, Islam has in many cases actually become an instrument of social change. When the 'young sheikhs' broke with the official establishment in the 1980s, they were able to do so from within Islam itself; when intellectuals today speak of the urgent need for political democracy and constitutionalism, they draw on such Islamic conceptual tools as shura and maslaha 'amma; and when women seek to liberate themselves from the social pressure of patriarchal norms, they achieve it by opposing God's law to the human law of their fathers, brothers and husbands, so that Islamic feminism paradoxically becomes the main vehicle for the self-affirmation of a better-educated and more 'liberated' younger generation. In the hands of a society now more aware of itself and the surrounding world, a society partly freed from the pressure of the religious establishment that used to subject it to the wishes of the Prince, the conceptual and symbolic apparatus of Islam has become since the 1980s an instrument of modernization – that is, a means of *criticizing social traditions*, through the invention of a religious tradition that is *new* precisely because it is *intended to be authentic*.

Individualization of values and behaviour, autonomization of religious discourse, Islamic critique of traditions: these three trends point to the emergence of a genuinely self-aware *political society* in Saudi Arabia, produced through liberalization both of the economy (since the oil boom of 1973) and of religious references (since the 1990s). Beyond the overblown media phenomenon of armed 'jihadist' militancy, this threefold evolution demonstrates that Islam is no longer the monopoly of those whose obsession with 'ablutions, childbirth and the washing of feet in the absence of water'[17] sealed off religious discourse by making it depend on the agreement of the royal regime. The demand for the independence of religion goes hand in hand with the demand for freedom of expression, since a society which believes that modernity can be not only formulated in Islamic terms (in accordance with the overused alternative, 'modernization of Islam' or 'Islamization of modernity') but entirely derived from Islam will make free interpretation of the Holy Text a cardinal political and cultural issue.

Arabia will certainly remain Saudi, and the reforms imposed from above by the royal family are mainly designed to preserve the foundations of the monarchy and national unity. The fact that in the process it has allowed a free debate to burst forth, and itself acquired a progressive and reformist hue, may be seen as a kind of cunning of monarchic reason. But we may ask ourselves whether Saudis will know how to take advantage of this opportunity, or whether, discouraged by the recent authoritarian impulses of a government more concerned with security than with a political loosening, they will refrain from taking part in the political reform process that was launched in 2003. It is still possible today to imagine a constitutional, democratic *and* Islamic Arabia, similar to Kuwait or Bahrain – or the Islamic Republic of Iran – although it is more likely that the inertia of the 'magical kingdom', together with a concern to preserve national unity and to avoid frightening the patron across the Atlantic, will stretch out the process of change.

We hope at least to have shown that, today more than ever, no support of even a verbal kind should be given to the local version of Western security fever, and that Saudis themselves should be left to open up their polity, society and economy, in their own language and with conceptual instruments of their own choosing. Jacques Berque once said that independence is 'the right to problems',[18] and it is by no means clear that Saudis are unable to solve their problems by drawing on foundations that are not so much contrary as different from our own. In any event, since 11 September 2001 we can be quite sure that such independence is not only crucial to the fate of 23 million men and women; it is also an important element in the peace and stability of the whole world.

Chronology

1744   Muhammad ibn Abd al-Wahhab settles in Diriya and enters the service of the emir Muhammad ibn Saud.

1789   The Saudis complete their conquest of Najd.

1806   The Saudis annexe Hijaz and expel Ottoman agents.

1809   British troops drive the Saudis from Bahrain.

1818   Having occupied Hijaz, the Egyptians lay siege to Diriya, which surrenders on 11 September. The emir is taken to Istanbul and beheaded. Occupation of Najd and end of the first Saudi state.

1824   Turki Al Saud liberates Najd at the head of a tribal coalition and chooses Riyadh as his capital.

1838–40 The Egyptians occupy Najd a second time.

1860   The British bombard Dammam.

1866   The British bombard Al-Qatif and Dammam.

1871–1913 The Ottomans occupy the eastern coast of Arabia.

1884   Muhammad Al Rashid, emir of Hail and vassal of the Ottomans, conquers Najd. End of second Saudi state.

1891   The Sauds emigrate to Kuwait, where they receive a pension from the Ottomans.

1902   Abdelaziz Al Saud, with British support, retakes Riyadh from the Rashids and confronts the Ottomans.

1913   Founding of the first Ikhwan settlement. Abdelaziz re-captures the east coast from the Ottomans.

1915	Signing of the Treaty of Darain; Najd becomes a British protectorate.
1916	Sharif Husain declares Hijaz independent and himself king of Arabia.
1918	The Ikhwan protest against British influence in Arabia.
1921	Abdelaziz annexes Jabal Shammar and has himself proclaimed 'sultan of Najd and its dependencies' by an assembly of tribal chiefs and ulema.
1922	Signing of the treaty of Al-'Uqair: delimitation of the Saudi northern borders.
1924	Conquest of Mecca by the Saudis. Abdelaziz organizes municipal elections in Mecca.
1925	Jeddah surrenders to the Saudis. Abdelaziz is proclaimed king of Hijaz by an assembly of ulema and merchants. Creation of a tax system.
1926	The first international Islamic Congress proclaims Abdelaziz 'Servant of the Holy Places'. A constitution is promulgated, the Consultative Assembly (Majlis al-Shura) is reopened, and municipal councils are created. Protectorate treaty between Najd and Asir. The Ikhwan protest against administrative centralization and British influence.
1929	Abdelaziz crushes the Ikhwan revolt with British help.
1932	The Saudi provinces merge into the Saudi Kingdom of Arabia. The American geologist Karl S. Twitchell discovers oil near Dhahran.
1933	Standard Oil of California (SOCAL, later Aramco or Arabian–American Oil Company) obtains a sixty-year concession over 50 per cent of Saudi territory.
1934	Annexation of Asir and signing of the Treaty of al-Taif with Yemen.
1938	Founding of Arabia's first bank, the National Commercial Bank.
1943	US President Roosevelt extends the lend-lease scheme to Saudi Arabia.
1945	Meeting between Abdelaziz and Roosevelt in Egypt. First Aramco strike.
1946	Opening of the US military base at Dhahran.

1947   Aramco strike and publication of an Egyptian-style labour
            code.

1949   Creation of the first university and training college.

1951   Signing of a treaty of assistance and mutual defence with
            the United States.

1952   Founding of Saudi Arabian Monetary Agency and creation
            of the rial.

1953   Aramco strike and attack on the US consulate in Dhahran.
            Army officers and workers create a Front of National
            Reforms. Abdelaziz dies and is succeeded by his son,
            Saud.

1956   Oil embargo against Britain and France following the
            Suez operation. General strike in the Eastern Province: the
            workers demand a constitution and American withdrawal;
            repression and banning of the Front of National Reforms.
            Creation of a student union in Qasim; clashes between
            students and the religious police.

1957   Saudi Arabia joins the International Monetary Fund (IMF).
            Opening of the first 'lay' university along Egyptian lines.

1958   Opposition between Saud and his brother Faisal within
            the royal family. Faisal is appointed prime minister and
            undertakes the reforms urged by the IMF.

1960   Prince Talal, at the head of the 'free princes', proposes a
            constitution. Saud and Faisal oppose the idea, but Talal is
            appointed finance minister. Creation of the Organization
            of Petroleum Exporting Countries (OPEC).

1961   Kuwait becomes independent.

1962   Abolition of slavery and creation of the General Petroleum
            and Mineral Organization (Petromin). The 'free princes' go
            into exile in Egypt. Revolution in Yemen: Arabia supports
            the royalists against Egyptian-backed republicans.

1963   Strikes in the Eastern Province. Dismantling of a socialist
            network.

1964   Helped by the ulema and the National Guard, Faisal
            deposes his brother Saud and has himself proclaimed
            king. Talal returns to Arabia.

1965   A new agreement with Aramco allows the government to double its oil revenue. First major purchase of American and British weapons.

1967   Aramco strike, anti-Israeli demonstrations and attack on the US consulate in Dhahram. Independence of South Yemen and creation in Aden of a People's Democratic Republic of Yemen.

1968   Creation of the first university for women.

1969   Two attempted military coups are foiled with CIA help. Creation in Jeddah of the Organization of the Islamic Conference (OIC).

1970   Saudi–Yemeni agreement and end of the war in North Yemen.

1971   Independence of Bahrain, Qatar and the emirates of the Trucial Coast, which become the United Arab Emirates.

1973   Because of the Israeli–Arab war, oil production is cut and the reference price of crude rises 70 per cent. The embargo on the United States is quickly lifted.

1974   Abolition of taxes and dismantling of the revenue service. Recognition of the Palestine Liberation Organization (PLO) and financial support for al-Fatah.

1975   Faisal is assassinated by a distant relative. Khaled is pro-claimed king. Creation of the Communist Party of Saudi Arabia and the Shiite Reform Movement. Normalization of relations with the People's Democratic Republic of Yemen, which receives financial support and oil from Riyadh.

1979   Rebellion in the army and the tribes of Hijaz. On 20 November, Juhaiman al-Utaibi and an armed group occupy the main mosque in Mecca and publicly denounce the US presence and the corruption of the princes. The rebels are captured after a two-week siege, with the help of a French GIGN rapid deployment force. Against the background of revolution in Iran, Shiites demonstrate in Eastern Province. Soviet troops enter Afghanistan.

1980   Restriction of women's freedoms. Crown Prince Fahd promises a constitution. Creation of non-governmental religious organizations. Start of the first Gulf War, between Iraq and Iran.

1981   Creation of the Gulf Cooperation Council (GCC). The Fahd
          plan for peace in Palestine recognizes the existence of the
          State of Israel.
1982   Khaled dies and is succeeded by his brother, Fahd.
1985   Islamic Jihad claims responsibility for a wave of assassina-
          tions in Riyadh.
1986   King Fahd announces on television that falling oil prices
          make it impossible to predict the state budget. Public
          spending cuts.
1988   Nationalization of Aramco. Launching of the anti-Soviet
          jihad in Afghanistan, with support from the American
          services.
1990   Iraqi invasion of Kuwait and second Gulf War. American
          troops are sent to Saudi Arabia. Forty-six women take the
          steering-wheel in Riyadh and are temporarily dismissed
          from their jobs. Unification of Yemen.
1991   Islamist intellectuals around Safar al-Hawali and Salman
          al-Auda address a petition for reforms to King Fahd.
1992   Promulgation of a Basic Law and a statute for the regions;
          creation of a Consultative Assembly (Majlis al-Shura). The
          Islamists publish a reform programme (the Memorandum
          of Advice).
1993   Muhammad al-Masaari creates in Riyadh the Committee
          for the Defence of Legitimate Rights. First agreement
          between the government and the Shiite minority.
1994   Civil war in Yemen; Riyadh supports the secessionists on
          both sides. Osama bin Laden creates in London an Advice
          and Reform Committee (ARC). Buraida intifada in Qasim;
          arrest of Islamist sheikhs and militants.
1995   King Fahd suffers an embolism and has to hand over de
          facto power to his brother, Abdullah. Attack on a US-run
          military training centre in Riyadh.
1996   Saad al-Faqih creates the Islamic Reform Movement in
          London. Attack on a US military complex in al-Khobar.
2001   Terrorist attacks in New York and Washington (11
          September) and revival of Saudi–American anti-terrorist
          cooperation. Abdullah carries out a general consultation
          of the constitutional bodies of the Saudi state.

2002   Prince Abdullah proposes an Israel–Arab peace plan (February) and publishes a draft Reform Charter for the Arab World (December). Islamists and liberals publish their manifesto ('How to coexist') in April.

2003   104 Islamist and liberal intellectuals send a petition for reforms and democracy to Prince Abdullah (January). Withdrawal of US troops stationed in Arabia (April). Terrorist attacks in Riyadh (12 May). Reforms become part of the government programme (June).

Notes

Introduction

1. Jean Baudrillard, 'L'esprit du terrorisme', Le Monde, 1 November 2001.
2. Here we shall mention only some of the works published in French: Claude Feuillet, L'Arabie à l'origine de l'islamisme, Lausanne: Favre, 2001; Antoine Basbous, L'Arabie saoudite en question, Paris: Perrin, 2002; Abdelwahab Meddeb, La Maladie de l'islam, Paris: Seuil, 2002; Stéphane Marchand, Arabie saoudite, la menace, Paris: Fayard, 2003; Laurent Murawiec, 'Arabie saoudite: l'ennemi public no. 1', interview with Amir Taheri, Politique internationale 98, Winter 2002–03. A few French and English-speaking journalists do stand out, however, for their more sophisticated approach.
3. See Chapters 4 and 8.
4. Legal opinion issued by a ulema. Being an opinion, not a law, a fatwa has no religious value, as the Muslim's relationship with God is strictly personal.
5. The equivalent of excommunication for a Muslim.
6. Islamic law.
7. The few exceptions include Fred Halliday, Arabia without Sultans, London: Penguin Books, 1974 (revised edn, London: Saqi Books, 2002); Paul Bonnenfant, ed., La Péninsule arabique d'aujourd'hui, 2 vols, Paris: CNRS Éditions, 1982; Saddeka Arebi, Women and Words in Saudi Arabia: The Politics of Literary Discourse, New York: Columbia University Press, 1994; Kiren Aziz Chaudhry, The Price of Wealth: Economies and Institutions in the Middle East, New York: Cornell University Press, 1997; Alexei Vassiliev, The History of Saudi Arabia, London: Saqi Books, 1998.
8. In Arabic the war between Iran and Iraq (1980–88) is called the first Gulf War, so that what is known in the West as the 'Gulf War' becomes

in Arabic the second Gulf War, and the war of 2003 against Iraq the third Gulf War.

9. Robert Fisk, 'Oussama Ben Laden par Robert Fisk', *Le Monde*, 19 September 2001 (reprinted from the London *Independent*). See also François Burgat, 'Des islamistes pas si "fous de Dieu" que ça?', *Le Figaro*, 27 September 2001, and bin Laden's statements on the Qatari Al-Jazeera television station (reprinted in *Le Monde*, 5 November 2001: 'Oussama Ben Laden: 'L'ONU est un instrument de crime')'.

10. Stephen Zunes, *Tinderbox: US Foreign Policy and the Roots of Terrorism*, London: Zed Books, 2003, p. 77.

11. From the Arabic *ulama*, the plural of *'alim* (theologian).

12. Fisk, 'Oussama Ben Laden par Robert Fisk'.

13. In 1995 and 1996 two bombings of American military installations, in Riyadh and Khobar (on the east coast of the kingdom), killed a total of twenty-four Americans.

14. Fisk, 'Oussama Ben Laden par Robert Fisk'.

15. See Chapter 4.

16. Fisk, 'Oussama Ben Laden par Robert Fisk'.

17. See Jean-Michel Foulquier, *Arabie séoudite, la dictature protégée*, Paris: Albin Michel, 1995.

18. See Chapter 6.

Chapter 1

1. Ibrahim Abdel-Méguid, *L'Autre Pays*, trans. C. Tissier-Tomas, Arles: Actes Sud, 1994.

2. Ibid., p. 208.

3. Ibid., pp. 121, 128.

4. This is the literal translation of the term for the Arabian Peninsula in classical Arabic: *Jazirat al-'Arab*.

5. Qahtan denotes the mythical line of the southern Arabs (of Yemeni descent) and encompasses what are thought of as the 'genuine' Arabs. (Today the term is used for a tribe in the south-eastern Assir region of Arabia.) Adnan covers the northern Arabs: that is, the 'Arabized' Arabs.

6. Jihad Al-Zein, 'Enough stereotypes!', in the Beirut daily *Al-Nahar*, quoted from *Courrier international*, 25 October 2001.

7. The phrase is quoted from Antoine Basbous, *L'Arabie saoudite en question*, Paris: Perrin, 2002, pp. 10–11.

8. Ibid.

9. It was a top US official who admitted that Saudi Arabia was a 'black hole': 'We have huge gaps in our understanding of what is going on there' (quoted by Alain Gresh, 'Mystères d'un attentat en Arabie saoudite', *Manière de voir-Le Monde diplomatique*, November–December 2001).

10. Thomas L. Friedman, 'Dear Saudi Arabia', *New York Times*, 12 December

2001, reprinted in Friedman, *Longitudes and Attitudes: Exploring the World after September 11*, New York: Farrar, Straus & Giroux, 2002, p. 127.

11. Ahmad Abodehman, *La Ceinture*, Paris: Gallimard, 2000, p. 11. This fine novel is the first written in French by a writer from the Arabian Peninsula.

12. Stéphane Marchand, *Arabie saoudite, la menace*, Paris: Fayard, 2003, pp. 269–70.

13. See Madawi al-Rasheed, *A History of Saudi Arabia*, Cambridge: Cambridge University Press, 2002, p. 15.

14. Marchand, *Arabie saoudite, la menace*, p. 127.

15. Ibid., pp. 315–16. The view that Marchand echoes was put forward by the great Syrian poet Nizar Qabbani, who called the Saudi people *Abu Jahl* (the 'father of ignorance') because of its wealth, hypocrisy and ostentatious bad taste. The characterization is all the more scathing if we remember that the pre-Islamic and pre-Saudi periods are both called *jahiliya* ('age of ignorance').

16. Ibid., p. 44.

17. Ibid., pp. 298–9.

18. François Burgat, *Face to Face with Political Islam*, London: I.B. Tauris, 2003, pp. 22–3; translation modified.

19. Abdolhassan Bani Sadr, 'Duplicité de l'Occident', *Le Monde*, 29 October 2001. On the way in which the United States encouraged the emergence of (sometimes terrorist) Islamist movements, especially in Afghanistan, Lebanon and Pakistan, see Stephen Zunes, *Tinderbox: US Foreign Policy and the Roots of Terrorism*, London: Zed Books, 2003, ch. 5: 'The Rise of Extremist Islamic Movements', pp. 171–93.

20. See Chapters 2 and 4 below.

21. Quoted in Alexei Vassiliev, *The History of Saudi Arabia*, London: Saqi Books, 1998, p. 32.

22. Jacques Benoist-Méchin, *Ibn Séoud ou la naissance d'un royaume*, Paris: Albin Michel, 1955, p. 7.

23. 'The Spirit of Christianity and Its Fate', in G.W.F. Hegel, *Early Theological Writings*, Philadelphia: University of Pennsylvania Press, 1971, p. 186. The words in square brackets are translated from the first version of Hegel's text (to be found in the Nohl edition of his works): see *L'Esprit du christianisme et son destin*, trans. F. Fischbach, Paris: Presses Pocket, 1992, p. 53.

24. See Mamoun Fandy, *Saudi Arabia and the Politics of Dissent*, London: Macmillan, 1999, pp. 18–19.

25. Georges Corm, *Fragmentation of the Middle East: The Last Thirty Years*, London: Hutchinson, 1998, Introduction and chs 1–3.

26. See, for example, the chapter 'Un islam rétrograde' in Jean-Michel Foulquier, *Arabie séoudite, la dictature protégée*, Paris: Albin Michel, 1995, pp. 59–78.

27. See, for example, Basbous, *L'Arabie saoudite en question*, ch. 3: 'Le wahhabisme,

islam belliqueux', pp. 123–59; and Marchand, *Arabie saoudite, la menace*: 'L'université, laboratoire de l'intolérance', pp. 207–13.

28. Ibn Khaldun, *Discours sur l'histoire universelle*, Arles: Sindbad–Actes Sud, 1997, p. 7.

29. Xavier de Planhol, *Les Nations du Prophète. Manuel géographique de politique musulmane*, Paris: Fayard, 1993, p. 3.

30. See Jacques Berque, *Arab Rebirth: Pain and Ecstasy*, London: Saqi Books, 1983, ch. 3: 'Ishmael and the Desert'.

31. Benoist-Méchin, *Ibn Séoud ou la naissance d'un royaume*, pp. 15–16.

32. A pre-Islamic poet. See *Les dix grandes odes de l'Anté-islam*, trans. J. Berque, Arles: Sindbad-Actes-Sud, 1995; *Seven Arab Odes (Muallaqat)*, trans. Desmond O'Grady, London: Agenda, 1990.

33. Marchand, *Arabie saoudite, la menace*, p. 269.

34. The total population is today estimated at 22.67 million, of which 16.52 million are Saudi citizens (72.9 per cent of the whole population).

35. Laurent Murawiec, 'Arabie saoudite: l'ennemi public no. 1', interview with Amir Taheri, *Politique internationale* 98, Winter 2002–03, p. 309.

36. Marchand, *Arabie saoudite, la menace*, p. 144.

37. Ibn Khaldun, *Discours sur l'histoire universelle*, p. 188.

38. See Marcel Kurpershoek, *Arabia of the Bedouins*, London: Saqi Books, 2001, pp. 194–5.

39. Georges Corm, *La Proche éclaté*, Paris: La Découverte, 1988, pp. 33–4.

40. See Chapter 3.

41. On the complex relations between state Islam and the Shiite minority, see Chapter 4 and the Conclusion below. See Fandy, *Saudi Arabia and the Politics of Dissent*, ch. 7: 'Sheikh Hassan al-Saffar and the Shi'a Reform Movement', pp. 195–228.

42. See Chapter 4.

43. Founded on 26 May 198 in Abu Dhabi, capital of the United Arab Emirates, the Gulf Cooperation Council (GCC) comprises the six monarchies of the Peninsula: Saudi Arabia, Kuwait, Bahrain, Qatar, United Arab Emirates and Oman. This 'community of oil and petrodollars' has operated a customs union since 1 January 2003, and a single currency is planned to come into circulation on 1 January 2010.

44. See Chapter 6.

45. I owe this fine expression to my friend Carl Poirier.

46. The Arabic translation of his book *La Ceinture* was banned in Arabia because of a few slightly risqué passages and a very precise description of how peripheral tribes reacted to the centrally imposed modernization.

47. The curved *janbiya* is a sign of virility and tribal identity.

48. That is, classical Arabic – a universal language in comparison with the tribal dialect.

49. And no longer *fulan bin fulan*, so-and-so son of so-and-so: that is, a member of a particular tribe or branch of a tribe.

50. Abodehman, *La Ceinture*, pp. 34–5.

Chapter 2

1. That is, Muhammad, son of Abd al-Wahhab. The personal identity of nationals of the Peninsular states consists of their first name, followed by the names of their father, grandfather and great-grandfather.
2. See the pages on Ibn Taymiyya in Sabrina Mervin, *Histoire de l'islam. Doctrines et fondements*, Paris: Flammarion, 2000, pp. 157 and esp. 245–7.
3. Muhammad ibn Abd al-Wahhab, *Kitab al-Tawhid*, Riyadh: Dar-al-Salam, 1998, pp. 11–12.
4. See ibid., p. 158: 'Draw attention to the aim of this practice, which consists of achieving oneness in the choice of terms to be used.'
5. See, for instance, Abdelwahab Meddeb, *La Maladie de l'islam*, Paris: Seuil, 2002, ch. 2: 'Généalogie de l'intégrisme', pp. 55–78.
6. Abd al-Wahhab, *Kitab al-Tawhid*, p. 101.
7. Ibid., p. 12.
8. Ibid., p. 43.
9. Ibid., p. 89.
10. Ibid., p. 143.
11. Ibid., p. 128.
12. Ibid., p. 116.
13. Jacques Berque, *Arab Rebirth: Pain and Ecstasy*, London: Saqi Books, 1983, p. 12.
14. Alexei Vassiliev, *The History of Saudi Arabia*, London: Saqi Books, 1998, p. 82.
15. Quoted in Madawi al-Rasheed, *A History of Saudi Arabia*, Cambridge: Cambridge University Press, 2002, p. 17.
16. The descendants of Abd al-Wahhab are the Al al-Shaikhs (literally 'those from the scholar's family'). The grand mufti of the kingdom today is Abdelaziz Al al-Shaikh; the minister of religious affairs is Salih Al al-Shaikh; and the justice minister is Abdallah Al al-Shaikh.
17. See Chapter 3.
18. Uthman bin Bishr, *'Unwan al-Majd fi Tarikh Najd* [The signs of glory in the history of Najd], vol. 1, Riyadh: Dar al-Habib, 1999, pp. 37 and 342.
19. Vassiliev, *The History of Saudi Arabia*, p. 83.
20. Letter from Italinski, the Russian consul, dated 1803. Quoted in ibid., p. 101. The *Kitab al-Tawhid* (pp. 176–7) outlines a system of 'international' law, in the form of exhortations to clemency and, above all, incorporation of the vanquished into the nation of the victors.
21. Vassiliev, *The History of Saudi Arabia*, p. 80.
22. Abd al-Wahhab, *Kitab al-Tawhid*, p. 143.
23. Bin Bishr, *'Unwan al-Majd fi Tarikh Najd*, vol. 1, pp. 23–4; emphases added.
24. Berque, *Arab Rebirth*, p. 35.
25. Jean Raymond, *Mémoire sur l'origine des Wahabys, sur la naissance de leur puissance et*

sur l'influence dont ils jouissent comme nation, Cairo: Institut français d'archéologie orientale, 1925, p. 34.

26. Stéphane Marchand, *Arabie saoudite, la menace,* Paris: Fayard, 2003, p. 32. The author continues: 'Wahhabism is the thoroughly reactionary Bedouin version of that aspiration to original purity which is so widespread in the Muslim world and is sometimes exploited to justify terrorist violence.' We have seen what to make of the 'Bedouin' and 'reactionary' character of Wahhabism. As to the link with terrorism, see Chapter 4.

27. See Guido Steinberg, *Religion und Staat in Saudi-Arabien. Die wahhabitischen Gelehrten, 1902–1953,* Würzburg: Ergon, 2002, pp. 28ff.

28. Quoted in Vassiliev, *The History of Saudi Arabia,* p. 99.

29. Ibid., p. 101.

30. Jean Baptiste-Rousseau, *Description du Pachalik de Bagdad, suivie d'une Note historique sur les Wahhabis,* Paris: Treutel & Würtz, Paris, 1809.

31. Louis Alexandre de Corancez, *The History of the Wahhabis: From their Origin until the End of 1809,* Reading: Garnet, 1995.

32. See the preface by C. Edel to William Gifford Palgrave, *Une année dans l'Arabie centrale* (1862–1863), Paris: France-Empire, 1992, p. x – this being the French translation of Palgrave's *Personal Narrative of a Year's Journey through Central and Eastern Arabia* (1862–63), London: Darf, 1985.

33. See Vassiliev, *The History of Saudi Arabia,* p. 75.

34. Corancez, *The History of the Wahhabis,* p. xiii; emphases added.

35. The equivalent of 'Islamism' in Arabic is *harakat islamiyya,* 'Islamic movement', or to a lesser extent *islam al-siyasi,* 'political Islam'. (Originally, of course, eighteenth-century Europeans coined the word 'Islamism' as a synonym of 'Islam'.)

36. Mamoun Fandy, *Saudi Arabia and the Politics of Dissent,* London: Macmillan, 1999, p. 19.

37. Mai Yamani, *Changed Identities: The Challenge of the New Generation in Saudi Arabia,* London: Royal Institute of International Affairs, 2000, p. 130.

38. Ibid., ch. 2: 'National Identity and Political Aspirations', pp. 26–48.

39. Fandy, *Saudi Arabia and the Politics of Dissent,* p. 11.

40. See Chapters 4, 7 and 8.

41. Raymond, *Mémoire sur l'origine des Wahabys,* p. 9.

42. See Chapters 3 and 4.

43. See Gilbert Grandguillaume, 'Valorisation et dévalorisation liées aux contacts de cultures en Arabie saudite', in Paul Bonnenfant, ed., *La Péninsule arabique d'aujourd'hui,* vol. 2, Paris: Éditions du CNRS, 1982, pp. 623–54.

44. Meddeb, *La Maladie de l'islam,* p. 67.

45. Bernard Cohen, 'Lawrence d'Arabie avait raison', *Libération,* 17 February 2003.

46. Laurent Murawiec, 'Amérique–Arabie saoudite: le divorce', *Le Figaro,* 23 May 2003.

47. Antoine Basbous, 'Les métastasies de la tumeur wahhabite', *Le Figaro*, 28 May 2003.

48. Mervin, *Histoire de l'islam*, p. 162.

49. Ibid., p. 163.

50. Ibid., p. 167.

51. Ali al-Umaym, 'Man al-mas'ul 'an hadi 'ashir september? Riwaiya ba'dh ma jara' [Who is responsible for 11 September? An account of a few events], *Al-Sharq al-Awsat*, 13 September 2002.

52. See Olivier Carré, *L'Utopie islamique dans l'Orient arabe*, Paris: Presses de la Fondation nationale des sciences politiques, 1995, ch. 5: 'Arabie saoudite: norme et normes'. See also Chapter 3 below.

53. Ibid., p. 105.

54. See 'Conclusion' below.

Chapter 3

1. Madawi al-Rasheed, *A History of Saudi Arabia*, Cambridge: Cambridge University Press, 2002, p. 144.

2. See Chapter 4.

3. Jean-Michel Foulquier, *Arabie séoudite, la dictature protégée*, Paris: Albin Michel, 1995, p. 125.

4. Helen Lackner, *A House Built on Sand: A Political Economy of Saudi Arabia*, London: Ithaca Press, 1978; Saïd K. Aburish, *The Rise, Corruption and Coming Fall of the House of Saud*, London: Bloomsbury, 1994.

5. *Lam al-Shihab fi Sirat Muhammad b. 'Abd al-Wahhab* [The brilliance of the meteor in the life of Muhammad ibn Abd al-Wahhab], anonymous manuscript preserved in the British Library, pp. 510–17; quoted in Alexei Vassiliev, *The History of Saudi Arabia*, London: Saqi Books, 1998, p. 35.

6. Jacques Benoist-Méchin, *Ibn Séoud ou la naissance d'un royaume*, Paris: Albin-Michel, 1955, p. 85; Lackner, *A House Built on Sand*, preface, p. ii.

7. Nazih Ayubi, *Over-stating the Saudi State: Politics and Society in the Middle East*, London: I.B. Tauris, 1995.

8. Ibid., p. 128.

9. For a complete panorama of foreign domination in Arabia, see Modjta-ba Sadria, *Ainsi l'Arabie est devenue saoudite*, Paris: L'Harmattan, 1989, pp. 45–84, and Vassiliev, *The History of Saudi Arabia*, pp. 83–111 and 140–286.

10. Vassiliev, *The History of Saudi Arabia*, p. 207.

11. Ibid., p. 275.

12. See Henry Laurens, *L'Orient arabe, arabisme et islamisme de 1798 à 1945*, Paris: Armand Colin, 2000, ch. 2: 'L'époque des Tanzimat'.

13. The Hashemite sharifs of Mecca are direct descendants of the Prophet. One member of the Hashemite family, King Abdullah II, still reigns in Jordan.

14. The Arab name for Saudi Arabia, which the British whispered to Abdelaziz in 1932, is *al-Mamlaka al-'arabiya al-sa'udiya* (Saudi Arab kingdom), but in

the media, private conversation, number plates, road signs and airports this is abbreviated to *al-Sa'udiya* ('Saudia').

15. Reconstruction aid that the United States accorded to its wartime allies.

16. Memorandum from Standard Oil of California, sent on 8 February 1943 to US Secretary of State Harold Ickes; quoted in Vassiliev, *The History of Saudi Arabia*, p. 324.

17. Quoted from Benoist-Méchin, *Ibn Séoud*, p. 402.

18. These are three key government posts – defence minister (Sultan ibn Abdelaziz), foreign minister (Saud ibn Faisal ibn Abdelaziz) and interior minister (Nayef ibn Abdelaziz) – plus the technical post of minister of public works and housing (Mutib ibn Abdelaziz).

19. For example, the Sauds bought two pan-Arab papers – *Al-Hayat* and *Al-Sharq al-Awsat* – and no longer needed to censor them. The same has been true *mutatis mutandis* of political oppositions: see Chapter 4.

20. King Fahd, as well as his six direct brothers (the most important of whom are Sultan, Nayef and Salman), are the sons of a Sudayri woman; King Faisal was the son of an al-Shaikh; and Crown Prince Abdullah's mother was a Shammar. Although these different tribal origins do not explain everything about the relations among members of the royal family, they do play a decisive role in certain friendships and enmities.

21. Al-Rasheed, *A History of Saudi Arabia*, p. 79.

22. See Madawi al-Rasheed, 'Dynasties durables et non durables. Les Rachid et les Sa'ud en Arabie centrale', *Maghreb–Machrek* 147, January–March 1995, pp. 13–25.

23. Marcel Kurpershoek, *Arabia of the Bedouins*, London: Saqi Books, 2001, pp. 62–3.

24. See Chapter 4.

25. Muhammad ibn Abd al-Wahhab, *Al-'Usul al-thalatha wa Adilatuha* [The three sources and their proofs], Riyadh: Ministry of Religious Affairs, 1419 AH, p. 30.

26. See E.E. Calverly, 'The Doctrine of the Arabian Brethren', *The Muslim World*, vol. 11, 1921, p. 354; quoted by Modj-ta-ba Sadria in *Ainsi l'Arabie est devenue saoudite*, pp. 131–2.

27. Quoted in Benoist-Méchin, *Ibn Saoud*, p. 248; emphases added.

28. In 1920, the Conference of San Remo established under British mandate the states of Transjordania (the present-day Jordan, occupying the left bank of the River Jordan) and Iraq, which were entrusted to two sons of Sharif Hussein: Abdullah for Jordan and Faisal for Iraq.

29. Kiren Aziz Chaudhry, *The Price of Wealth: Economies and Institutions in the Middle East*, New York: Cornell University Press, 1997, p. 69.

30. The Ikhwan have been seen in the West as a socialist or even Bolshevik movement, because of the egalitarian norms in force in their kolkhoz-style *hijra*. 'The Ikhwan brethren are more or less communistic', wrote one American journalist in the 1920s.

31. François Pouillon and Thierry Mauger, 'Un État contre les bédouins', *Maghreb–Machrek* 147, January–March 1995, p. 138.
32. Ibid., p. 132.
33. Ibid., p. 146.
34. See Chapter 6.
35. 'Letter from the Directorate of Finance to the Newly Appointed Financial Secretary of Bisha: Special Instructions', 1352/3/25 (1933–34 AD); quoted in Chaudhry, *The Price of Wealth*, p. 58.
36. After Abdelaziz's death in 1953 his son Saud ascended the throne, only to be toppled by his half-brother Faisal in 1964 following a four-year period of internecine strife. When Faisal was murdered in 1975 by one of his nephews, his half-brother Khaled took over as ruling monarch, and was succeeded by his half-brother Fahd in 1982. Since being felled by an embolism in 1995, Fahd has been gradually replaced by his half-brother Abdullah, crown prince, regent and 'vice-guardian of the two holy places', as the Saudi press sometimes calls him.
37. Chaudhry, *The Price of Wealth*, p. 61; emphases added.
38. In 1954, it was estimated that 8 per cent of children were in full-time education, and that 95 per cent of the population were illiterate. In 1957 a total of 600 Saudi students were enrolled in foreign universities, and by the mid-1970s the figure had climbed to 5,000. In 1960 some 143,000 pupils were in primary and secondary education, compared with 800,000 (600,000 boys and 200,000 girls) in 1973. See Alexei Vassiliev, *The History of Saudi Arabia*, pp. 433–5.
39. Quoted in ibid., p. 370.
40. Ibid., p. 361.
41. This system, in which every foreign company has to pay to be represented by a Saudi sponsor (*kafil*), has allowed sizeable fortunes to be amassed in a short space of time.
42. See Chapter 5.
43. The Arabian–American Oil Company, the new name of what had before 1945 been Standard Oil of California, secured a sixty-year concession in 1933 to exploit Saudi oil over more than 50 per cent of the territory. See Chapter 5.
44. See Chapter 4.
45. Olivier Carré, *L'Utopie islamique dans l'orient arabe*, Paris: Presses de la Fondation nationale des sciences politiques, 1995, p. 109.

Chapter 4

1. See Introduction.
2. Interview, Jeddah, 20 May 2002.
3. Ghazi Al Qusaybi, *Hatta la takun fitna* [To prevent dissension], Beirut: Dar al-Kikma, 1991; quoted by Madawi al-Rasheed, 'La couronne et le

turban: l'État saudien à la recherche d'une nouvelle légitimité', in Bassma Kodmani-Darwish and May Chartouni-Dubarry, eds, *Les États arabes face à la contestation islamiste*, Paris: Armand Colin–IFRI, 1997, p. 81.

4. François Burgat, 'De l'islamisme au postislamisme, vie et mort d'un concept', *Esprit*, August–September 2001, p. 83.

5. Nilüfer Göle, *Musulmanes et modernes. Voile et civilisation en Turquie*, Paris: La Découverte, 2003, p. 11. (Cf. Nilüfer Göle, *The Forbidden Modern: Civilization and Veiling*, Ann Arbor: University of Michigan Press, 1996.)

6. A perfect example of this is the assertions of Laurent Murawiec in 'Arabie saoudite: l'ennemi public no. 1', interview with Amir Taheri, *Politique internationale* 98, Winter 2002–03.

7. An excellent introduction to the study of Saudi Islamist movements may be found in al-Rasheed, 'La couronne et le turban', and in Mamoun Fandy, *Saudi Arabia and the Politics of Dissent*, London: Macmillan, 1999.

8. This oil cartel, distinct from OPEC (Organization of Petroleum Exporting Countries), comprises Algeria, Bahrain, Egypt, Iraq, Kuwait, Libya, Qatar, Saudi Arabia, Syria and United Arab Emirates.

9. On the principles of US energy policy, see Louis Blin, *Le Pétrole du Golfe. Guerre et paix au Moyen-Orient*, Paris: Maisonneuve & Larose, 1996, ch. 1, pp. 9–19.

10. Alexei Vassiliev, *The History of Saudi Arabia*, London: Saqi Books, 1998, p. 401.

11. Georges Corm, *Fragmentation of the Middle East: The Last Thirty Years*, London: Hutchinson, 1998, p. 349. On the 'semiology' of the embargo, see ibid., pp. 346–53.

12. As expressed by theoreticians of the rentier economy, this principle links the authoritarian character of the oil states ('no representation') to the fact that they have only one source of revenue and to the lack of input from citizens into the state budget ('no taxation'). See Chapter 5.

13. Chaudhry, *The Price of Wealth*, p. 144.

14. Ibid., p. 152.

15. A decree of 1975 permitted state officials to engage in business activity, and this was followed up in 1978 by a decree on 'the regulation of service officials' (that is to say, 'sponsors').

16. Statistics collected in Chaudhry, *The Price of Wealth*, pp. 156–8.

17. See Chapter 6 below.

18. The period between 1973 and 1983 witnessed the construction of 74 airports, 2 harbour installations, 30,000 kilometres of asphalt roads, 30 hospitals, 7 seawater desalination plants and 100 dams. Farhad Rad-Serecht, *Les États du Golfe. De la prospérité à l'implosion*, Paris: Eska, 1991, p. 8.

19. See al-Rasheed, *A History of Saudi Arabia*, pp. 144–5.

20. Quoted in François Burgat, 'Les Salafis au Yémen ou ... la modernisation malgré tout', *Chroniques yéménites* 11, Sanaa: CNRS–CEFAS, 2002, n 16.

21. Commemoration of the martyrdom of the Shia saints Hassan and

Hussein, which the Saudi state tolerates only as a private practice.

22. See Chapter 7.

23. See Chapter 2.

24. History of Dissent, collective of the Movement for Islamic Reform in Arabia (MIRA – al-Harakat al-islamiya li-l-islah), n.d., www.miraserve.com/english. new.htm, ch. 2, pp. 7–8; emphases added.

25. Ibid., ch. 1, p. 3; emphases added.

26. François Burgat, Face to Face with Political Islam, London: I.B. Tauris, 2003, p. 49.

27. See Robert Vitalis, 'Aramco World: Business and Culture on the Arabian Oil Frontier', in Madawi Al-Rasheed and Robert Vitalis, Counter-Narratives: History, Contemporary Society and Politics in Saudi Arabia and Yemen, New York: Palgrave Macmillan, 2004, pp. 151–81.

28. Quoted in Vassiliev, The History of Saudi Arabia, p. 357.

29. La Révolution [Paris], 22 February 1985.

30. Quoted in Jacques Benoist-Méchin, Ibn Séoud ou la naissance d'un royaume, Paris: Albin-Michel, 1955, p. 486.

31. Burgat, Face to Face with Political Islam, p. 91.

32. Interview, Riyadh, May 2002.

33. See Chapters 2 and 3. Cf. Burgat, Face to Face with Political Islam, ch. 4; and Abdou Filali-Ansary, Réformer l'islam?, Paris: La Découverte, 2003, esp. chs. 6, 8, 9 and 16.

34. Jacques Berque, Il reste un avenir, conversations with J. Sur, Paris: Arléa, 2002, p. 85.

35. See Chapter 8.

36. Rad-Serecht, Les États du Golfe, p. 189.

37. See Muzhakkarat al-nasiha (Advisory memorandum), a programme addressed to King Fahd in 1992. See Chapter 8: 'The Army', www.miraserve. com/documents/islahdocs2.htm, pp. 28–9.

38. Fandy, Saudi Arabia and the Politics of Dissent, pp. 67–8.

39. 'Asbab Suqut al-Duwal' [Why do states disintegrate?], a tape-recorded sermon; quoted in Fandy, Saudi Arabia and the Politics of Dissent, p. 97; emphases added.

40. The Arabic text of this letter may be found on the website of the Movement for Islamic Reform in Arabia: www.miraserve.com/documents/ islahdocs1.htm.

41. Quoted in al-Rasheed, A History of Saudi Arabia, p. 168; emphases added.

42. Khitab al-matalib, www.miraserve.com/documents/islahdocs2.htm.

43. See Olivier Roy, Globalized Islam: The Search for a New Ummah, London: C. Hurst, 2002, esp. Introduction and ch. 8.

44. See Burgat, Face to Face with Political Islam, ch. 5: 'Revolutionary violence and unofficial violence', esp. pp. 77f.

45. See Ali al-Umaym, 'Man al-mas'ul 'an hadi 'ashir september? Riwaiya ba'dh ma jara' [Who is responsible for 11 September? An account of a few events], Al-Sharq al-Awsat, 13 September 2002.

46. See Conclusion below.
47. Mansur al-Nuqaidan, 'Kharitat al-islamiyyn fi al-Sa'udiya wa qissat al-takfir' [The road map of the Saudi Islamists and the history of the idea of excommunication], Ilaf, 27 February 2003.
48. On the social dimension of the Islamist critique, see Chapters 7 and 8.
49. MIRA, History of Dissent, ch. 6, p. 1; emphases added.
50. Ibid., ch. 2, p. 3; emphases added.
51. Jazirat al-islam (The Islamic Peninsula), a sermon distributed on cassettes, n.d.; quoted in Fandy, Saudi Arabia and the Politics of Dissent, p. 101.
52. Göle, Musulmanes et modernes, p. 11.

Chapter 5

1. Unless it is stated otherwise, we have relied in this chapter on data and estimates contained in the Economist Intelligence Unit, Saudi Arabia: Country Report, London: The Economist, February 2003.
2. Michel Chatelus, 'La situation économique des pays producteurs de pétrole de la Péninsule arabique', Maghreb–Machrek 174, October–December 2001, p. 60.
3. On the concept of a rentier state, see Hazem Beblawi and Giacomo Luciani, eds, The Rentier State, London: Croom Helm, 1987; especially Luciani's contribution 'Allocation vs. Production States: A Theoretical Framework'.
4. Giacomo Luciani, 'Arabie saoudite: l'industrialisation d'un État allocataire', Maghreb–Machrek 129, July–September 1990, p. 77.
5. See Chapter 6.
6. In Chapter 3.
7. See Luciani, 'Arabie saoudite: l'industrialisation d'un état allocataire', p. 76. Cf. Michel Chatelus, 'Policies for development: attitudes towards industry and services', in Beblawi and Luciani, eds, The Rentier State, pp. 123–4.
8. Kiren Aziz Chaudhry, The Price of Wealth: Economies and Institutions in the Middle East, New York: Cornell University Press, 1997, p. 152.
9. Ibid., p. 177.
10. Farhad Rad-Serecht, Les États du Golfe. De la prospérité à l'implosion, Paris: Eska, 1991, pp. 12–15.
11. Robert E. Looney, 'Internal and External Constraints on Saudi Arabian Economic Growth: The Role of Defence Expenditures and Remittances', in J.W. Wright, ed., The Political Economy of Middle East Peace: The Impact of Competing Trade Agendas, London: Routledge, 1999, p. 212.
12. Chaudhry, The Price of Wealth, pp. 274–5.
13. See Rad-Serecht, Les États du Golfe, pp. 27–48 and 132–4; and Luciani, 'Arabie saoudite: l'industrialisation d'un État allocataire', p. 76.

14. If we add in subsidies and the pay of seconded civil servants, 34 per cent of the state budget is devoted to public corporations. Half of the subsidies in question are earmarked for pension funds, in anticipation of privatization and early retirement.

15. See Alain Gresh, 'Balbutiements de l'opinion publique en Arabie saoudite', *Le Monde diplomatique*, May 2002, pp. 14–15.

16. See Chapter 8.

17. See International Monetary Fund, 'IMF Concludes 2002 Article IV Consultation with Saudi Arabia', Public Information Service No. 02/121, 25 October 2002, available at www.imf.org/external/np/sec/pn/2002/pno2121.htm.

18. See Omar Bagahr, 'Why Did Seventy-Three Deputies Vote "No"' [in Arabic], *Al-Madina*, 18 January 2003.

19. Michel Chatelus, 'La situation économique des pays producteurs de pétrole de la Péninsule arabique', *Maghreb–Machrek* 174, October–December 2001.

20. This executive body, created in 1999 and chaired by Crown Prince Abdullah, has the task of implementing the broad lines of the economic reform.

21. See Rad-Serecht, *Les États du Golfe*, pp. 25–6.

22. Lamʻ al-Shihab fi Sîrat Muhammad b. ʻAbd al-Wahhab, quoted in Alexei Vassiliev, *The History of Saudi Arabia*, London: Saqi Books, 1998, p. 35.

23. Montesquieu, *De l'esprit des lois*, XX, 2, Paris: Gallimard–Pléiade, 1951, vol. 2, pp. 585–6.

Chapter 6

1. See Chapter 7.

2. See Germaine Tillion, *The Republic of Cousins:Women's Oppression in Mediterranean Society*, London: Saqi Books, 1983, esp. ch. 1: 'The Noble Mediterranean Peoples', pp. 13–35.

3. Ahmed Abodehman, *La Ceinture*, Paris: Gallimard, 2000, p. 105.

4. See Jacques Seguin, 'L'aménagement du territoire en Arabie saoudite: ses enjeux politiques', *Maghreb–Machrek* 156, April–June 1997, pp. 23–35. See also Paul Bonnenfant, 'La politique urbaine en Arabie saoudite', in *Politiques urbaines dans le monde arabe*, Lyons: CNRS–EMA, 1984; and Paul Bonnenfant, 'Villes moyennes et petites en Arabie saoudite' and Ahmed K. Amrouche, 'La mutation urbaine en Arabie saoudite', both in *Petites villes et villes moyennes dans le monde arabe*, Tours: CNRS–URBAMA, 1986.

5. Alexei Vassiliev, *The History of Saudi Arabia*, London: Saqi Books, 1998, p. 459; *L'État du monde 2003*, Paris: La Découverte, 2002, p. 236.

6. Mai Yamani, *Changed Identities:The Challenge of the New Generation in Saudi Arabia*, London: Royal Institute of International Affairs, 2000, p. 37.

7. Ibid., p. 8.

8. Ahmed Abodehman, "'Ayn al-nass' [People's eye], *Al-Riyadh*, 14 June 2002.

9. On Unaiza, for example, see Soraya Altorki and Donald P. Cole, 'Unayzah, le 'Paris du Nadjd': le changement en Arabie saoudite', *Maghreb–Machrek* 156, April–June 1997, pp. 3–22. And, on the history of Riyadh, the reader may refer to William Facey, *Riyadh: The Old City*, London: Immel Publishing, 1992.

10. Ibn Khaldun, *Discours sur l'histoire universelle*, Arles: Sindbad–Actes Sud, 1997, p. 33.

11. On the Riyadh property market in the 1970s, see Paul Bonnenfant, 'La capitale saoudienne: Riyad', in *La Péninsule arabique d'aujourd'hui*, PARIS: CNRS–CEROAC, 1982, pp. 682–700.

12. Interview, Riyadh, May 2002.

13. See Pascal Ménoret, 'Les murs de Riyad. Islam et modernité urbaine en Arabie saoudite', *Chroniques yéménites* 9, 2001, pp. 161–8.

14. Marcel Roncayolo, *La Ville et ses territoires*, Paris: Gallimard, 1997, pp. 92–3; emphases added.

15. See Chapter 3.

16. Yamani, *Changed Identities*, p. 8.

17. See Xavier de Planhol, *Les Fondements géographiques de l'histoire de l'islam*, Paris: Flammarion, 1968.

18. Yamani, *Changed Identities*, p. 22; emphases added.

19. See Chapter 8.

20. A couple of examples: 'Sulukiyat shabab al-battalat al-salbiya in'ikas li-l-waqi' al-lazi ia'ishunahu' [The negative attitude of the young unemployed to the situation in which they live], *Al-Watan*, 4 February 2002; and 'Sabab iqla'i 'an al-mukhdarat: wafat al-fatat al-lati kuntu ata'ata ma'aha amami' [How I broke the addiction: the girl I used to take drugs with died before me], *Al-Jazira*, 3 May 2002.

21. See Youssef Courbage, 'L'Arabie saoudite: une démographie en changement', *Maghreb–Machrek* 174, October–December 2001, p. 33.

22. Ibid., p. 35.

23. *Al-Iqtisadiya*, 27 May 2002.

24. Courbage, 'L'Arabie saoudite: une démographie en changement', p. 34; emphases added.

25. See Chapter 4; and cf. Kiren Aziz Chaudhry, *The Price of Wealth: Economies and Institutions in the Middle East*, New York: Cornell University Press, 1997, pp. 156–8.

26. See Stéphane Marchand, *Arabie saoudite, la menace*, Paris: Fayard, 2002, pp. 159–61.

27. See Chapter 5.

28. See, for example, Hosham Dawod and Hamit Bozarslan, eds, *La Société irakienne. Communautés, pouvoirs et violence*, Paris: Karthala, 2003.

29. See Chapter 1, section 'Bedouin and sedentary', and Chapter 3, section 'Twilight of the Bedouins'.

30. Fawziya Abu Khalid, 'Heritage and heritage', Al-Yawm 5409, 8/19/1408
    AH; quoted in Saddeka Arebi, Women and Words in Saudi Arabia: The Politics of
    Literary Discourse, New York: Columbia University Press, 1994, pp. 57–8.
31. See Hannah Arendt, Between Past and Future, London: Penguin, 1993, esp.
    the Preface: 'The Gap between Past and Future', and ch. 6: 'The Crisis
    in Culture: Its Social and Its Political Significance'.
32. See Pierre Bourdieu, Sociologie de l'Algérie, Paris: Presses universitaires de
    France, 1961, esp. ch 5: 'Le fonds commun'.

Chapter 7

1. Jean-Michel Foulquier, Arabie séoudite, la dictature protégée, Paris: Albin Michel,
   1995, p. 99.
2. Alexis de Tocqueville, Democracy in America, vol. 1, trans. Phillips Bradley,
   New York: Vintage Books, 1954, p. 4.
3. See Chapter 4.
4. See, for example, the series of articles on women that the daily Al-Riyadh
   published in January and February 2003 under the title: 'Al-Riyadh taftah
   al-milaf al-sha'ik li-l-ahwal al-shakhsiya li-nisf al-mujtama'' [Al-Riyadh
   opens the vexed issue of the personal situation of half of society].
5. Juhayer Al-Musa'ed, 'Creator and victim', Al-Jazira 6033, 5 April 1989;
   quoted in Saddeka Arebi, Women and Words in Saudi Arabia: The Politics of Literary
   Discourse, New York: Columbia University Press, 1994, pp. 185–6.
6. Ibid., p. 269.
7. Fatna Shaker, Nabt al-ardh [The plant of the earth], Jeddah: Tihama, 1981,
   p. 10; quoted in ibid., p. 207.
8. Mona al-Munajeed, Women in Saudi Arabia Today, London: Macmillan, 1997,
   ch. 4: 'The Veil', pp. 47–57.
9. The Koran, XXIV: 30–31; translated from J. Berque's French version,
   p. 375.
10. Ibid., XXXIII: 59; p. 454.
11. Germaine Tillion, The Republic of Cousins: Women's Oppression in Mediterranean
    Society, London: Saqi Books, 1983, esp. ch. 1: 'The Noble Mediterranean
    Peoples', pp. 13–35.
12. Ibid., p. 30.
13. Arebi, Women and Words in Saudi Arabia, p. 17.
14. Shaker, Nabt al-ardh; quoted in ibid., p. 207; emphases added.
15. Arebi, Women and Words in Saudi Arabia, pp. 30–35.
16. See Chapter 4.
17. See Mai Yamani, Changed Identities: The Challenge of the New Generation in Saudi
    Arabia, London: Royal Institute of International Affairs, 2000, p.106.
18. US Department of State Report, March 1996; quoted in ibid., p. 102.
19. Arebi, Women and Words in Saudi Arabia, p. 50; L'État du monde 2003, Paris: La
    Découverte, 2002, p. 236.

20. Sharifa al-Shamlan, 'Perfect Calm', in Abubaker Bagader, Ava M. Heinrichs-dorff and Deborah S. Akers, eds, *Voices of Change: Short Stories by Saudi Arabian Women Writers*, Boulder: Lynne Rienner, 1998, p. 48.

21. Juhayer Al-Musa'ed, 'Women journalists and women's liberation' [in Arabic], *Al-Jazira* 4395, 10 October 1984; quoted from Arebi, *Women and Words in Saudi Arabia*, pp. 189–90.

22. Arebi, *Women and Words in Saudi Arabia*, p. 283.

23. See Yamani, *Changed Identities*, 'Legitimate role models and the growth of islamic feminism', pp. 99–102.

24. Quoted in Alain Gresh, 'Balbutiements de l'opinion publique en Arabie saoudite', *Le Monde diplomatique*, May 2002, pp. 14–15; emphases added.

25. Interview, Riyadh, May 2002.

26. See Nilüfer Göle, *The Forbidden Modern: Civilization and Veiling*, Ann Arbor: University of Michigan Press, 1996; and Fariba Adelkhah, *La révolution sous le voile. Femmes islamiques d'Iran*, Paris: Karthala, 1991; *Being Modern in Iran*, New York: Columbia University Press, 2000.

27. Alain Gresh, 'Balbutiements de l'opinion publique en Arabie saoudite', *Le Monde diplomatique*, May 2002.

Chapter 8

1. Bashar al-Assad in Syria, Mohammed VI in Morocco, Abdallah II in Jordan, Hamad Al Khalifa in Bahrain and Hamad Al Thani in Qatar.

2. Mai Yamani, *Changed Identities: The Challenge of the New Generation in Saudi Arabia*, London: Royal Institute of International Affairs, 2000, pp. 130–31.

3. This chapter takes up and develops ideas published elsewhere: see Pascal Ménoret, 'La ré-islamisation de la jeunesse saoudienne', *La Pensée*, third quarter, 2003.

4. See Marcel Kurpershoek, *Oral Poetry and Narratives from Central Arabia*, vol. 2: *The Story of a Desert Knight: The Legend of Shlewih al-'Atawi and Other 'Utaybah Heroes*, Leiden: E.J. Brill, 1995.

5. See Chapter 4.

6. Interview, Riyadh, June 2002.

7. Yamani, *Changed Identities*, pp. 136–7; see also Chapter 4 above.

8. Yamani, *Changed Identities*.

9. Badriya al-Bishr, 'Un jeudi', in *Le Mercredi soir. Femmes de Riyad*, trans. Jean-Yves Gillon, Paris: L'Harmattan, 2001, pp. 45, 46 and 51–2.

10. Paul Nizan, *Aden, Arabie*, New York: Columbia University Press, 1987, p. 59.

11. See Pierre Bourdieu, 'La "jeunesse" n'est qu'un mot', in *Questions de sociologie*, Paris: Minuit, 1984, pp. 143–54, esp. p. 151: 'Many generational conflicts are conflicts between systems of aspirations that have been constituted at different ages.'

12. It has spread so far, in fact, that the most commercial part of Syrian and Lebanese musical production is sung in Saudi dialect!

13. Yamani, *Changed Identities*, p. 148.

14. See Conclusion.

15. See Michaela Prokop, 'Saudi Arabia: The Politics of Education', *International Affairs* 79, 2003, p. 79. Cf. Yamani, *Changed Identities*, ch. 3: 'Education', pp. 49–69.

16. Prokop, 'Saudi Arabia: The Politics of Education', p. 89.

17. See Jacques Berque, *Arab Rebirth: Pain and Ecstasy*, London: Saqi Books, 1983, ch. 5: 'A Linguistic Model', pp. 23–8.

18. See Conclusion.

19. Quoted in Prokop, 'Saudi Arabia: The Politics of Education', p. 89.

20. Interview, Riyadh, January 2002.

21. During the first few months of 2003, editorial writers and intellectuals debated *inter alia* the teaching of English in primary schools and the problem of the teacher's authority.

22. Contrary to the view of Stéphane Marchand, for one. See his *Arabie saoudite: la menace*, 'L'université, laboratoire de l'intolérance', Paris: Fayard, 2003, pp. 207–13.

23. Unesco and Planning Ministry statistics, quoted in Prokop, 'Saudi Arabia: The Politics of Education', p. 87.

24. Ibid.

25. See Chapter 5.

26. Yamani, *Changed Identities*, p. 115.

27. See Yamani, ibid., pp. 125–30, where she adopts roughly the same typology: 'modernist liberals' and 'Salafist radicals' at the two extremes; 'traditionalists' and 'conservative Salafists' in the middle.

28. Interview, Riyadh, June 2002.

29. Yamani, *Changed Identities*, p. 131.

30. Bourdieu, 'L'art de résister aux paroles', *Questions de sociologie*, p. 13.

Conclusion

1. See François Burgat, 'Introduction', *Face to Face with Political Islam*, London: I.B. Tauris, 2003.

2. Interview with Robert Baer, *Atlantic Unbound* [online edition of *Atlantic Monthly*], 29 May 2003.

3. Interview with Robert Baer, *BuzzFlash*, 12 September 2003.

4. Madawi al-Rasheed and Robert Vitalis, eds, *Counter-Narratives: History, Contemporary Society and Politics in Saudi Arabia and Yemen*, London: Palgrave, 2004, esp. pp. 1–33.

5. On the economy, see Kiren Aziz Chaudhry, *The Price of Wealth: Economies and Institutions in the Middle East*, New York: Cornell University Press, 1997. On

the pluralism of legal norms and the council responsible for Saudi Islamic law, the reader may consult Thabet Koraytem, 'Le pluralisme juridique en Arabie saoudite. Essai de systématisation', thesis in comparative law, Paris–II Panthéon–Assas, 2000.

6. See Eric Hobsbawm and Terence Ranger, eds, *The Invention of Tradition*, Cambridge: Cambridge University Press, 1984.

7. Jacques Berque, *Arab Rebirth: Pain and Ecstasy*, London: Saqi Books, 1983, pp. 67–8.

8. See Jean-François Seznec, 'The Perils of Privatization in the Gulf', lecture given on 19 March 2001 at Georgetown University; and 'Prospects for Democratization in Saudi Arabia', lecture given on 26 September 2002 at Columbia University.

9. Bruce Berman and John Lonsdale, *Unhappy Valley: Conflict in Kenya and Africa*, London: James Currey, 1992, p. 5. Cf. Jean-François Bayart, *Le gouvernement du monde. Une critique politique de la globalisation*, Paris: Fayard, 2004, p. 30 and chs 1, 2 and 3.

10. 'Ru'iya li-hadhir al-watan wa mustaqbalihi', *Al-Quds al-'Arabi*, 30 January 2003. Cf. Pascal Ménoret, 'Les manifestes saoudiens de réforme, 30 janvier et 1er mai 2003', *Maghreb–Machrek* 177, Autumn 2003, pp. 107–11.

11. 'Shuraka' fi al-watan', *Al-Quds al-'Arabi*, 1 May 2003. Cf. Ménoret, 'Les manifestes saoudiens de réforme', pp. 111–15.

12. 'What we are fighting for', the American text, is available at www.americanvalues.org, while the Saudi response, "Ala ay asas nata'aiyish' [On what basis we live together] is available at www.islamtoday.net.

13. See Fariba Abdelkhah, Jean-François Bayard and Olivier Roy, *Thermidor en Iran*, Brussels: Complexe, 1993.

14. See Laurence Louër and Sabrina Mervin, 'Les chiites d'Irak: renaissance à Nadjaf', *Esprit*, July 2003, pp. 87–8 and 96–7.

15. A third text, published in late September 2003 by 305 liberal intellectuals (including 50 women), reaffirmed the demands of the Manifesto of the 104 in the security context of the fight against terrorism.

16. François Burgat, 'Les élections présidentielles de septembre 1999 auYémen: du "pluralisme armé" au retour à la "norme arabe"', *Maghreb–Machrek* 168, April–June 2000, pp. 67–75.

17. Ghazi Al Qusaybi, *Hatta la takun fitna* [To prevent dissension], Beirut: Dar al-Hikma, 1991.

18. Berque, *Arab Rebirth*, p. 119.

Select bibliography

Social and political sciences

Altorki, Soraya, and Cole, Donald P., *Arabian Oasis City: The Transformation of 'Unayzah*, Austin: University of Texas Press, 1989.

Anscombe, Frederick F., *The Ottoman Gulf: The Creation of Kuwait, Saudi Arabia and Qatar*, New York: Columbia University Press, 1997.

Arebi, Saddeka, *Women and Words in Saudi Arabia: The Politics of Literary Discourse*, New York: Columbia University Press, 1994.

Ayubi, Nazih N., *Over-stating the Arab State: Politics and Society in the Middle East*, London: I.B. Tauris, 1995.

Blin, Louis, *Le Pétrole du Golfe. Guerre et paix au Moyen-Orient*, Paris: Maisonneuve & Larose, 1996.

Bonnenfant, Paul (ed.), *La Péninsule arabique aujourd'hui*, Paris: CNRS–CEROAC, 1982.

Burgat, François, *Face to Face with Political Islam*, London: I.B. Tauris, 2003.

Carré, Olivier, *L'Utopie islamique dans l'Orient arabe*, Paris: Presses de la FNSP, 1991.

Chartouni-Dubarry, May, and Kodmani-Darwish, Bassma, *Les États arabes face à la contestation islamique*, Paris: Armand Colin/IFRI, 1997.

Chaudhry, Kiren Aziz, *The Price of Wealth: Economies and Institutions in the Middle East*, New York: Cornell University Press, 1997.

Detalle, Renaud (ed.), *Tensions in Arabia: The Saudi–Yemeni Fault Line*, Baden-Baden: Nomos Verlagsgesellschaft, 2000.

Facey, William, *Riyadh: The Old City*, London: Immel Publishing, 1992.

Fandy, Mamoun, *Saudi Arabia and the Politics of Dissent*, London: Macmillan, 1999.

Field, Michael, *The Merchants: The Big Business Families of Saudi Arabia and the Gulf States*, Woodstock: Overlook Press, 1985.

Al-Ghazzami, 'Abd Allah Muhammad, *Hikaiya al-hadatha fi al-mamlaka al-'arabiya al-sa'udiya* [The story of modernism in Saudi Arabia], London: Al-Markaz al-Thaqafi al-'Arabi, 2004.

Hajrah, Hassan Hamza, *Public Land Distribution in Saudi Arabia*, London: Longman, 1982.

Halliday, Fred, *Arabia without Sultans*, revised edn, London: Saqi Books, 2002.

al-Hamad, Turki, 'Tawid al-Jazira al-'arabiya' [The unification of the Arabian Peninsula], *Al-Mustaqbal al-'Arabi* 93 (1986): 27–40.

Herb, Michael, *All in the Family: Absolutism, Revolution and Democracy in the Middle Eastern Monarchies*, New York: State University of New York Press, 1999.

ibn 'Aqil, Abu 'Abd al-Rahman, *Masa'il min tarikh al-jazira al-'arabiya* [Issues from the history of Saudi Arabia] Riyadh: Mu'assasa dar al-Asala li-l-thaqafa wa-l-nashr wa-l-i'lam, 1993.

Kurpershoek, Marcel, *Arabia of the Bedouins*, London: Saqi Books, 2001.

Lackner, Helen, *A House Built on Sand: A Political Economy of Saudi Arabia*, London: Ithaca Press, 1978.

al-Munajjed, Mona, *Women in Saudi Arabia Today*, London: Macmillan, 1997.

al-Naqeeb, Khaldoun Hasan, *Society and State in the Gulf and Arab Peninsula: A Different Perspective*, London: Routledge, 1990.

Rad-Serecht, Farhad, *Les États du Golfe. De la prospérité à l'implosion*, Paris: Eska, 1991.

al-Rasheed, Madawi, *Politics in an Arabian Oasis: The Rashidi Tribal Dynasty*, London: I.B. Tauris, 1991.

al-Rasheed, Madawi, *A History of Saudi Arabia*, Cambridge: Cambridge University Press, 2002.

al-Rasheed, Madawi, and Vitalis, Robert (eds), *Counter-Narratives: History, Contemporary Society and Politics in Saudi Arabia and Yemen*, New York: Palgrave Macmillan, 2004.

Sadria, Modj-ta-ba, *Ainsi l'Arabie est devenue saoudite*, Paris: L'Harmattan, 1989.

Seccombe, Ian, and Lawless, Richard, *Work Camps and Company Towns: Settlement Patterns and the Gulf Oil Industry*, Durham: University of Durham, 1987.

Steinberg, Guido, *Religion und Staat in Saudi-Arabien. Die wahhabitischen Gelehrten, 1902–1953*, Würzburg: Ergon, 2002.

Vassiliev, Alexei, *The History of Saudi Arabia*, London: Saqi Books, 1998.

Yamani, Mai, *Changed Identities: The Challenge of the New Generation in Saudi Arabia*, London: Royal Institute of International Affairs, 2000.

Literature and travel narratives

Les dix grandes odes de l'Anté-Islam, trans. J. Berque, Arles: Sindbad–Actes Sud, 1995.

Abdel-Méguid, Ibrahim, *L'Autre Pays*, trans. C. Tissier-Thomas, Arles: Actes Sud, 1994; *The Other Place*, trans. Farouk Abdel Wahab, Cairo: AUC Press, 1997.

Abodehman, Ahmed, *La Ceinture*, Paris: Gallimard, 2000.

Abu-Khalid, Fawziya, Qira'a sirriya fi tarikh al-sumt al-'arabi [Secret readings in the history of Arab silence], Beirut: Dar al-adab, 1985.

Bagader, Abubakr, et al. (eds), Voices of Change: Short Stories by Saudi Arabian Women Writers, Boulder: Lynne Rienner, 1998.

al-Bishr, Badriyah, Le Mercredi soir. Femmes de Riyad [short stories], trans. J.-Y. Gillon, Paris: L'Harmattan, 2001.

Doughty, Charles M., Travels in Arabia Deserta, 3rd edn, London: Constable, 1979.

al-Hamad, Turki, Al-'Adama [novel], London: Dar al-Saqi, 2000.

al-Hamad, Turki, Al-Shumaiysi [novel], London: Dar al-Saqi, 1999.

al-Hamad, Turki, Al-Karadib [novel], London: Dar al-Saqi, 1999.

Kurpershoek, Marcel (ed.), Oral Poetry and Narratives from Central Arabia, vol. 1, The Poetry of ad-Dindan. A Bedouin Bard in Southern Najd, Leiden: E.J. Brill, 1994; vol. 2, The Story of a Desert Knight: The Legend of Shleweih al-'Atawi and Other 'Utaybah Stories, Leiden: E.J. Brill, 1995; vol. 3, Bedouin Poets of the Dawasir Tribe: Between Nomadism and Settlement in Southern Najd, Leiden: E.J. Brill, 1999.

Palgrave, William G., Personal Narrative of a Year's Journey through Central and Eastern Arabia (1862–1863), London: Darf, 1985.

al-Qusaybi, Ghazi Abd al-Rahman: Shiqqa al-Hurriya [The apartment of liberty – novel], London: Riad al-Rayyes Books, 1994.

Shaker, Fatna, Nabt al-ardh [Plant of the earth], Jeddah: Tihama, 1981.

Sowayan, Saad Abdullah, Nabati Poetry: The Oral Poetry of Arabia, Berkeley: University of California Press, 1985.

al-Subaiyi, Nasir, and al-Khalidi, Ibrahim, Hadith al-Sahra' [Speech of the desert – verse collection], Kuwait: Sharika al-Mukhtalif li-l-Nahr wa al-Tawzi', 2002.

Thesiger, Wilfred, Arabian Sands, Harmondsworth: Penguin, 1991.

Index